Praise for *Singing in the Lifeboat*

"Written with warmth, charm and a great deal of humour. Not only a memoir, but an homage to times gone by. I was captivated by Mr Bain's reminiscences, and his skill as a professional writer shines through in every paragraph."

– **RJ Ellory**, multi-award-winning author of *A Quiet Belief in Angels* and a dozen other best-sellers.

"Unsettlingly honest."

– **Brian Freemantle**, best-selling author of the Charlie Muffin series of espionage novels.

"Really excellent writing and compelling story-telling. Ian Bain displays a journalist's eye for the telling detail as he lays his life bare in this extremely readable memoir. From a broken childhood via Fleet Street and alcoholism to business success in the Middle East and finally self-discovery, Bain tells it all with forensic honesty and a deal of good humour."

– **Richard McNeill**, author of *What Genius Wrote This?*

"This is the extraordinary story of an extraordinary man. An impoverished Scottish upbringing and an alcoholic absentee father dealt Ian Bain a rotten hand. But he progressed from a junior reporter at fifteen, merchant seaman and big-time booze smuggler to night editor of a South American daily newspaper at twenty-three and a Fleet Street career before heading for Dubai. Fired for his drunken exploits, he sobered up to launch what became one of the most successful PR firms in the Middle East, later embarking on a remarkable journey of self-discovery. Ian's story is poignant, funny, startling and beautifully written."

– **Tony Boullemier**, author of *The Little Book of Monarchs.*

"Ian Bain tells a gripping story with drama and a keen sense of the absurd. He's experienced the rougher side of journalism and the smooth and sometimes not-so-smooth side of public relations, and he casts a sharp, ironic eye on each of them. There's the tough personal story of a writer's life here – the story of a professional, told by a professional. You finish the book with a deep breath, and the feeling that you've been in the company of a good friend."

– **Andrew Taylor**, author of *Books That Changed the World* and others.

"Ian Bain had a tough upbringing and a rollercoaster life. This is the unvarnished memoir of a survivor."

– **Brian Izzard**, author of *Glory and Dishonour* and others.

SINGING IN THE LIFEBOAT

IAN BAIN

MOSAÏQUEPRESS

Published by
MOSAÏQUE PRESS
Registered office:
70 Priory Road
Kenilworth, Warwickshire CV8 1LQ
www.mosaïquepress.co.uk

Cover design by Paul Tomlinson (2Can Design)

ISBN 978-1-906852-42-9

To my grandchildren
Madeleine and Oliver

and in memory of my grandfather
Alexander 'Sandy' Macdonald

Contents

"Life is a shipwreck, but we must not forget to sing in the lifeboats."

"La vie est un naufrage, mais nous ne devons pas oublier de chanter dans les canots de sauvetage."

– Voltaire

The author, aged eighteen months.

Introduction

MY GRANDFATHER was the inspiration for this book. He was long gone when I realised how little I knew about him. From my own sparse memories and the few threadbare accounts I pieced together, it became clear he was a fascinating man who lived in fascinating times. But it was a source of sadness to me that there were no records of his life, no list of achievements, no copies of his occasional writings.

So this book came about largely because I wanted my grandchildren to know more of me than I know of him. There was the thought, probably fanciful, that in the years well beyond me they might hand a battered copy to their grandchildren and tell them that their great-great-grandpa was an interesting man. Or maybe I'm just trying to grab a tiny scrap of immortality.

What I do know about Grandpa is that he arrived in this world before the motor car, before domestic electricity and long before radio or motion pictures. In the year of his birth, 1876, Disraeli was the British Prime Minister and, in America, Custer made his last stand at the Little Bighorn. He spent his entire working life in the age of steam, a railwayman through and through. When he retired because of an eye injury in the late 1930s he had reached the respected height of superintendent of locomotives at Ladyburn Running Sheds in Greenock, Scotland.

Alexander 'Sandy' Macdonald, my mother's father, used to tell me stories that were never written down and are mostly long forgotten. There are a few notable exceptions such as the time as a young child sitting on his father's shoulders, he watched the immediate aftermath of the Tay Bridge Disaster of 1879 or when he caught saboteurs trying to blow up a munitions train during the First World War. Sadly, these are bare-bone recollections, absent of any colour or depth.

Very early in my life, according to tales related by others, Grandpa used to strap me in a push-chair and navigate the steep paths up Mount Schiehallion. We went for many long walks in that fashion but perhaps it's because he was such a quiet and uncomplaining man that he remained a background figure during my turbulent childhood.

My primary memory of him is as an old man sitting in his armchair in front of the television, his pipe and tobacco pouch on a side table along with a box of Swan Vestas matches, a large ashtray and tools for scraping out the pipe and damping down the tobacco, all the *accoutrements* of a serious pipe smoker. His tobacco came in solid blocks from which he would carve shavings with a pocket knife. Altogether, it was quite an operation. His shirts and pullovers bore burn marks from enthusiastic lighting that invariably sent sparks flying in multiple directions. Sometimes, when he put the pipe in his jacket pocket, hot ash would burn through the material, sending up little tell-tale curls of smoke and giving rise to my mother's much-repeated warnings that one day he would set himself and the rest of us on fire.

He was a delightful old man with some novel eccentricities. He would talk to the television newsreader, thanking him for each announcement and bidding him good evening at the end of the bulletin. I might say to him "Come and get your dinner, Grandpa" and he would shush me and tell me not to interrupt the gentleman. At that time he was into his eighties and still in fairly good physical health, in spite of his smoking. His conversations with newsreaders were endearing and while they suggested his mind was slipping, I often felt he was inwardly chuckling at the rest of us for thinking he was a little mentally adrift. Or maybe, as the product of a much earlier era, he never did come to terms with pictures that travelled through the air and appeared in a little box.

On many Sundays, he and I would go to the local Baptist church, not because either of us particularly wanted to but because my mother sent us, representing the family, so to speak, and avoiding any requirement for her to attend. Occasionally, we would skip church, spend the plate money on cinema tickets and report back on the quality of the service.

Grandpa had an elder sister. I don't recollect her being called by any name other than Sissie. She was, by all accounts, an exceptionally wealthy widow who was prone to miserliness. When her husband died, she telephoned my mother. "I wondered if you would like to have any of John's suits for your John," she said. "I could let you have them at a good price."

When she died, she left her fortune to her lawyer and her doctor. We encouraged Grandpa to fight the will but he wouldn't hear of it. "If that's what Sissie wanted to do with her money, I'm not going to interfere," he said.

That is about the extent of my knowledge of Sandy. It's something of a tragedy because his life and loves and his achievements deserve to be better remembered. My paternal grandfather died before I was born and I know absolutely nothing of him other than that his was a hard existence on the Isle of Skye as head of a family of thirteen children, the youngest of whom was my father. Sandy was the one I knew and it's a cause of much sadness to me that I didn't know him well enough.

He was in a hospice in the final days of his life. It was 1963 and I had just returned from a year-long trip to sea. I went to see him and took with me his beloved pipe. I had scraped out the bowl, run a pipe-cleaner through the stem to remove the gunge and packed it firmly with his tobacco. He was propped up in bed, his eyes closed and not entirely of this world. He was suffering from leg ulcers that were not responding to the little treatment they had been given. I held the pipe to his mouth. He said nothing but a hand came up and grasped it with some urgency. I struck a match and held it to the tobacco. He drew hard and the flame bent into the bowl. It took a second match to get it going but he began to puff away vigorously and pretty soon the room was filled with smoke. I opened a window before it attracted the nursing staff. After a while I took the pipe from him. He let it go willingly and the suggestion of a smile crossed his beautiful, tired face. Grandpa died early the next morning.

WHEN I was three, we lived for a while with my grandparents in a cottage called Whitebridge on the road from Aberfeldy in Perthshire to Rannoch Moor. Across the narrow country road, a small stream ran alongside a stone wall into which someone in times past had built half a Belfast sink, presumably to provide drinking water for horses.

To my delight, the sink was frequently visited by a sizeable trout. I would collect small worms from the garden and drop them in. The trout would pop out of the stream and claim them.

We had few passers-by but I showed this wonderful trick to anyone who walked the road, including a couple of anglers on their way to fish the waters of Rannoch.

I never saw the trout again.

– 1 –

Sins of the father

THE LARGE manila envelope stares at me open-mouthed from the bottom drawer of my desk as if ready to defy any attempt to put it in the rubbish basket. It contains all that is left of my father – his death certificate, a savings book, a Merchant Navy seaman's card and a handful of small square photographs with black-and-white images of times long gone and people I never knew.

My father was, to put it as kindly as I can, a near-hopeless drunk with no sense of responsibility or moral integrity and for whom the regular abandonment of his family was just something that some men do. I was twelve when he left us for the last time. He had shown up after a long absence saying he was dying of cancer and had less than six months to live. While my older sister Katherine and I went into grief, my mother, whose experience of the marriage disinclined her to believe anything he said, checked with the hospital and discovered the lie.

His eviction from my life at that point was an immediate relief but also something of a tragedy. Years later, a psychiatrist told me that I'd spent my childhood in a war zone – domestic turmoil, constant upheaval, moonlight flits, nine schools in the ten years of my education as my father lost one job after another or we struggled to stay one step ahead of the bailiffs, not always successfully. But with him went the hope – admittedly a forlorn hope – that he might one day become the father I so desperately wanted, a dad who would stand on the sidelines of the football pitch and yell encouragement, who would show me how to make a kite and teach me to fish and hold me in his arms when I was sad.

The dynamics of our household changed. The female domination of my mother, grandmother and my sister became more perceptible. My gentle and unquestioning grandfather had long been emasculated and I sensed, even then, that the remaining male energy generated an unconscious discomfort in the family. If I argued with or upset my mother, she would sometimes wag a finger in my face with the stern warning: "You're going to turn out just like your father!" I felt at times as if I had become my father *in absentia*.

When she found a hidden picture book of nudes in statuesque poses, she dragged me into the back garden and shouted to the neighbours to come and look at "this disgusting boy".

My mother, Flora, was a product of a time when there was little or no understanding of adolescence at family level and she judged in the way that she herself would have been judged. Living through two world wars and with a husband who created only dreadful insecurity, she was on familiar terms with austerity, deprivation and grief. Before I was born, she had lost a child, Joyce, to diphtheria at the age of six. After my birth, she became pregnant again and had a backstreet abortion for economic reasons.

But she did her very best and she showed her love by creating a certain stability – putting a roof over our heads, clothes on our backs and food on the table. In that way, she was quite wonderful and in my adult years I came to love and appreciate her much more than I had in my youth.

IT WAS twenty-five years before I encountered my father again. A cousin had made the connection and I went to see him with some curiosity and more than a little trepidation. We agreed to meet at noon in a car park in Crawley in Sussex where he lived on social security in a one-bedroom council flat in an ugly part of a town distinguished only by its proximity to Gatwick Airport. Clearly, I also wanted to show him what I had achieved in my life without any help from him.

Leaning against a battered old Vauxhall with a blue disabled badge on the dashboard, this once distinguished marine engineer looked grey-skinned and frail and much shorter than I remembered. We shook hands and I stepped back in case he tried to hug me.

"Hello, son," he said. "It's been a long time."

"You've been drinking," I said.

"I needed some Dutch courage," he replied. He looked over my shoulder.

"That's a nice car, son. What is it? A Mercedes?"

"It's just a car… John."

We drove to a nearby hotel where we sat in the lounge and ordered coffee. He couldn't walk more than a dozen paces without pausing to rest. "I've only got one lung," he said, lighting the remains of a thin roll-up cigarette. "Damn things," he said. A laugh became a hacking cough and his eyes watered.

I tried to take him in, this man responsible for my presence in the world and for so much of the pain and trauma I had endured in my early life and that, to a degree, I still suffer from today.

There were patches of stubble where he hadn't shaved properly and he'd stuck a tiny piece of paper over a nick from the blade. His grey flannels had long since lost any crease and his shoes were scuffed and dirty. An anger momentarily rose in me and I thought: This pathetic old man is my dad.

"How," I asked him, "could you have been such a dreadful father?"

He went immediately into blame. "It wisnae all my fault! It was that old bizzim of a grandmother of yours! She never liked me from the beginning." And he went on: "Anyway, look at you. It doesn't look as if it did you any harm."

I put my head in my hands. If you only knew, father. If you only knew.

Picking up his cup with shaking hands, he spilled coffee on his already stained trousers and on the table. It embarrassed and flustered him and he tried to mop it up with a paper napkin. I suddenly felt sorry for him.

"Would you like a drink?" I asked.

"Now that's not a bad idea!" he laughed.

After a while, as I got ready to take him back to his car, he asked me for a handful of my business cards to give to his friends at the British Legion. He was proud of me.

Over the next three years until his death, most of which time I spent working in Dubai, we remained in contact and I saw him irregularly, giving him money and letting him meet his six-year-old granddaughter. But I kept him at arm's length, never allowing him to know my UK address nor to see Natalie more than once or twice a year.

Sometimes he would phone me in Dubai in the middle of the night, drunk and crying, accusing me of neglecting him and denying him access to his grandchild.

When he died from lung disease at the age of seventy-three, I arranged the funeral and notified relatives on Skye. I didn't collect the ashes.

But guilt has a grip like a bulldog's and as I moved further along my own path, exploring the inner self and finding deeper meaning to my life, I began to regret my harsh indifference. There are gifts in even the worst of happenings and I could see that our abrupt departure from Scotland to the south of England contained elements worthy of gratitude. It was an accidental blessing, but the move provided me with far greater opportunities to become a journalist. And in Gravesend, when I needed to learn shorthand and typing, two basic essentials of that trade, I only had to walk down the street to the local training college. You couldn't do that in Portree or Pitlochry, at least not then.

My father also gave me a certain self-sufficiency, an ability to be with myself without craving company or becoming too introspective. But whatever words I may use – or however long I may spend – professing acceptance or even forgiveness, there are still some wounds that may never heal.

IN THE New Year of 2017, my wife and I went over to Skye and as I drove along the narrow single-track road that runs down to our village of Carbost, my first time back in fifty years or more, I felt a distinct unease, as if it was all too long ago and much too late and there was nothing there for me now.

Even in the gentle rain, with the tops of the Cuillins obscured by hanging cloud – pretty much the normal state of island weather – Skye looked beautiful. The white-painted crofts and houses of Carbost – too many of them holiday homes these days – form a curve along the hills that slope down to the clear waters of Loch Harport, an inlet from the sea. I looked at the stony beach and a hazy memory emerged of my father landing boxes of giant crabs from a boat onto the shore and the infant me squealing in terror as they waved their claws.

To take in the view, I stopped the car half-way down the hill towards the Talisker distillery and beside a flat square of ground where a few teenage boys were playing football. Suddenly he was there among them, running and yelling with the rest, pulling and jostling as they chased the ball and each other, crashing to the ground and picking himself up again, wiping the mud from his knees and laughing loudly.

Tomorrow he would be hauling in the salmon nets on his uncle's boat or climbing his beloved Cuillins just for the thrill of having the world at his feet.

Standing by the roadside, I heard a female voice shout: "John, come away in for your tea." As the boys dispersed, I experienced a sudden emptiness and I wondered if Thomas Wolfe was right. You can't go home again.

I NEVER thought I'd be grateful to my father for much and especially not for going off to the pub, an activity that ruined his life and caused so much grief to his family.

During the last war, he was an engineer in the Merchant Navy, the branch of the armed services that suffered a greater casualty rate than any other. Twenty-seven per cent of merchant seamen are believed to have died because of enemy action. So there has always been a grudging admiration for his courage.

In 1941, a couple of years before I was born, he was sent to Liverpool to await a ship that was due in port. The shipping company put him up in a depressing boarding house near the docks. I don't really blame him for spending his evenings in the local bars.

The air raid sirens went off one night and the clientele of the pub just went down to the cellar where they carried on drinking until the all-clear sounded. When he got back to where he'd been staying, the house wasn't there. Neither was the rest of the street. I don't know what my father did then. Probably went straight back to the pub.

– 2 –

Something of an education

IF YOU LEAN towards the bright side of life, you might imagine that the name – the Gordon School for Boys – carried the suggestion of a preparatory establishment for young gentlemen. In reality, the school lay at the opposite end of the educational spectrum, a few degrees short of a correctional institution.

It specialised in metalwork and woodwork, and the administration of corporal punishment; all stick and little carrot. The teaching staff included a few gentle souls like Mr Swan who took our class to the cinema, and a sizeable gang of bad-tempered bullies like Mr Noble who would throw the whole box of chalk at you and Mr Rowlands who once sneaked up behind me in the classroom and hit me so hard on the side of the head that he knocked me off my chair – the origin, I sometimes think, of the tinnitus that has plagued me all my adult life.

The Gordon was the receptacle for any boy expelled from all the other schools in the Gravesend district, a regular intake that swelled the impressive ranks of its own home-grown hooligans. The four educational streams ranged from A for children of reasonable literacy to D for those who, back then, were classed as being of sub-normal intelligence. The school didn't do O-levels or any such exams. It didn't think anyone would pass them. When, at eleven years old, I arrived there without paperwork from any of my previous schools in Scotland, they put me in the C stream.

It didn't strike me at the time that I was paying a terrible price for my father's alcoholic meanderings around the country, dragging his family with him or forcing us to chase after him and whatever earning capacity he had left. That was just the way it was and I'd never known any other life. But it still demanded a certain resilience and constant alertness. Sometimes, after he'd disappeared without warning, it took us a while to catch up. Such had been the case with the move to Gravesend on the industrial reaches of the River Thames.

The three years until the Gordon turfed me out at the age of fifteen was the longest period I'd spent at any of the nine schools I attended in the ten years of an education (for want of a more appropriate word) that began at Tarbert Primary School on Loch Fyne. That was where – in a playground altercation on my first day – I collected a black eye and delivered a bloody lip and where we annoyed our teacher, the quite lovely Miss Heron, by insisting on calling her Miss Herring, a word with which we were much more familiar. After a while, she gave up correcting us.

Recollections of my next school in Skelmorlie, Ayrshire, are vague. I wasn't there for long but I remember we used chalk and wood-framed slates instead of pen and paper. It was also the only school where they tried – unsuccessfully – to make me write with my right hand.

From our next home, a damp pre-fab in Dunstaffnage, Argyll, it was a bus ride into Oban where I attended the Rockfield Primary School. My sister and I once missed the bus and accepted a lift from a stranger who drove us all over the place until I opened the car door and threatened to jump. Sweating, nervous and clearly undecided, he eventually stopped outside the school and told us to get out. The teacher wanted to call the police but I didn't understand the fuss. I'd never heard of paedophiles.

It was a pretty tight squeeze when the four of us went to live with my grandparents in their small cottage in Easdale, well south of Oban. To get to the local school, we twice a day crossed what locals proudly called the only bridge over the Atlantic. The whole school was contained in a large single room with two rows of desks, from the back to the front, for each of the five age groups. The miracle was that we were all taught by the one teacher, a middle-aged beanpole of a woman who seemed to possess a time-machine quality in that she could leap effortlessly from one year to another. Quite the discipli-

The old Gordon School for Boys is now a community centre but it still looks like a prison block.

narian, she also served school lunch and refused to let us leave the table until our plates were clean. I have had a powerful aversion to tomatoes ever since.

There may be a couple of other, very temporary, schools so distant in my memory that I can't remember them. Or maybe I'm just shutting them out. I recall well enough Auchtermuchty in Fife, where I spent nearly a year and where I listened on the radio to Dick Tracy and the coronation of the Queen. It was 1953 and we all got the day off school.

It was also a time of particular hardship for the family. My father had gone to sea for a year but stopped sending home money after the first month. My mother, a one-time semi-professional actress, made a little cash from elocution lessons which helped us survive. I used to cut shapes from cereal packets and stuff them into my shoes so that my socks avoided direct contact with the ground. It worked well enough until it rained.

The next stop was Glenrothes, a depressing new town with row after row of council houses and where my father found a job down the mines, working as an engineer on the big machines that cut the coal from the face. One of the peculiarities of that place was that the school dentist would come to your home in the evening, sit you in an armchair and stick a chloroform mask over your face. He only did extractions.

Our class was beginning to prepare for the Qualification Test, the

Scottish equivalent of the English 11-Plus, and a vital exam that determined if you would follow the fairly elite Grammar School path or go down the road of what is now known as a comprehensive education with all the other test failures. It was a year away and there was time.

I enjoyed acting, maybe something I'd got from my mother or because of all the real drama in my life, and I was to be the star of the school production, a role I'd rehearsed for weeks. On the eve of the play, I had to tell the drama teacher I wouldn't be able to do it. We would be flitting that night, as soon as my father could borrow a van. Sure, it was unfair that the teacher screamed his anger into my face, but who else within shouting distance could he blame?

That time we ended up in Methven in Perthshire, an undistinguished, basically one-street village between Perth and Crieff, although the surrounding area where we lived in a dilapidated country house that had been split into flats was pleasant enough. I loved helping on the next door farm where I learned to drive a tractor but I spent most of my free time roaming the hills and woods and fishing the streams.

On arrival in Methven, I discovered the Qualification Test was not a year away but the following week. Many of the questions could have been in another language. The letter to my mother didn't actually say I'd failed; just that my next school would be of the secondary kind.

Our financial situation remained critical and for some time I suffered the crippling embarrassment of being the only boy in school still in short trousers. I begged my mother repeatedly to end my misery and she eventually found a second-hand pair of long ones for a shilling or so in a jumble sale. It was the happiest day of my young life.

I remember only ever having one school friend and that was in Methven. His name was Milne Pullar. I tried looking him up online a few years ago, to no avail, although I did find on Friends Reunited a sixty-year-old group photograph of the class that I'd never seen before.

The major problem with this nomadic existence was that I was forever the new boy in school with all the unwelcome attention that attracted. A frequent target for the school bullies, I would enlist support from Katherine whose superior height and muscle power ensured they rarely troubled me again. Of course, she didn't always attend the same school and on many occasions I had to fend for myself.

PRESUMABLY, no-one in the Gordon School had previously heard a Highland accent. It generated great hilarity among my classmates and I had to make rapid adjustment.

During my time there, I suffered a hip problem that required five hours of surgery, two months in hospital and a year on crutches. When I returned to school, the younger delinquents found some sport in trying to kick the crutches from under me.

With a little practice, I developed a way of swinging a crutch fast and hard against the sides of their heads before they could flee. I would lure them in by leaning against a wall and leaving one clutch tantalisingly hanging out. When they took the bait I'd catch them with the other. What surprised me was the degree of pleasure I found in doing it and how much I anticipated their continued but less frequent attempts.

When I finally left school for good in the winter of 1958, shortly after my fifteenth birthday, I could breathe freely for the first time in a decade. But it took many more years for me to understand how I had turned my rage against the world and the grief over my lost childhood in on myself. For a long time I was hell-bent on self-destruction – drinking heavily and smoking two packs of cigarettes a day while my physical self-care was non-existent.

Many years later, my haphazard schooling finally caught up with me when I applied to a US college to study psycho-dynamics on a part-time basis. The college wanted to see proof of education. With only emotional scars to offer, it meant that at the age of fifty-six I had to sit what was basically a high school diploma along with a lot of much younger folk. It was the first exam I ever passed. Although at that time I was chairman of a successful company, it filled me with delight and a sweet sense of achievement.

– 3 –

The house in Parrock Street

THE ESTATE agent's particulars for the house in Parrock Street contained one defining sentence – 'In need of complete modernisation'. This was something of an understatement. The four-storey townhouse had changed little in the hundred years or so since the terrace of eight had been built for the river pilots who guided ships on the River Thames between Gravesend and the London docks. In 1956, completely unmodernised meant no electricity, no hot water, no bathroom and no indoor toilet. Heating was by coal fires. Lighting was by gas mantle, thin filigree cotton bags stiffened with chemicals that clipped over the wall-fitted mains gas points and had to be hand-lit carefully.

My father, when he wasn't in the pub or doing occasional shifts as an engineer on the river tugs, eventually installed electricity. Then he would disappear, sometimes for months. I would take the opportunity of his absences to raise the floorboards and rip out the old gas lead piping to sell for the only pocket money I was ever likely to receive.

Irrespective of its basic condition, the house was solid and, with a sale price of £400, gave every appearance of a bargain – were it not for the giant cuckoo in the nest. But even then, well, it was a roof over our heads and there was some pride in that it was the first property my family ever owned – even if my mother had had to borrow the money from her brothers.

It is only a small exaggeration to say that the council abattoir lay at the bottom of the garden. It didn't sit benignly alongside the potato patch. It stood, or rather squatted, hugely and meanly just ten feet beyond the back gate, the other side of the narrow access lane that ran behind the garden wall, a malevolent presence that dominated the immediate neighbourhood. With little more than three strides, I could walk from our garden gate and stand in the large double doorway that always seemed to be open, even during much of the grim business conducted within. It was a place of terrible fascination.

At the age of eleven, I had little moral indignation or enough experience of the world to be repulsed by the slaughterhouse. It was just there. It had been there when we arrived and, presumably, would be after we'd gone. And, clearly, my father and mother knew of it before they bought the house. Our acquiescence was included in the price. Neither did our neighbours seem especially bothered. Occasionally, on hot windless days when the smell of blood hung thickly and the flies congregated in intimidating clouds, the old man next door might turn up his nose and say "A bit pongy today, eh?" and carry on weeding his vegetables.

On summer nights I would lie in bed and hear the hiss of the steam hose or the terrified bellowing of the animals as they smelled their imminent despatch. From my bedroom window, I could watch through that open doorway as they hauled a pig's carcass up on block and tackle and attacked it with knives and steam, its skin stripped in minutes, perhaps destined to become handbags or gloves.

The slaughterhouse wasn't operational all the time. Sometimes it would sit for days in brooding silence. Then a cattle truck or pig transporter would appear, reversing down the narrow back street that linked at right angles with the alleyway. It always seemed to arrive in the evening. The alley would be sealed off, the truck ramp lowered and the animals driven noisily into an interior pen next to the killing room. Local children gathered to watch, all of us hoping for the great escape. Occasionally, if a gap had been left by the surrounding workmen, a bullock would make a bid for freedom and we would chase after it whooping excitedly as it ran for its life down the street, scattering cyclists and pedestrians. Sadly, I don't recall one that wasn't recaptured or, if deemed enough of a danger, brought down by a marksman. We never stopped hoping. Maybe the next one would make it.

Within a short time, the killing would begin. Perhaps it was a kindly thing to do, rather than leave them lamenting through the night. We were never allowed to watch, nor would we have wanted to. The animals were stunned first and then shot by a gun with a heavy steel spike that penetrated the skull through the front of the head. The foreman sometimes showed us the guns they used.

Only in later years did I feel the horror of those events. At the time, I accepted them because they were part of the trauma of my sudden departure from the hills and forests of the Scottish Highlands, from the streams and lochs, and my arrival in this dilapidated town with its busy, dirty streets and foreign language.

The abattoir is long demolished, its site now covered by a road, on the other side of which lie blocks of council flats. Gone too is the house in Parrock Street and its contents of hardship, confrontation and struggle, bulldozed with the rest of the old terrace to make way for a row of modern townhouses. But I wonder if the residents, lying awake at night, sometimes hear the distant cries of animals.

– 4 –

Read all about it

I HAVE LITTLE in the way of meaningful objects from times long gone – a few newspaper and magazine cuttings, some old photos, a fifty-year-old address book and a couple of letters in a well-worn wallet, plus bits and pieces that I've put away for reasons I can't now remember. These and more are contained in a large square orange and red box my wife has labelled 'Ian's Special Things.'

One of the letters has some significance. Well, they both do, but we'll stick with the first. It reads:

> Dear Ian,
> I am pleased to offer you the position of junior reporter with the *Kent Messenger* at a salary of £3.6s.6d. per week. Please telephone me to arrange a convenient start date. I look forward to welcoming you to the team.
>
> Yours sincerely,
> Henry Cohn, editor,
> Gravesend and North Kent edition

When I first opened it, expecting the worst, I let out a yell that brought the family running and possibly had the neighbours across the street peeking from behind their curtains. After passing it around amid showers of congratulations, I folded the letter carefully back into its crisp white envelope, said I'd be back in a while and caught the bus to the town library where I found my usual seat in the reading room, the place where I could always guarantee space and peace. I took the file of the *Kent Messenger*, a large circulation weekly, from the rack and laid it on the table in front of me.

I sat, head down, shedding tears silently, betrayed only by an occasional soft sniffle and a quiet blowing of the nose. But no-one looked up or paid any attention. Maybe they thought I had a cold.

I might have wondered at the tears, but not for long. The whole gamut – or maybe in my case gauntlet – of emotion was present: An enormous sense of joy and achievement mixed bizarrely with the profound sadness and pain and loneliness that had claimed so much of my life until that point. All the failures, mine and my father's, all the humiliations, gathered in on me, needing acknowledgment. All the anguish and distress of school and home life rose up in protest as if resisting the push from their tightly-held compartments of my consciousness by the waves of delight that were coursing through me.

For here, in this little envelope, was a freedom I had never known, a powerful promise of a whole new and exciting world. How incredibly smart, how bloody brilliant of me, I thought, to have taken a secretarial course immediately after leaving the Gordon School for Boys. At the North Kent Technical College I learned 130 words per minute Pitman's shorthand, fifty words a minute touch typing, domestic science and a lot more about girls than I had previously imagined. In our class there had been thirty of them and me.

The shortlist had come down to a grammar schoolboy and me. Henry, a round, bald-headed man in his mid-forties, told me later that my arrival in the interview room with the vital tools of the trade already in my pocket had overcome his understandable misgivings about the Gordon School. And I had sold myself well.

I've occasionally wondered about the boy who didn't get the job. Did he continue to seek work in newspapers? Or did he abandon the idea of journalism in his disappointment and do something boring, like accountancy?

My mother, by then a teacher, loaned me the price of a new suit and a couple of weeks later I sat on the bus to the office for the first time. I could not have been happier. In my mind, I was the defender of Press freedom, the exposer of crime and corruption, the protector of public rights, the conscience of the local authorities. I was Clark Kent looking for a phone box. I was still fifteen years old.

The first job Henry gave me was rolling up the subscription copies of the newspaper and licking the address labels, more than fifty of them every week. It would get better, I thought, and it did. I was assigned to cover the magistrates' court every other morning and also given my own geographical districts around Gravesend, two fifteen-mile circuits that each encompassed two or three villages. Twice a week, I would borrow my sister's bicycle and claim the bus fares, my first lessons in the great journalistic tradition of fiddling expenses. There had been an office motor bike but the previous junior reporter had written it off and nearly himself with it and there would not be another. At least my mother was pleased.

In each village I would call on the vicar, the women's institute, the local Nosy Parkers in the hope of a scandal, the pub, the police station – if there was one – and the teashop in hope of a free cream bun. The landlord of the pub in Longfield, where I got a free half-pint, said to me one day: "Hey, Ian, I might have a story for you."

"Really, Bill. What's that?"

"I'm building a forty-foot motor cruiser," he explained. "Taken me five years and it's nearly finished."

"Where is it?" I asked. "Down on the coast?"

"Naw," he said. "It's in the back yard. Come and have a look."

There was a magnificent sleek-lined vessel, surrounded by a high and solid stone wall.

"Fantastic, Bill!" I said. "How are you going to get it out without knocking down the wall?"

"Ah," he replied. "I'm working on that."

Obviously, it was a brilliant story.

"Well done, boy," said Henry, who always called me boy. "Just put the facts together and I'll knock it into shape."

I had sleepless nights before the paper appeared with a big picture and story and my first ever byline. But on that same day, I also saw the story and picture in all three of the London evening newspapers. I knew how they'd got it. Henry and chief reporter Roy were their local correspondents and probably made more money from their freelance work than from their regular jobs.

"Once a story is published," said Henry, "it's in the public domain and there's no copyright," indicating that I wouldn't see a penny of the proceeds.

"That's theft," I said.

"No, boy," said Henry. "That's life."

I DID LEARN one important lesson on the perils that lie within complacency. The Southfleet village council met on a Wednesday evening once a month and the eight miles along dark country lanes with a dim and faltering front light made it a fraught bike ride. Once, in a bitterly cold wind and unrelenting rain, I gave up pretty quickly and turned back, phoning the clerk of the council the next morning for the usual uninteresting bits and pieces on motions passed or denied.

On the Friday, Henry called me in. He said nothing but shoved across his desk the *Gravesend and Dartford Reporter*, our bitter rival. 'VILLAGE COUNCILLORS IN MASS BRAWL!' screamed the main headline, exclamation mark and all.

"I got a puncture halfway there and had to wheel it back," I lied. "Honestly."

Henry looked at me. "Have you ever considered another career?" he asked. "You might want to give it some thought. I don't think you're cut out to be journalist."

We had, briefly, the services of a third reporter. Dennis was an elderly homosexual and a drunk so life for him was difficult in the unenlightened era of the late 1950s and early '60s. I once had to cover a case at the magistrates' court where it was Dennis in the dock and where a policeman was reading from his notes:

"I was lying on the roof of the public convenience on Windmill Hill observing the accused engage in an illegal activity with a sailor. I shouted to them to stop but as I tried to get down from the roof, I fell and broke my ankle. The two gentlemen were very concerned for my welfare, made me comfortable and stayed with me until assistance arrived, whereupon I told the accused: 'You're nicked!'"

The chairman of the magistrates was so impressed by Dennis's selflessness that he gave him a conditional discharge, thereby saving his job. It proved, however, to be only a stay of execution. Called in on his day off to cover the annual Girl Guides *fête*, Dennis had spent all morning in the pub and by the time he got to this major local event he was desperate for a pee. With no toilet in the immediate vicinity and being totally blitzed, he urinated in the middle of the lawn, exposing himself to parents, Guides and the chief inspector's wife.

Court reporting was pleasant and fairly easy, although at times I was consumed by embarrassment. Sex cases were presented meticulously and I would blush fiercely. In those days, child victims had to take the witness box, face their abusers and describe the assault in precise detail. If it was excruciating painful for me to hear them, it was undoubtedly a terrifying ordeal for them. Yet they usually did it with great courage, if not composure, while I had my head buried in my hands, or carving my initials on the desktop with my ballpoint pen.

The *Kent Messenger* was a wonderful launch pad for my career and even if Henry was never much of a teacher, he will always have my gratitude for the opportunity and for the guidance he did give me. Some years after I left, I was in Gravesend again and invited him out for a drink.

He hadn't changed much, maybe a little rounder. Roy, he said, was now a senior executive at headquarters in Maidstone but he preferred the little office and the quiet life, not to speak of the freelancing proceeds.

"And what are you up to these days, boy?" he asked, sipping his half-pint of bitter.

"I'm a senior sub-editor with the *Daily Express* in Fleet Street," I replied with unrestrained glee.

"Well, there you go," said Henry. "Didn't I always say you'd make it to the top?"

– 5 –

My role in the Cuban missile crisis

I HAD BOUGHT the small red transistor radio for seven dollars plus sales tax in one of the multitude of electronics shops that dominated the area around Times Square, New York. It had one wheel that controlled the volume and another that sought to navigate through the plethora of commercial radio stations squeezed into a narrow AM bandwidth. It wasn't easy to isolate one station without overlap from another. The radio had been made in Japan – not entirely a guarantee of quality back in 1962 – and sounded as if the speaker had been formed from a squashed tin can. But it worked, mostly, even if the back fell off repeatedly until I kept it closed with sticky tape.

I propped it up against the window of my surprisingly spacious cabin on the SS *City of Brisbane*, a 10,500-ton British cargo ship that plied its trade between Montreal and Australasia, calling at multiple ports in between.

My presence on the ship owed everything to a regular contact on my rounds as a junior reporter with the *Kent Messenger*. Bill Richardson, owner of the Nelson Hotel on the corner of Windmill Street and one or two other relatively upmarket hostelries around the town, used to regale me with tales of life on the ocean waves as a senior purser with Ellerman Lines. In his sixties, silver-haired and retaining a Cary Grant smoothness that charmed his female clientele and infuriated his ever-watchful wife Pam, Bill took a shine to me and filled my head and my dreams with images of tropical climes, distant horizons and maidens fair and foul.

"I can have a word with my friends at Ellerman if you fancy giving it a go," he ventured.

"Can you call them today?" I replied without hesitation. I'd have said yes to a cross-Channel ferry if it would get me away from Gravesend and all the town held for me.

And so it was that as a junior assistant purser with one thin gold band on a white background on the sleeve of my brand new officer's uniform, I flew out of Heathrow on an aged propeller-driven Douglas DC-6 to join the ship in Montreal via a refuelling stop in Gander, Newfoundland.

When my even more ancient suitcase tumbled down the conveyor in Montreal and smashed against the wall of the carousel, it burst open and scattered its contents. Our captain, Tommy Kirk, and the other officers waited patiently as I scrambled around collecting socks and underwear and pleading with baggage handlers for bits of string to tie it back together.

Since this was a cargo ship without passengers, there was only the purser and myself running the department.

"You take charge of the cooks and officers' stewards," he said. "Draw up the menu for the next day's service in the officers' dining room, keep stock of the provisions and make lists of whatever we need to buy in each port."

I also had to issue tobacco and wage advances to the seventy-strong crew of deckhands, oilers and firemen, cooks and stewards, all Asians. The government of India had decreed that British shipping firms trading there had to carry crews of that nationality. This suited the companies since the men were genuinely hard-working and were paid less than British crewmen.

The purser continued: "You can look after the surgery as well."

He handed me the keys and a copy of the *Ship Captain's Medical Guide* and offered to consult if anything tricky came up.

"Just pray we don't get an appendicitis in the middle of the Pacific."

That was how I happened to be allocated the otherwise empty doctor's cabin with its sizeable bunk, daybed, writing desk, armchair and hand basin. And why I was able to lean my little radio against a proper window that overlooked the main deck.

We set sail from Montreal down the great St Lawrence River, call-

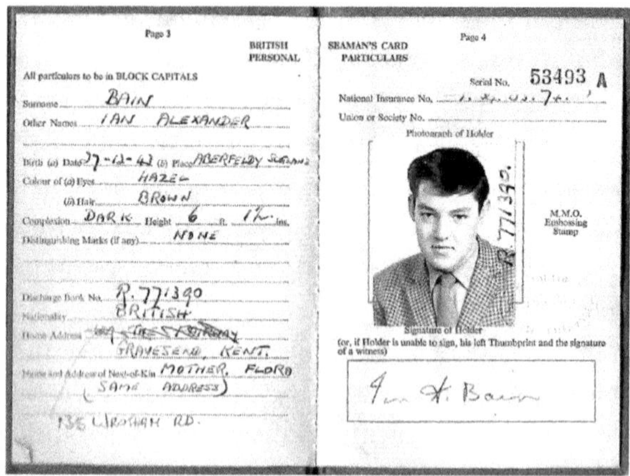

Page 3

BRITISH PERSONAL

All particulars to be in BLOCK CAPITALS

Surname: BAIN

Other Names: IAN ALEXANDER

Birth (a) Date: 27-12-42 (b) Place: ABERFELDY SCOTLAND

Colour of (a) Eyes: HAZEL

(b) Hair: BROWN

Complexion: DARK Height 6 ft. 1½ ins.

Distinguishing Marks (if any): NONE

Discharge Book No.: R.771390

Nationality: BRITISH

Home Address: GRAVESEND, KENT.

Name and Address of Next-of-Kin: MOTHER, FLORA (SAME ADDRESS)

135 WROTHAM RD.

Page 4

SEAMAN'S CARD PARTICULARS

Serial No. 53493 A

National Insurance No.

Union or Society No.

Photograph of Holder

R.771390.

M.M.O. Embossing Stamp

Signature of Holder (or, if Holder is unable to sign, his left Thumbprint and the signature of a witness)

Ian A. Bain

ing at Quebec and Three Rivers, then out into the wild Atlantic, rounding Cape Breton Island for Portland, Boston, New York, Philadelphia and onwards south, places of absolute delight to an eighteen year old more familiar with the views across the Thames to the Tilbury power station.

These were the days long before containerisation and each stop seemed a leisurely affair, taking days to load cargoes of steel tubing, automobiles, heavy equipment and manufactured goods.

We were rarely more than twenty miles from shore, about the outer limit of my little radio's reception and it sang to me all day and into the night, helped by a regular supply of batteries from the chief electrician. *I can't stop loving you,* warbled Ray Charles while Johnny Tillitson implored his girl to send him the pillow that she dreamed on and Elvis lamented 'she's not you'.

In Brooklyn, we bought a record player and a pile of 45s and invited the nurses from the local hospital to a party in the officers' mess at the end of which, chivalrous as I was, I offered to accompany a pretty young nurse to her home. She said she lived in Queens. "No problem," I said, unaware that Queens was about ninety minutes away by subway.

After a semi-chaste kiss on her doorstep, I set off again on the long haul back to the ship which was docked at the end of Brooklyn's 40th Street, only to discover that at that time of the morning, the subway trains didn't venture beyond the Brooklyn Bridge.

The gang warfare that had brought notoriety to Brooklyn in the 1950s had given way to an uneasy truce in the early 1960s but taxi drivers at night apparently didn't take fares into the still-disputed territory that lay along the forty blocks that lay in front of me. It was like one of those movies where humanity has been wiped out and the only life that existed belonged to stray cats and wild dogs. That was until I saw a group of youths standing under a lamp post.

I could cross the street and reveal my terror or carry on towards them and try to hide it in bravado, I thought. I chose the latter and as I approached, there was the sound of song. They were harmonising in the old barbershop tradition.

From the tables down at Mory's
To the place where Louie dwells
To the dear old Temple bar we love so well
See the Whiffenpoofs assembled
With their glasses raised on high
And the magic of their singing casts its spell.

It was utterly beautiful and I might have stopped for a moment if it hadn't seemed like tempting fate. Why they were in that place and at that time were questions that didn't, in the circumstances, urgently require answers.

In Newport News, Virginia, the third mate and I headed for a dancehall renowned for the presence of large numbers of unaccompanied young ladies. We invited two of them to dance and they stood bemused as my friend and I started doing the Twist – until we looked around and saw that everyone was doing something else and we hadn't a clue what it was. The Twist, we realised, had come and gone.

Out of Newport News with a load of precision tools for New Zealand, we headed for Charleston, South Carolina, and on to Savannah, Georgia, where I was threatened with arrest for insisting on sitting next to an Indian crewman on the bus from the port to the city. The driver refused to move until I did. It was my first experience of the ugliness of segregation.

My little radio continued to belt out tinny but recognisable tunes. Bob Pickett headed the charts with *Monster Mash*, The Four Seasons had us believe that *Big girls don't cry* and Marcie Blane wanted to be Bobby's girl.

But in between the numbers, and with increasing frequency, came alarming news bulletins. Off the coast of Florida, we heard: "The government has confirmed the presence of nuclear missile silos both complete and under construction on Cuba."

The newsreader added breathlessly: "The Governor of Florida has asked all citizens to remain calm, and advises there is no need for panic buying," while at the same time revealing that some supermarkets were already bare of essentials like tinned goods, sugar, flour and frozen foods. Tempers frayed as long lines of cars formed at filling stations and off-duty military personnel were instructed to return to their bases immediately.

There was something surreal about our ship ploughing onward through a calm sea of an amazingly light blue while dolphins danced alongside and towering cotton wool clouds punctuated an otherwise featureless seascape. The only sounds came from the constant and comforting throb of the steam turbine engine and the gentle swish of the bow wave. Yet, just beyond the horizon, America was nearing chaos.

As Fort Lauderdale radio slipped away, I re-tuned to WAXY Radio South Miami to hear President John F Kennedy tell the nation of the imminent possibility of a nuclear war unless Soviet ships carrying missiles to Cuba were turned around. On 22 October, the US Strategic Air Command was ordered to DEFCON 2, the stage before a nuclear war. Long-range US Air Force bombers circled over the North Atlantic and Europe, constantly refuelling in the air while missiles were prepared for firing from silos throughout the United States.

Meanwhile, listeners were invited to buy a new Chevrolet from South Florida's favourite dealer and told that nobody served better key lime pie than Alfredo. Duane Eddy wanted listeners to *Dance with the guitar man*, Antony Newly wondered what kind of fool he was and Tony Bennett left his heart in San Francisco. All might have seemed right with the world.

English-language broadcasts from Florida and the Bahamas gave way to outpourings of hysterical Spanish as we neared Cuba, intent on making our way around the north of the island, through the Windward Passage and on to the Panama Canal for the twenty-one-day voyage across the Pacific to New Zealand and Australia.

In the officers' mess, we gathered round the short-wave radio for news from the BBC that sounded more menacing by the hour. Captain Kirk told us of wax-sealed instructions in the ship's safe that were to be opened in the event of war.

Cuba appeared on the starboard side, the Sierra Maestra range – where Fidel Castro had planned his revolution – rising directly from the sea in a blue haze. As we stood on deck, an American warship approached rapidly on the port bow. It came within a few hundred metres, its men lining the decks and its guns trained on us. Then in a minute it was gone. A US Navy jet sent us to the deck as it roared in at sea level, turning on its side at the last moment so that a wing-tip passed between the foremast and the bridge and leaving behind shattered eardrums. Almost immediately, all was quiet again. The sky remained blue and the sea calm. It was as if nothing had happened.

We heard on the BBC, with great relief, that Soviet leader Nikita Khrushchev had blinked first and agreed to remove all missiles from Cuba. We later learned that, in return, the US would dismantle missile sites in Turkey.

A couple of weeks later we were in mid-Pacific on a course for Auckland. Some evenings I would sit out on deck watching the stars or the mesmerising phosphorescence cast up by the bow wave, still a little amazed at how far I had travelled, not just in distance.

I don't know why one night I turned on my AM-only transistor radio with its very short range reception limit. But thanks to the peculiarities of the atmosphere at night, I heard a sparklingly clear voice from more than 3,000 miles way: "This is KTKZ 1380 AM Sacramento, the station for slow and easy listening," said the DJ, after which Gene Pitney sang how *Only love can break a heart*, Brenda Lee lamented she was all alone and the velvet voice of Nat King Cole recalled the charms of *Ramblin' Rose*.

My little red radio eventually gave way to a super all-singing-and-dancing multi-band extravaganza and a sound quality to dream of. But I wish I'd kept it… as a reminder of interesting times.

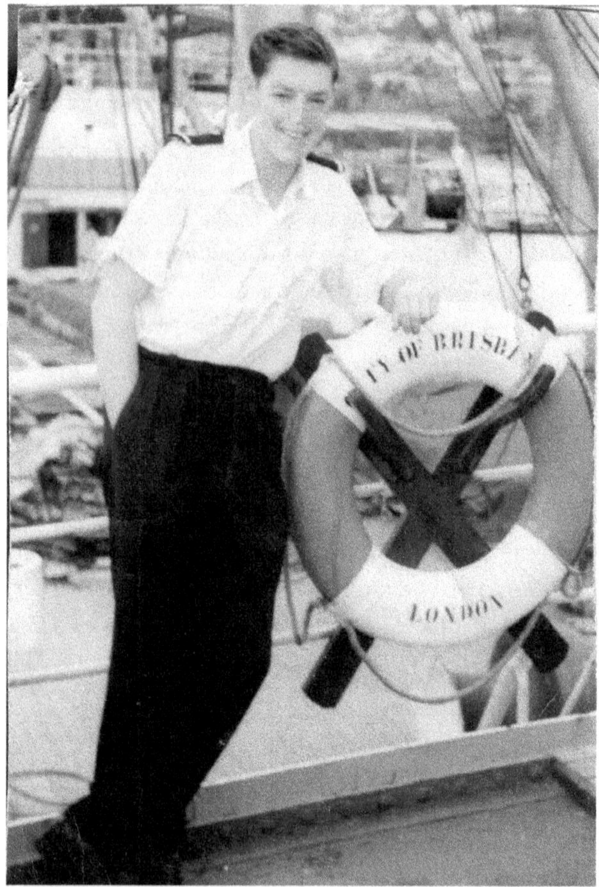

On the SS City of Brisbane *in Wellington Harbour, 1962.*

– 6 –

Smugglers three

IT WOULD be tempting, but not totally correct, to claim that I come from a long line of big-time booze smugglers. In truth, it's a pretty short one. There was an ancestor, distant in both time and kinship, who reputedly made his fortune in South America from nefarious activities that included the illicit movement of alcohol, an uncle who outran or outwitted the US Coastguard during the glory days of prohibition in the 1920s – and myself.

What the three of us had in common, apart from the obvious, was that our adventures were conducted in exotic, far-away places. Not for us any amateurish campervan-across-the-Channel caper. We were in the big-money league… well, maybe I was more on the edge of it, but each of us could have gone to jail for a long time in not very hospitable parts of the world.

The ancestor, whose name I completely forget, centred his operations in Brazil and returned with his riches to Scotland where he enjoyed a long and very comfortable retirement and judged his expiration perfectly, his money running out at about the same time as he did.

My uncle, Farquhar Macdonald, my mother's eldest brother, was the engineer on a small but fast freighter that shipped great quantities of Scotch and Canadian whiskies from the Bahamas along the Eastern seaboard of the United States, what was known in the prohibition days as Rum Row.

I'm uncertain how he found the job, but he once told me: "It got too dangerous trying to bring the cargo ashore ourselves so we used to stop just outside the three-mile limit anywhere up the coast from

Florida to New Jersey. It would be picked up by very speedy flat-bottomed cruisers that could zip it right up onto the beach.

"Other rum runners could be more of a problem than the Coastguard because they sometimes tried to hijack our load. But they didn't come near us after we mounted a machine gun on the deck."

Farquhar, who said he once featured on an FBI wanted list under the name of 'Farter' Macdonald, was made redundant when the US extended its maritime limit to twelve miles, making it much more difficult for the smaller vessels in heavy seas. In any case, prohibition was nearing its end. He enjoyed a long career as an engineer and went on to run a remnants shop in Brechin. What an interesting obituary the *Dundee Courier* might have had.

As for myself, I didn't set out to be a smuggler but I did nothing to avoid it. Nor did I really consider the risks. I was a nineteen-year-old assistant purser on the SS *City of Hull*, a freighter sailing from the UK to India with cargoes of heavy machinery and agricultural equipment. The year was 1963 and there was, shall we say, a window of opportunity. It was a time when all manufacturing, purchase, transport and consumption of alcohol in the state of Maharashtra had been prohibited, creating an enormous appetite for contraband.

The purser, who had put me in charge of catering, stores, crew wages, the ship's accounts, first aid and a few other things, suggested I should also take command of the smuggling operation, including whatever requirements arose for bribery and corruption. It was a nice little set-up shared only by the two of us until, that is, the captain caught me lowering cases of whisky into small boats in the dead of night and indicated that a ten-per-cent cut would be a reasonable reward for a blind eye.

Only afterwards did I realise that by removing himself from any physical activity, Ted the purser could deny all knowledge and if anyone was to go to jail, it would not be him.

On the India route, most ships stopped at Aden at the southern end of the Red Sea for cheap fuel and to replenish supplies. A British protectorate and a free zone in what is now Yemen, Aden with its barren rocks was a port where you could purchase anything at fairly exceptional prices. Ted and I bought several hundred cases of Scotch at £7 a case and piled them into bonded and unbonded storerooms on board the ship, filling every available space within our control. You might wonder where the money came from. Since we managed the ship's funds, we simply borrowed it from the safe without really considering that doing so was, in fact, a serious criminal offence.

My personal shopping consisted of a hundred or more leather-cased Sanyo short-wave radios which were subject to heavy import duty in India and on which I'd been told by old India hands that I could triple my outlay. The stacks of boxes took up an inordinate amount of space in my cabin.

THE RANN of Kutch was a short voyage from Aden across the gentle swell of the Arabian Sea, following the mountainous coastline of Oman for part of the way. The Rann is a flat desolate area of salt marshes where the temperature reaches fifty degrees in the summer and zero in the winter and where fishermen in humble boats were casting nets for small sub-surface fish. With a pilot on board to keep us off the mudflats, the ship edged nervously along the narrow dredged channel. There were no docks nor even a distinguishable port. We anchored half a mile offshore, opened the forward hatches and prepared to unload our cargo into battered wooden barges towed alongside by a tug that belched thick black smoke into the hazy sunshine.

A Customs launch approached on the port side. Sailors lowered the gangway and a group of four heavily braided officials came on board. After tea and niceties in the purser's office, they inspected the bonded storeroom with its stacks of booze and, with a smile and a wave of dismissal that seemed to reinforce the expectation of a gift, declined to check its contents against the manifest.

The excisemen asked for a gluepot and brush and pasted a sheet of paper across the edge of the steel door and its frame. Signed and stamped, it was a simple but effective seal since opening the door would tear the paper and land us in a lot of expensive trouble. Customs officers in our next port, Bombay, would have to be present when the room was next unlocked.

A bottle of Scotch and a carton of two hundred cigarettes per man was the usual consideration. Failure to participate in the traditional expression of goodwill might have resulted in a search of the entire ship, a delay in leaving port and a very angry captain. They left happily but not without planting an idea in my head for the next encounter with their colleagues.

THE BOMBAY Roads is not a network of streets but a large area of sea a few miles off this most cosmopolitan of all India's cities. It's a vast holding area where cargo ships laid up, often for several days, while waiting for a berth in the busy port. In that age before containerisation, unloading and loading were comparatively long processes and much of the ship's business with port officials, shippers, agents and Customs officers was conducted while we remained at anchor.

On a bright and sticky summer's morning, I emerged on deck and looked around in amazement at possibly fifty or sixty ships of all sizes and nationalities, an armada that seemed to stretch to the horizon. How many of these, I wondered, were full of whisky.

Distant thunderclouds heralded the imminent arrival of the monsoon rains but the sea was relatively calm and dozens of small launches buzzed back and forth between the freighters and the shore. After breakfast, the purser summoned me.

"There's someone here you should meet, Ian," he said. "Why don't you take him into the office."

Pleasantries exchanged, my visitor got to the point.

"I understand you are the person to see about the purchase of certain commodities. Provided they are good brands, I'll pay £20 a case for as many as you want to sell."

"£30," I said, "money up front and any losses are yours."

"I can't go beyond £25," he replied.

"Agreed, but I'll also need you to take one hundred Sanyo radios at £20 each."

For the next two nights, a flotilla of small boats without lights approached on the shadow side of the ship and I recruited a few of my crew – with suitable compensation, of course – to lower the contraband onto tiny decks that skittered alarmingly in the swell. One case hit the water but a boatman quickly retrieved it.

On the journey from the Rann of Kutch I had experimented with how much Lyle's Golden Syrup I could add to the pot of glue without it looking suspicious. By the time we reached Bombay, I felt I had got the mixture just about right. Putting it to the test with the Customs officials was an experience fraught with anxiety but they didn't notice anything amiss and, on their departure, I was able to peel back the paper seal, giving me access to the rest of the merchandise.

It was considered wise to spread the trade among two or three buyers and when I agreed a sale with another visitor I asked casually if this was his full-time business. It was just a way of making conversation over coffee.

"Oh, no," he said. "I'm a Customs officer."

I still feel a sense of pride that I didn't instantly piss myself but I recall a vision of iron bars and a grim prison cell packed with unfortunates like me.

He saw the blood drain from my face and laughed. "Don't worry. This is my second job."

MANY, MANY years later my Indian wife-to-be introduced me to her parents who were visiting Dubai from their home in Chennai. They were not aware at the time that we were romantically involved.

"Have you been to India?" asked Sharadha's father.

"Oh yes," I replied, and regaled them with the tale of my smuggling adventures without noticing their growing discomfort or Sharadha's worried frown, so lost was I in the tale. When she told them some time later of our intention to marry, they were initially not at all pleased. It was understandable. Apart from cultural differences, who would want an unrepentant criminal in the family?

CAPTAIN BROADBENT was a nervous man, which was understandable after years in a Japanese prisoner-of-war camp. On his ship, safety was everything. Our weekly fire and lifeboat drills were carried out meticulously. I was in charge of the stretcher party and we sometimes had to strap a crew member into a special maritime stretcher and haul him up ladders from the depths of the hold. In hot and heavy weather, no-one ever volunteered to be the injured party so I always chose the smallest guy. He must have hated me.

The captain was a stickler for ensuring what is called a positive GM or metacentric height which determines the stability of the ship, empty or full. When we picked up a cargo in Mozambique of Zambian copper and Rhodesian tobacco, it was clear to him that all the copper had to be loaded into the very bottom of the holds.

We had come from the Arabian Gulf, steaming empty across the Indian Ocean at only six knots because the tobacco crop wasn't ready. It had been a dreadful three-week voyage through the monsoon but it wasn't until, fully loaded, we reached the Bay of Biscay homeward bound that the captain and the rest of us realised he may have been over-cautious.

We ran into an enormous swell from a storm in mid-Atlantic. The waves were forty feet and more and terrifying to look at. They came at us broadside and the ship would roll dreadfully one way, hover at an impossible angle, and roll back, doing the same at the other side. The copper was acting as a pendulum and it seemed that it wouldn't be long before we went over.

Eventually, the helmsman turned her head-on into the waves – a precarious movement in itself – and the captain reduced speed to a minimum so that we just held position while the huge waters crashed over the bow for many hours on end. If I learned anything it was how big ships in big seas really can disappear without trace.

– 7 –

Man of mystery

SEAN TOOLAN was one of those people who, once they've crossed your path, continue to do so again and again until you feel that coincidence is simply not a reasonable explanation.

I first met him when he was escorted by the editor onto the editorial floor of the *Western Morning News*, the Plymouth-based regional daily newspaper where I had recently begun work as a news sub-editor after leaving the Merchant Navy.

My three years at sea, even on reflection decades later, were among the happiest of my life, and I nearly stayed on because I'd enjoyed them so much and because getting back into journalism proved far from easy. I had chased a dozen jobs in the South of England without success – too long out of newspapers, most editors said – when I saw an ad in the *UK Press Gazette* for a sub-editor for the weekly *Cornish Guardian* in Truro. I was forlorn when I heard the vacancy had been filled so I went back to sea on a coasting trip – loading up the ship at different ports around the UK and Europe before handing over to a deep-sea crew. We were docked in Bristol when a letter arrived via my mother from the *Western Morning News* saying that the *Cornish Guardian*, a sister paper, had passed on my application and would I care to come down for an interview. I still wonder at times how my life might have unfolded had that not happened.

I took the next day off work, got the deck crew to unload my Lambretta scooter and putted off merrily to the city of Drake and the Pilgrim fathers where I was offered the job at a salary that seemed well beyond my expectations.

"Would seventeen-ten be acceptable?" the editor asked.

"That's fine, sir," I replied, resisting an urge to thank him for his generosity.

On receipt of the appointment letter, I realised he'd meant £17.10s a week and not £1,710 a year, requiring a reassessment that meant, to achieve a near-meeting of ends, I had to take a lunchtime job as a barman while working nights on the newspaper. Even then, I often had to pawn my suit and my record collection towards the end of each month. I wasn't yet twenty-two and the year was 1965.

With decent readerships, strong local advertising and a blend of national and local news, provincial daily newspapers had not then begun the sad decline that was to make journalism a precarious profession and newspaper ownership a very risky business. Most people got their news through the Press and there was plenty of it in the Sixties. Cases like the Profumo sex scandal, the Great Train Robbery and the dreadful Moors Murders doubled circulations overnight.

The latter particularly stays in my mind. Because of the very distressing evidence presented against killers Ian Brady and Myra Hindley, who were initially charged with the murders and sexual assault of three children, the Press Association news agency reported every word – even the full transcription of the tape of a child begging her abusers to stop hurting her – and left it to the individual newspapers to decide how much of this horrendous material to publish.

I had the task of editing the story over the fourteen days of the trial, making me the judge of what was – and what was not – appropriate for readers to know. Public interest was intense and there had to be a delicate balance. Too much detail would undoubtedly offend and too little could lead to accusations of unnecessary censorship. It was ridiculous for the editor to entrust someone of my age with that responsibility but we didn't have a single complaint, one way or the other.

Plymouth had long been maligned as a Navy town full of drunken sailors but I found it quite delightful. To the north, Dartmoor began where the city limits ended while the beaches and resorts of South Devon and Cornwall were reasonably short scooter rides away, journeys sometimes shared by some of those West Country girls whose rosy complexions and rounded vowels held equal charm. My basement flat on the Hoe cost five pounds a week and was the first real home I had to myself, other than my cabin at sea.

SEAN WAS introduced to us as being relatively new to journalism. He was to start as a junior sub-editor and the editor hoped he would be warmly welcomed by his new colleagues. In his mid-twenties, tall, handsome in an aristocratic way and with a shadow of a moustache long before designer stubble came into vogue, he'd had a short-term commission in the Irish Guards but spoke with that terribly English accent the BBC used to require of its announcers. None of us ever heard the hint of a brogue.

It was said that Sean was acquainted with the Rothermeres who owned the *Daily Mail* which, in turn, owned the *Western Morning News*, but there was never an indication that he wasn't up to the job. The consensus among us was that he'd been dropped into Plymouth to learn the trade before elevation to the big league in Fleet Street. He neither acknowledged nor denied it, perhaps because he was continually cultivating the air of mystery that held him apart from the rest of us.

Sean enjoyed being aloof and was, to some degree, a narcissist. While he gave little away in terms of himself or his possessions and was slow in buying a round, he would readily take advantage of the generosity of others. He borrowed my flat for a few days while I was on holiday and didn't apologise for leaving it in an utterly dreadful mess. That's not to say he wasn't likeable and easy to forgive; people wanted to be his friend. Sometimes he would show up in the pub with glamorous ladies from London which all added to the mystique, not to speak of the jealousy.

It wasn't too long before Sean announced he'd been offered a job on the *Daily Mail* which, we all agreed, was no surprise. Nor was it a surprise when he borrowed my large naval trunk and never got round to returning it.

After I'd also moved on, we bumped into each other in Fleet Street, had a drink, talked about fun times in Plymouth and promised to meet regularly but never did.

A few years later, on a flying visit to Chicago, I was reading the *Chicago Tribune* over breakfast in my hotel when I noticed a lengthy article about some famous dog sleigh race in the frozen north – by Sean Toolan. I managed to get through to him at the newspaper and we had a particularly drunken night touring Chicago's many Irish bars where he sang rebel songs. Once more we parted with promises but with little likelihood of ever meeting again.

I really didn't think much more about him until he turned up in the office of the *Observer* where I was working on the sports desk. He was his usual charming self, didn't look that much older although he must have been in his late thirties by then, and we repaired to the office pub, the Cockpit, for another night of gentle but serious inebriation.

It was at the time of the civil war in Lebanon, a particularly long and bloody conflict, and he was the *Observer*'s new Beirut correspondent, contracted on a freelance basis. It was an assignment of intense attraction to someone of Sean's character. His enthusiasm was such that it seemed as if being a war correspondent was the ultimate job in journalism, that all his years of minor adventure and desk-bound achievement were simply passing time.

He embraced it with enormous vigour. His descriptive writings, analyses, interviews with faction leaders and stories on the suffering of the people were insightful and well-produced and he was highly regarded on the editorial floors of the *Observer*.

In that time, I had moved to Dubai where I set up in public relations but continued to write occasionally for the newspaper. At one time or another Sean and I may well have had bylines on the same page, although my stuff was relatively pedestrian.

Even when people you know put themselves into dangerous situations, there's a tendency to believe that, regardless of the risk, they will come through unscathed so there was little to minimise the shock when I read the headline 'OBSERVER JOURNALIST SEAN TOOLAN KILLED IN BEIRUT'.

He had been stabbed four times in the chest and shot once in the back on the steps of the Commodore Hotel, the headquarters of the foreign press throughout the war. There was obvious speculation that he'd been murdered over something he'd written or that it was a targeted killing by an anti-Western group.

The truth that eventually emerged was quite different but curiously appropriate to Sean's cavalier nature. He and another man, unknown to each other, were having affairs with the wife of a Western diplomat. For Sean it was a deadly liaison. The other man was the leader of a local militia who, after discovering his rival's existence, lay in wait with some of his men outside the Commodore. From the nature of his defensive wounds, the medical examiner ventured that Sean "must have put up a hell of a fight."

After the war, I had to go to Beirut on business and my secretary told me she'd booked me into the Meridian. On arrival, I found it was the Meridian Commodore and it occurred to me that the story of Sean Toolan, even years after his death, was still ongoing.

On the steps where he died, I said a silent prayer for the man with whom I'd shared an unusual history and vaguely considered a friend, but paradoxically had never really liked. He was a good journalist but a lonely and troubled individual who could not endure closeness or deep personal relationships. There was no wife or child to mourn his passing, no-one who ever really got to know him.

But that's not the end of this sad story.

Meeting up in London with Ian Mather, defence correspondent of the *Observer* for many years, the conversation inevitably centred on our former colleague. Except, Ian told me, Sean Toolan never existed.

As they tried to organise his funeral, even the *Observer*'s most dogged investigative reporters could find nothing of his origins. There was no record of a Sean Toolan in the Irish Guards and no birth certificate in the UK or Irish Republic for a man of such a name and date of birth. There was a thought that he came from Manchester where he might have had a sister.

So the man who revealed so little of who he was in life remained a mystery in death. There's no doubt that's just how Sean, or whatever his name was, would have wanted it.

– 8 –

The night editor

THE PARAMEDICS may have been on a cigarette break or were awaiting instructions but I seemed to be lying on the gurney beside the ambulance for an inordinate amount of time. Thankfully, there was no rain or blinding sun. There were, however, plenty of onlookers who eyed me with curiosity and even suspicion because I didn't look damaged. I hadn't met with an accident so there was no blood or sticking-out bones and I lay there, mostly with my eyes closed, while a child poked at me to see if I was dead. What I'd encountered was a nasty case of dysentery or colitis or gastroenteritis; I was never quite sure of the exact diagnosis but I'll settle for whatever sounds the worst. And I felt at least half dead for it wasn't getting any better. Looking up at the faces, the tall buildings above them and the trees that formed canopies over the street, a sardonic thought occurred to me… 'Welcome to Buenos Aires.'

I had arrived from London forty-eight hours earlier on a British United Vickers VC10 that stopped in Madrid, Dakar, Rio de Janeiro and Montevideo. Everyone had to get off each time. At one of these points I may have ingested some contaminated food or liquid. I considered a glass of discoloured orange juice at Rio airport to be a prime suspect.

A paramedic reappeared, stuck a drip in my arm and clattered the gurney into the ambulance. The crowd drifted away, disappointed at the lack of drama, and off we went, siren blaring not because I was in danger of expiring but just to cut through the traffic. We arrived at the British Hospital where one might have assumed the staff spoke

English. With the exception of the doctor who examined me, they didn't. This was especially unfortunate because I sensed some reciprocation of my attraction to a lovely young nurse on my ward. Sadly, we simply could not communicate and I worried about attempting gestures that might have been misunderstood. The year was 1967 and English had not then become a priority in most Argentine schools.

That is by no means a criticism. My Spanish vocabulary at the time didn't extend to a handful of words. I learned later that the owner of the guesthouse where I'd found temporary accommodation had been on the phone to the office demanding my urgent removal because I was clearly dying and she didn't want a corpse on her hands.

The three days in hospital gave me time for self-reflection. What on earth was I doing here (here being Argentina and not just the infirmary bed)? Had my appetite for travel and adventure finally exceeded itself?

At twenty-three, I was the newly-appointed night editor of the *Buenos Aires Herald*, an English-language daily newspaper which, in the years after I left it, won international respect for its courageous fight against widespread government-sponsored abductions and murders. But in the latter half of the 1960s, life was quiet and people were reasonably prosperous. The country was between revolutions or, to be more correct, military coups. This gave the impression of some stability although the ambitions of junta chief Juan Carlos Ongania to create a new right-wing political and social order, with its shades of European fascism, generated an element of fear among workers and academics alike and may have sown the seeds for the terror that was to come. The buildings around the Casa Rosada, the presidential palace, stood pock-marked by cannon fire from multiple coups over the ages, reminders that the potential for violence and upheaval in Argentina is never to be discounted.

Almost fully recovered, I found a studio apartment in a modern block in the Barrio Norte, near the junction of Calles Uruguay and Arenales. This was an upmarket area of Buenos Aires – tree-lined streets with fashion boutiques and genteel tea rooms, elegant restaurants and expensive hair stylists.

Finances dictated that I furnished the flat in a minimalist way – just a desk, a chair and a bed that with a few cushions doubled as a sofa – but it was all I needed and while I intended to add more, I never got around to doing so. There were a couple of wicker chairs and a cane table on my balcony overlooking the back garden and I would drag them inside if required.

To get the best reception for my short-wave radio, I formed an aerial from a length of coated copper wire and tied an end to a potato which I hurled into a tree at the bottom of the garden. It held firmly and I picked up the BBC World Service with great clarity until an upstairs neighbour complained about the wire and I had to remove it.

It was spring when I arrived and the jacaranda blossom had turned the neighbourhood into a mass of blue and lavender and the local parks with their birdlife, fountains and flower gardens into havens of beauty and tranquillity.

Most mornings I would wander down Avenida Santa Fe where I'd find a pavement café, order coffee and *medialunes* – half-moons (a wonderful name for croissants) – and read the newspaper or, more usually, watch the girls go by. After fifty years and seventy countries, I've never doubted my original belief that the women of Argentina are the most beautiful in the world.

From my apartment, it was a twenty-minute walk to the office located in a new building on 25 Calle de Mayo in the heart of the red-light district. Perhaps the newspaper's owners felt that journalists and prostitutes had something in common and we certainly co-existed well enough once the ladies accepted we had no money for that kind of leisure activity. More of an enigma was the presence next door to us of the English Club. It was similar in style and attitude to an exclusive London gentlemen's club and the most important of the self-made Anglo-Argentines were members. Or maybe it was perfectly located for the old fellows.

It was a delightful walk, summer or winter, and only in heavy rain or bitter wind would I jump on a bus or grab a taxi. It took me across 9 de Julio, the widest avenue in the world, and through one of the most vibrant, raucous parts of the city, teeming with life and colour and car horns, where the smell of charcoal-roasted meat permeated the air and the flamboyant music of the tango blared incessantly from almost every doorway long into the night.

If I was lucky on my way to work, I'd encounter street tango dancers in the pedestrian Calle Florida, a bit like buskers in London. They were mainly professionals from night-time shows making a little tax-free cash on the side.

There is nothing quite like the tango. The music can be sad, joyous, often urgent, sometimes violent and the dance itself is a masterpiece of motion. These days, when I hear a snatch of tango on the radio or television, I am transported back to these magical moments and I allow myself to feel the warm embrace of far away and long ago.

Working from about four to eleven five nights a week, I was in charge of what news went into the paper. With a team of three, I edited the material, wrote the headlines and designed the pages. There were a fair number of local stories but it was mostly international news from Reuters, AP and UPI which was what the readership wanted in an era before CNN or any other global TV network.

I should say something about my colleagues, three of whom arrived at the same time as I did. My deputy was Alex from Glasgow whose attempts to emulate 1960s rock stars succeeded only as far as the haircut. "Call me Lex," he insisted but no-one did. I forget his surname.

Within a year, he had married a local girl, albeit a little reluctantly, and had become a father. He and I didn't mix much socially but I recall one evening when we'd enjoyed rather a few too many beers. His loudness attracted the attentions of the police who carted him off to the cells for the night. I followed on and remonstrated a little too successfully on his behalf, for they let him go and kept me.

My No 3 was John Prime, a bright young man about the same age as me who – if I recall correctly – went on to become part of the senior management of Financial Times Publications in London.

The fourth newcomer was Roy, a middle-aged sports journalist who constantly pointed out the shortcomings of Buenos Aires compared to his beloved London. A particular target of his wrath were the public lavatories, really just holes in the ground over which one had to squat. It was a dislike that soared in intensity after his braces once got in the way.

I never saw much of Norman Ingrey, the elderly editor who had often left the office by the time I arrived in the late afternoon, but my immediate superior was deputy editor Robert Cox, a talented and diligent journalist and a kindly man who would become a hero in the dark days over the horizon, ignoring death threats and leaving the country with his family only after an attempt to kidnap his wife. Andrew Graham-Yooll, an Anglo-Argentine whose father had arrived from Edinburgh in the 1920s, was the senior reporter and another who would risk his life defying attempts to silence the newspaper. The author of some thirty books in English and Spanish, he later worked in London for the *Guardian* and the *Daily Telegraph* and was a fellow at Wolfson College, Cambridge, before returning to the *Herald* in safer times as editor-in-chief.

My relationship with the Spanish language stumbled along. I didn't have the resources to hire a tutor and the only assistance I received was from a battered copy of *Teach Yourself Spanish* which read as if an extra degree of difficulty had been deliberately written in. Achieving some mastery over the menus of the inexpensive restaurants that abounded throughout the city was my immediate priority, talking to people a secondary consideration. The menus ran to great length and were entirely in Spanish. Stabbing a finger at some item really did not work for I could end up with something that both looked and tasted vile. A few times, I would wander among the tables until I saw a dish that looked attractive and that someone was clearly enjoying, then drag a waiter over and point to it excitedly, usually to the bewilderment of the people at the table and to the waiter himself.

When I'd perfected the pronunciation of *bife de chorizo con papas fritas y ensalada de lechuga y remolachas* and received in return an enormous sirloin steak that overlapped the plate, I was up and running. The steak would arrive with two large metal platters, one for the fries and the other for the salad of lettuce and beetroot. It could have fed a family. That and a half-carafe of red wine cost the equivalent of ten bob or fifty pence. When I'd expanded my linguistic skills into chicken, fish, pork and vegetable dishes and even sugar-saturated desserts like *dulce de leche* and *postre vigilante*, I turned my attention to conversational Spanish which had its pitfalls since the language of Spain could differ in some significant ways from the language of Argentina. For example, the verb *para cojer*, to take, would – according to my Teach Yourself book – apply to taking a road, a direction, a train or vehicle. In the idiom of the Buenos Aires *Porteño*, it meant to take a woman. I learned this one evening when I suggested to a girlfriend that we do something impossible to a taxi. She collapsed in hysterics while I stood on the pavement baffled.

When we finished work for the night, some of us would make our way to the Wembley Bar just around the corner in Calle Tucuman where we drank Quilmes beer, smoked Jockey Club cigarettes, ate *tostados de jamon y queso* and sometimes listened to Roy complain about some new irritation. The bar's only connection to Wembley was the owner's affection for football and he and his customers would quiz us on the English game, which only Roy knew anything about, and he couldn't speak Spanish.

One regular customer, a police lieutenant on his break, could be quite expressive in making his point which was not necessarily restricted to soccer. He would bang his fist violently on the bar on which he had also laid his submachine gun. With each thump, the barrel would edge round towards me. I would push it away until it was pointed somewhere else, often at the barman who would nudge it back in my direction. It quietly went back and forth and the policeman, in full flow, was quite oblivious. It eventually dawned that I should sit on the other side of him.

On nights off I would sometimes gravitate towards a folklore bar on Avenida Santa Fe, a few blocks from my apartment. It was owned and run by Henry, a middle-aged Anglo-Argentine, and frequented by university students and younger members of faculty who would play acoustic guitar and sing mournful laments, the contents of which were not unlike traditionally miserable Scottish songs. These were delightful, friendly people – happy, effusive, natural, somewhat amoral and about as left-wing as you could get without brandishing a Kalashnikov. Many were followers of Che Guevara, Argentina's most famous son who was fighting a revolution in Bolivia at the time. They welcomed me warmly and, when we'd all had enough to drink, occasionally invited me to deliver an off-key rendition of *Ae Fond Kiss* or *By Yon Bonnie Banks* or any Burns song and rewarded me with energetic but largely undeserved applause.

These days, I sometimes wonder what became of them. They and their kind were sitting ducks for the state death squads that ruthlessly picked off opponents of successive military dictatorships from 1974 to 1983. This was the so-called Dirty War, which resulted in the disappearance of as many as thirty thousand revolutionaries, political activists, trade unionists and others. One of the worst periods was around 1977 when intellectuals, priests, artists, journalists, students and professors were targeted. Only in recent years have the Argentine courts under a democratic government handed down long prison sentences to the generals and their henchmen responsible for the decade-long reign of terror that shamed a beautiful country and a wonderful people.

– 9 –

Me and Big Jock

JOCK STEIN, Celtic Football Club's legendary manager, apologised as he grabbed me by the collar with one hand, opened the door with the other and propelled me into the corridor. "Sorry, but no reporters in here at half-time!" he yelled after me. The policeman outside the away team's dressing room at Racing Club's El Cilindro stadium in Buenos Aires moved to apprehend me but hesitated when I flashed my pass and I scarpered back up to the Press box with my dignity a little bruised and an anecdote for the memoirs.

This was November 1967 and the second leg of the world club championship between the winners of the European Cup and South America's Copa Libertadores. Having taken time off from my job with the *Buenos Aires Herald* to help cover the match for the *Scottish Daily Mail*, I'd sneaked in to have a word with Celtic goalkeeper Ronnie Simpson who'd been knocked out of the game by a missile before it had even started.

Celtic had won the first leg 1-0 in Glasgow and went on to lose the second 1-2, forcing a deciding match across the River Plate in Uruguay, a game that's burned into football history as the infamous 'Battle of Montevideo' in which four Celtic and two Racing players were sent off. Tommy Gemmell would have joined them if the referee had seen him kick an opponent in the testicles. With obvious relish, Gemmell said later: "This Argentinian had been spitting at us through the game so when I saw a chance I got him right in the goolies." Down to seven men, Celtic lost 1-0 and went home in disgrace, each man heavily fined by the club for indiscipline.

Mixing with the great 'Lisbon Lions' – as that Celtic team were known after winning the European Cup in the Portuguese capital – and even playing snooker with a couple of them in the days leading up to the Buenos Aires encounter was heady stuff for a twenty-three-year-old journalist who was otherwise confined to a desk. Being paid well for it too was rather good. The value of the peso, always a fragile currency, continued to drift, and I took advantage of as many opportunities for freelance work as I could get. Since my *Herald* salary was in pesos, freelancing was my only means of accumulating savings in a hard currency.

The most prestigious work – if not the most lucrative – was for the *Economist*. The British-based magazine required a few hundred words every three weeks or so which meant I had to scour, with some difficulty, the Spanish-language media for interesting political or economic trends and events and weave in something of an analysis. The Falklands was always a popular subject, even back then. Decades later, I renewed the connection in the Middle East, resulting in at least one issue being banned in the Gulf while I hid behind the usual 'From Our Correspondent' byline.

My other major task for the British Press was covering, as best I could from Buenos Aires, yachtsman Francis Chichester navigating the hazards of Cape Horn on his single-handed voyage around the world. Today, such circumnavigations are almost every-day occurrences but Chichester was the first in his yacht *Gipsy Moth IV* and it was big news in the UK.

The *Daily Express*, for which I was writing, sent a team of reporters and a photographer from the New York office to Punta Arenas at the southern end of Chile. Leading it was David English who went on to become the acclaimed editor of the *Daily Mail* and received a knighthood for his services to journalism.

This heavy-handed and wildly expensive venture turned into one of those catastrophes for which Fleet Street is famous. Most of Chile had been struck by a massive communications blackout and the *Express* team could not file a word. In the meantime, I was getting some information from the Argentine Coastguard which was monitoring Chichester's progress and I duly reported it. Back came a cable from the *Express*:

> MANY THANKS YR SPLENDID EFFORTS WHICH GETTING YOU MAJOR PAGE ONE STORY STOP IF YOU CAN CONTACT OTHERS COMMA TELL THEM GO HOME COMMA THE PARTY'S OVER STOP"

I still have it somewhere.

IN THOSE days long before satellites, we communicated with Europe by undersea cable; telephone calls were never guaranteed, frequently failed and could take forever. For my mother's birthday, I had booked a call the required twenty-four hours in advance, giving the Buenos Aires operator the Gravesend number. Almost on time, the phone rang in my apartment.

"Hello caller," said Buenos Aires. "I have your call to the UK. I am putting you through to Miami." *Click, screech, kchunk.*

"Caller, this is Miami. Please hold the line while I connect you to New York." There followed a lengthy series of whirs, whistles and buzzes until the New York operator came on the line.

"Hello Buenos Aires… you there? Transferring you now to London." I could hear an impressive variety of noises as the signal pressed on valiantly down a further three thousand miles of transoceanic cable. The whole exercise was taking a sizeable amount of time and I was concerned the connection would break.

"Hello, this is London, caller. I'm putting you through to Gravesend." By this point, the voice was so faint I had to press the phone hard against my ear. Even so, it took only a minute for the Gravesend operator to come on the line: "Hold on, caller… dialling the number for you now."

Brr brr… brr brr… brr brr… brr brr. The subdued ringing went on and on until Gravesend came back on the line. "Sorry caller, there's no answer." It hadn't occurred to me that my mother might go out with friends to celebrate her birthday.

Naturally, I missed my family and friends but homesickness was never an issue, probably because I'd been a wanderer all my life and didn't consider any place to be home. There was too much in the world to see and explore and thoughts of Gravesend on the grimy lower reaches of the Thames did not encourage nostalgia. On a clear day, you could see across the river to the power station.

I loved being in Buenos Aires, but it wasn't as if the city was dangerously exciting, like Rio de Janeiro or São Paulo. To describe it as conservative and pretty safe, maybe even a little staid, might have caused some anxiety to tour operators and their like who preferred the projection of a wilder image. Yet there was, in my experience, little that was bizarre in the nightlife and the chances of being robbed in the street were fairly unlikely. The massive number of immigrants from Italy, Spain and other European countries in the late 19th and early 20th centuries brought with them old world attitudes that were largely still in place half a century later. Sadly, the great wealth that existed at that time had been squandered by subsequent military and elected governments.

The British had built a vast railroad network that brought Argentina's raw materials to the capital for processing and export to a hungry global market. The country ranked among the world's largest producers of beef, wheat and wool, encouraging massive investment and with it great prosperity, but this *belle èpoque* ended with the outbreak of the First World War, never really to return.

While the money had flowed, Buenos Aires spent it lavishly on great avenues to rival Paris, cultural extravagances like the Teatro Colon, still one of the greatest opera houses in the world, and on the redesign of the downtown streets in the style of a checker-board grid. One of the hazards in my time was the absence of traffic lights on many streets. Cars approached each junction with horns blaring and slowed only if the responding noise from a vehicle coming from a side street was clearly louder. At night, drivers added flashing headlights to their calculations. It could be quite terrifying in the back of a taxi, yet I saw very few serious accidents.

All cars in those days had locally-made bull-bars fitted to their front and rear bumpers, the purpose of which was to create a parking space by pushing whole lines of other vehicles backwards and forwards. Then they had to do the same again to get out. God help any pedestrian standing between two parked cars even a distance away. You could lose your legs.

AS THE months went by, I expanded my circle of friends. It wasn't my intention to socialise mainly with Anglo-Argentines but it worked out that way since I made most of my connections through newspaper colleagues and, in any case, maintaining conversations entirely in Spanish was always an effort.

I played cricket for Belgrano Cricket Club. Let me rephrase that: I kept score for the team and if they were ever desperately short of a man I might be asked to don a set of whites. My playing opportunities, however, ended in dramatic style. There could not have been a worse time for me to fail miserably or a better time to become the conquering hero and be carried off the field to tumultuous applause. I was sent in to bat – the last man to face the last ball of the last over needing two runs to win the championship.

The other side's fast bowler was an enormous Australian brute who looked like and probably was an ex-professional. He glared at me evilly all the way to the start of his long run-up then thundered down towards the wicket and hurled the ball at a terrifying speed. I took a mighty slash at where I thought it might be, heard a horrible clunk behind me and a great groan from the crowd. My middle stump had been knocked almost out of sight.

Belgrano were quite good about it and still let me keep score.

SOME WEEKENDS off I took a train out of town to where Henry, who ran the folklore bar I frequented in the Barrio Norte, owned a small *estancia*, or ranch, in *el campo* on the edge of a quiet town. There was nothing to do but sit by the pool under the jacaranda and eucalyptus trees, drink beer, eat barbecued *bifes* and chorizo sausages, talk with interesting people and sometimes play chess. With a constant background of chirping crickets and the southern stars shining brightly in the night sky, it was idyllic. I felt a little uncomfortable in that I had earlier formed a quiet relationship with Henry's twenty-two-year-old daughter, but that ended when she told me she was getting married – the following week.

These visits gave me a glimpse of the vastness of the Pampas, the seemingly infinite expanse of nearly 300,000 square miles of grass and scrub lands that stretched from the Atlantic coast to the edge of the Andes Mountains and I wanted to see more of this remarkable country that was home to monkeys in the north and penguins in the south.

I took a week's holiday and a train from the British-built Retiro station in Buenos Aires to Mendoza in the foothills of the Andes, a journey of nearly twenty-four hours and a thousand kilometres, stopping irregularly and for indeterminate periods at little stone-built stations that looked like sets for western movies. They would have been of wooden construction had there been any trees on the Pampas. It was said that a *gaucho*, the South American cowboy, would shoot a steer so that he could hitch the reins of his horse to its horns and cut a slice of meat from the animal's haunch for his meal.

I'm not sure how true that was but it seemed a shocking cruelty and, secondly, a terrible waste. Yet such wastage, albeit on a much smaller scale, occurred every day on the street where I lived. Popping into the local butcher's shop for a couple of pork chops or whatever, I watched the maids from all the fine apartments buy several kilos of meat at a time. Substantial amounts left by the family at the end of each day all went down the waste chute. In Buenos Aires, people often ate beef for breakfast, lunch, dinner and – after a trip to a movie or show – late supper. They were chomping their way through valuable exports at such a pace that the government took the extreme measure of banning the sale of beef two days a week and causing uproar in the process, although heart attacks were said to have decreased.

From the train, the grasslands appeared mostly featureless and unfenced, like a green or yellow ocean moving in the wind all the way to the horizon. Very occasionally, a house with a number of barns around which horses grazed interrupted the singularity of the view. Yet the landscape was extraordinarily compelling. Tribes of native people used to ride these ranges until they were wiped out in the 1850s by the brutal Argentine dictator Rosas who, incidentally, ended up as a small farmer near Southampton.

The train arrived in Mendoza at night and only in the morning did I see the stunning grandeur of the Andes dominated by Aconcagua – at nearly 23,000 feet, the highest mountain outside the Himalayan ranges. After all the flatness of Buenos Aires and its surrounds, these magnificent snow-capped peaks were heart-lifting. I felt like singing as I walked down the street from my hotel.

I have a special love of mountains. I wanted not just to be near them, but to be among them, so I took a small bus that crossed the Andes into Chile at 12,000 feet by a pass that was open only a few months of the year. At the time, I wouldn't have missed the experience for the world. Looking back at it now, it was certainly foolhardy. I recall looking down from halfway up a mountain directly onto a tiny thread of silver that was actually a raging white river a kilometre or two below. The bus had to accelerate to get around countless steep hair-pin bends notable for the absence of marker stones. Meeting another on the way down was heart-in-the-mouth stuff as we scraped past with nothing to spare and wheels right on the edge, an inch or two from oblivion.

Our driver was clearly exhausted. At one point, he shouted to me to come up front and sit beside him. "Talk to me," he said. "I'm falling asleep." He did the sixteen-hour trip every day and had to check, clean and refuel the vehicle before he could eat and go to bed. At every rest halt on the journey someone had to shake him awake when it was time to go. My Spanish improved remarkably. In any case, my incessant chatter must have helped him focus because he couldn't understand what I was saying and kept asking me to repeat it.

– 10 –

Express delivery

THERE WAS a time when news was not about the size of Kim Kardashian's bum, when scoops came from hard digging and not from tapping the phones of so-called celebrities or through the unethical chicanery of a fake sheikh. And if editors ever did yell "Hold the front page!" it wasn't in order to insert yet another non-story about the search for Madeleine McCann.

It was a time when printed news was still king and when the *Daily Express*, now a parody of its former self, sold more than three million copies a day and was the paper that attracted the best of journalists.

Everyone at the small reunion of old friends and colleagues who once worked for the *Express* was all too aware of its crumbling circulation and disintegrating reputation. Our conversation centred less on the deplorable state of the newspaper today and more on the tribulations of getting old, on times past, the quality of our lunch and, inevitably, on absent friends. I asked about some of the people from my time on the foreign desk, among them John Moger, Jim Nichol, Stewart Steven and Jim Thurman. And Les Diver, Bill Montgomery and Douglas Orgill in the news sub-editors' domain. All long dead, I was told. Yesterday's news.

Among the living that November afternoon was David Eliades, a former night foreign editor who co-wrote a number of successful books, including one that became a Disney movie and another that was turned into a stage musical still running in one part of the world or another some forty years on. We have remained friends for all that time.

Journalism back in the glory days of Fleet Street, once the physical but now only spiritual home of what was the great national newspaper industry, was a decent, even respected, profession and to some extent it still is. But the public perception of it changed for the worse due partly to a man with whom I once shared a desk in the black glass art deco building immortalised by *Private Eye* as the Black Lubyanka.

It was near darkness when the gathering came to a close and I wandered somewhat sadly down the Street past the *Daily Telegraph* with its huge Gothic columns and crossed the side streets where the *Daily Mail*, the *Sun*, the *Evening News* and the *Evening Standard* used to live. The Black and White milk bar had been over there and the Press Association's headquarters, designed by Lutyens, on a corner further down.

Not for nothing was Fleet Street called the Boulevard of Broken Dreams. To borrow from Sinatra's song about New York, if you could make it there, you could make it anywhere. But for all those who did, many did not. In spite of its magnetic, romantic allure, the Street was an unforgiving master with no tolerance for fools or much room for sentiment. I recall one journalist who was fired after a couple of days and another who walked out three hours into his first shift, never to return.

For the first time in more than forty years, I dropped in at the Old Bell, the *Express* pub across the road from the office and just up from Ludgate Circus. It used to be packed with journalists and printers but this time there was only a handful of City types drinking Mexican bottled beer. My memory of sawdust on the floor may be a little faulty but the place no longer smelled of stale tobacco and spilled ale. Otherwise, it had barely changed.

"I've not been in here since I was your age," I told the Eastern European barmaid. "It used to be full of people from the *Express*."

"Express?" she asked. "What is Express?"

The Poppins next door to the *Express* had gone, as had Poppins Court in which it was situated. Actually the pub was called the Red Lion but no-one referred to it as that – just as the *Daily Mirror* pub, the White Hart, was only ever known as the Stab (in the Back). Halfway up Fleet Street, the 400-year-old Cheshire Cheese where Dr Johnson once held court and where Dickens scribbled away assiduously – at different times of course – was useful if you wanted to drink in neutral territory.

Led by Rupert Murdoch, the newspapers began moving out of Fleet Street when new technology ended decades of being held hostage by the powerful print unions. In 1986, the *Sun* and its sister paper, the *News of the World*, set up in 'Fortress Wapping' surrounded by barbed wire and high fences while staff had to run the picket lines of printers protesting bitterly over the end of the restrictive practices that had nearly bankrupted the industry. The great offices they left are now occupied by banks and insurance companies and by an awful lot of ghosts.

I turned up my coat collar against the chill wind that swept up Blackfriars Street from the river. It whistled around the side of St Bride's Church, creating little swirls of dust, and I stood for a while in a doorway opposite the old *Express* building, its black glass shining in the street lights, experiencing a flood of memories until it all got a bit overwhelming and I had to leave.

IT WAS November 1968 when I presented myself at the front reception and was escorted to the office of Eric Raybould, the managing editor, who had hired me as a news sub-editor partly as a result of my work for the *Express* from Buenos Aires. But if my previous jobs in journalism had demanded reasonable levels of ability, this one raised the bar substantially. While I was up for the challenge, I questioned if I had the talent.

I could hear the large open-plan editorial room before we entered it. Half a dozen phones rang simultaneously while reporters shouted into others. Rows of typewriters, linked by chains to prevent their theft, clattered ceaselessly and a bank of teleprinters carrying news from Reuters and other agencies chugged out streams of paper. Cries of "Copy!" rang across the floor as sub-editors waved stories ready for typesetting and messengers rushed to collect them. Heavy wooden boards twelve feet long hung from the ceiling exhorting staff to MAKE IT EARLY, MAKE IT ACCURATE! and to GET IT TO THE PRESS ON TIME! The noise, the buzz was electric and intimidating. It looked like a movie set but no-one yelled "Cut!" and the seemingly frenzied – but actually quite organised – activity continued with little hesitation. In the midst of it all, an elderly woman pushed a trolley. "Tea? Anyone want tea?"

Eric left me with Douglas Orgill, the chief sub-editor, a delightful man who didn't raise his voice or lose his temper in the five years I worked with him. In his spare time, Douglas wrote authoritative books on tank warfare; some excellent fiction too. He smiled, shook my hand and pointed to an empty chair at a double desk. "Get yourself settled in and come back and see me. Oh... and welcome to the *Daily Express*."

A sub-editor is basically a rewrite man. He or she is handed a reporter's story and told the length required and the width and point size of the headline. Since reporters tend to overwrite, a story often has to be cut heavily to fit the space available, particularly so in the popular Press. Therein lies the art of the sub who must reduce it, say by half, yet not lose salient points. It also wasn't uncommon for a reporter to innocently bury the best angle on the story in the fifth or sixth paragraph, necessitating a major rewrite. These days it's all done on screen but in my time it was typewriters for the reporters and biros for the subs. We had 'cut and paste' long before Microsoft was born – paper, scissors, a paste-pot and a brush. The end result had to be a tight, crisply written story with a strong intro and a good, even clever, headline that drew the reader in. The other vital element was time; it had to be done in minutes.

The *Express* was known throughout the Street as a subs' newspaper. Rewrite men ruled. It was said that on occasion a reporter might only recognise his or her story from the byline.

The sub-editor in the other chair was younger than me by a year or two. "I've not been long here myself," he said as I sat down, "but if you have questions I'll help if I can." What a nice chap, I thought. "We work a straight six-hour shift without a break," he added. "You can send up to the canteen for something to eat and if it gets quiet you can nip out for a five-minute pint but leave your jacket on the chair." He paused. "Sorry... I should introduce myself. I'm Kelvin Mackenzie."

It was clear that Douglas was initially giving me stories only difficult enough to provide him with an indication of my subbing skills. A month or so later I was getting the heavy stuff.

"This Middle East situation looks like blowing up," said the editor in charge of the foreign news page. He handed me lengthy stories from reporters in Tel Aviv, Beirut, Damascus, Amman, Cairo, Washington and London. "I need ten paragraphs in total. You've got fifteen minutes. Send it down to the print room one paragraph at a time and don't use the word 'meanwhile.'" By the seventh hand-written paragraph I was struggling to remember what I'd said in the third but somehow it got done on time and to the editor's satisfaction. Such was the pressure that I, like many of my colleagues, generally smoked a full packet of cigarettes each shift.

As for Kelvin, he was an exceptional sub-editor with a great talent for writing headlines. After a couple of years, he left for the soon-to-be-published Murdoch *Sun*. "Why don't you come with me?" he suggested. "They need subs." I was offered a job but changed my mind when the *Sun* first hit the streets. I wrote to Derek Marks, the *Express* editor, asking if he could match the offer. He replied giving me more than I'd sought, adding: "This is an indication of the value I place upon the work you are doing for the *Daily Express*." I knew it was a standard letter but it was nonetheless an endorsement of something that, throughout my life, I could never hear too often and have never truly believed – that I was good enough.

Kelvin became the *enfant terrible* of Fleet Street when he eventually took over as editor of the *Sun* and his notoriety grew with each outrageous headline. 'GOTCHA!' said the *Sun* front page when the Argentine cruiser Belgrano was sunk in the Falklands war with the loss of 323 lives. 'FREDDIE STARR ATE MY HAMSTER!' read another famous headline which, like the allegations of Liverpool FC supporters robbing the dead at the Hillsborough disaster, was quite untrue. He had also gone from a convivial colleague on the *Express* to an abusive tyrant at the *Sun*, feared and loathed by many of his staff. Years later, he was to admit that his editorship of the newspaper had had a "positively downhill effect on journalism."

As Kelvin had demonstrated, the effect of power on personality

On the Foreign Desk of the Daily Express, 1972. *The author is the pipe-smoker.*

could be dramatic and he was not alone in unleashing his Mr Hyde. The young, mild-mannered *Express* reporter Paul Dacre with whom I sank many a pint in the Old Bell became – from a journalistic viewpoint – the brilliant editor of the *Daily Mail* and – from a human perspective – a foul-mouthed bully who terrorised his subordinates.

I was never going to be a high flyer in the style of Kelvin, but I did a variety of interesting jobs on the *Express* including that of copy-taster. It sounds a weird title but it meant reading through the never-ending supply of stories from reporters, news agencies and accredited freelancers across the country and selecting a core number that would probably make it into print. I once suffered the embarrassment of spiking a story that developed into the main lead on page one. On the other hand, I remember seeing the potential in a one-paragraph brief that the newsdesk had missed. Sent back for a staff reporter to follow up, it went on to lead the front page. When I moved over to the foreign desk, I did pretty much the same work.

The role I really didn't like was what they called late stop. You're the last man on the floor, hanging around until 4.30am in case a big story breaks, like an air crash or terrorist bombing (the IRA was blowing up London in those days). Then you would stop the presses and change the front page. Such incidents rarely happened in the wee small hours so it was wise to bring a good book. When they did it was tragic but, my God it was exciting! Well, so I'm told. It never actually happened to me.

And if you fancied a pint after that you could go the Press Club or nip up the road to Covent Garden where the pubs opened before dawn for workers in the huge flower and fruit market. It wasn't unusual to find nearly as many journalists as market porters at the bar.

DRINKING WAS a enormous part of the Street culture, much more so than it is today, and is the stuff of legend. Most memoirs of Fleet Street contain multiple stories of alcoholic misadventure, often hilarious and usually attributed by the author to other people. My own small contribution to any collection of such tales would be the time I unintentionally circumnavigated the county of Kent.

The *Express* had booked the vast ballroom of the Waldorf Hotel in London for a lunch for hundreds of editorial staff and the presentation of a new-look paper by its impeccably-suited Old Etonian managing director, Jocelyn Stevens. I didn't think it was much of an improvement and it did nothing to lift the circulation, but that's beside the point. I don't remember too much of the event except there was no limit to the flow of wine and many imbibed freely, particularly those of us who had come in on our day off. I do recall interrupting Jocelyn at the start of his presentation by shouting to a waiter: "Bring us another bottle! This one's corked!"

Later, in search of further refreshment, several of us repaired to the Press Club and it was around 9pm when I left to catch a train to Tonbridge where I was living at the time. Unsurprisingly, I slept through Tonbridge, Ashford, Folkestone, Dover and Deal and was shaken awake by a guard when the train reached its destination at Ramsgate. By then it was midnight and there was to be a twenty-four-hour rail strike the coming day. The station staff persuaded a driver who was repositioning a train along the North Kent coast to Sittingbourne to let me ride along. There I was able to hop another to Chatham where I took a taxi to Gravesend, turning up on a cousin's doorstep at around 2am.

After a night on the couch and with a hangover memorable for its severity, I endured a three-hour bus ride to Tonbridge, arriving home in time to shower, pick up my car and drive to the office for the 3pm start to my shift that, I hoped, would not be too demanding.

Another train journey involving the *Express* was brief but traumatic and left me shaken to the extent that the noisy clatter and the throwing around of carriages as they cross points at speed still induce a momentary anxiety.

It happened in one of those heatwaves that periodically engulf southern England. For more than a week, Saharan temperatures had caused roads to liquefy, pets to fry and elderly folk to keel over in droves. Rails on the main route from Tonbridge into London had gone all wobbly in the intense heat and trains were being routed via Reigate, a longer journey. But the 2pm departure would still get me into town in time for my shift. I had a travelling companion that day, Jack Atkinson, another *Express* sub-editor who also lived in Tonbridge. I'd always thought of him as the laid back, almost academic type until I learned he was a serious gun collector and fitness fanatic. We sat at a table in the buffet car with the windows open, drinking tea and running down the *Express* management. The Surrey countryside thundered past and it looked as if the driver was trying to make up lost time.

I was nodding off when there was an ear-splitting shriek of twisting metal, followed instantly by the front of our carriage rising sharply, like an aircraft taking off. Jack and I, the only two passengers in the buffet car, were thrown against the side then hurled along the floor, only to be propelled forward again as the rear carriages, still on the rails, slammed into ours. I remember trying to cling to a table leg, terrified of being thrown through the window and subsequently crushed.

Our carriage, still nose in the air, hesitated then toppled on its side with a crash and slid down an embankment, coming to rest against a fence. Thankfully, it hadn't completely rolled. It seemed like an age but the whole incident probably took no more than a minute. I checked myself over. I was hurting in many places but there was no blood that I could see and my right wrist felt sprained rather than broken.

"How are you doing, Jack?" I asked.

"I've spilt my tea," he said.

The carriage door was now awkwardly positioned above our heads. With the help of the buffet car attendant, who also appeared to be relatively unhurt, we managed to lever it open, climb out and drop to the ground. Passengers from the other carriages that had come off the rails began to emerge, some weeping and in shock but, miraculously, there were no obvious serious injuries.

Sure that our help wasn't needed, and rather than wait for the emergency services, Jack and I clambered over the fence to the road beyond and thumbed a lift back to Tonbridge. In my head, I was already writing the story: 'EXPRESSMEN IN RAIL CRASH TERROR', or words to that effect. I rang the newsdesk to let them know.

"Don't worry, old boy," came the cheery reply. "The electricians are on strike and there's no paper tomorrow."

– 11 –

Messing about in the Channel

WHEN YOU pick up £5,000 in voluntary redundancy and get a new job before you've left the old one, there's only one thing to do with such a windfall – invest it wisely. So I bought a boat. Not any old boat, but a thirty-five-foot steel-hulled workboat that I could hire out for fishing parties or as a support vessel for cross-Channel swimmers. Of course, to be near the boat I had to move to Folkestone where a precious mooring in the harbour was available, even if that meant a daily commute of 140 miles. But I'd be driving up to London against the traffic and coming back in the early hours.

I managed to register her as a commercial fishing vessel, enabling me to sell any catches on the market, and called her the *Iolaire*, sea eagle in Gaelic. It was an unfortunate choice of name. I was unaware at the time that on New Year's Day of 1919 the steam yacht *Iolaire* went down off the Isle of Lewis with the loss of 205 lives, nearly all of them troops returning home from the war.

Folkestone didn't have the flamboyance of Brighton or as many well-heeled retirees as Eastbourne or Bournemouth while the old part of the town looked more worn out than quaint. Its cliffs were not white like those down the road at Dover but it had its attractions, the greatest of which was a sandy beach and, of course, the sea. I liked the place. My small house was only fifteen minutes' walk from the harbour. The smell of the sea was ever-present in the prevailing south-westerly breeze and I never tired of it.

The prospect of slipping the moorings, opening the throttle and heading out into the English Channel (maybe Calais for lunch?)...

imagining the spray in my face as the bow hits the first of the swells, only served to increase my impatience while I waited for the *Iolaire* to be fitted out. I needed wooden benches for the open deck aft of the wheelhouse… radar and navigation equipment… a dozen life-jackets… bedding for the two bunks… a small gas cooking range… cutlery and crockery… tools and ropes… buckets and boxes… and much, much more.

I also needed a skipper.

Terry was an experienced sailor. He knew boats and engines and fishing and was as familiar with our part of the English Channel, its tides and shallows, weather and eccentricities, as he was with every pub in town. The big drawback with Terry was his fondness for the drink.

"Give him a chance," said the people who sold me the boat. "When he's working, he really cuts down on his intake."

That wasn't exactly a job-clinching reference, but I was getting desperate. Advertising had produced nothing and most potential skippers I spoke to in the harbour were already in employment. More money would not entice them to give up a steady jobs for a newcomer who might, as they say, be here today and gone tomorrow.

Terry did try to behave himself but he had that ability of certain drunks to appear functional while being well pissed – in the way that drunks who can hardly stand can get into cars and drive away smoothly. To get onto the boat in the inner harbour, you had to climb down a wooden ladder. I didn't realise there was anything wrong until Terry missed his footing and plunged twenty feet into the water between the wall and the boat without touching either and therefore avoiding serious injury.

All things considered, our association went quite well for months and angling groups liked him. And to be fair, the big accident wasn't his fault.

We were out at night, a couple of miles offshore and laying about half a mile of long lines across the tide. It was dark with no moon which made the work more difficult. Long-lining is a traditional way of catching fish. It involves a continuation of ropes with baited hooks attached by nylon every six feet or so. At each end of the rope is a small anchor and a brightly coloured buoy. Little lead weights tied at various points ensure that the rope sits on the seabed. So you drop one anchor, making sure the buoy bobs to the surface, then motor slowly towards the shore playing out the rope and the baited hooks before you toss the other anchor in the sea. It's a delicate job because a hook getting caught in the coil of rope produces one hell of a mess. You also keep an open knife right next to you. If a hook gets into your flesh, you have to cut the nylon or the rope instantly or risk being dragged over the side.

Some fishermen would go back into harbour then come out again when the tide had turned. Needing to keep Terry out of the pub, I just anchored the *Iolaire* within sight of the first buoy and fished with rod and line while we waited, but caught little in the way of decent fish.

When the time came, we motored over to the buoy, hooked it aboard, lifted the anchor at the end of the rope and began the slow process of hauling in whatever catch there might be. The rope had to be laid into a basket in near-perfect loops with the nylon lines and hooks hanging outside. A few dogfish began to come up, followed by a good cod, a couple of flatfish, then a series of empty hooks until more fish appeared. We were doing this more for fun than money but at that rate we might get a few pounds for the night's catch.

Above the quiet ticking of our own engine, I could hear the increasing thump, thump, thump of a big diesel. Approaching from our stern quite fast was a trawler about three times our size. She was still a distance away and I wasn't immediately concerned. We had our navigation lights on and would be clearly visible to anyone in the wheelhouse. She was heading for Folkestone and, a little worryingly now, wasn't changing course.

I lifted the binoculars. The foredeck was lit up and three men were gutting fish and throwing them into stacked boxes. Flocks of seagulls spiralled behind the boat, swooping down on discarded remains. There was a figure in the wheelhouse so I began to feel better.

Then the figure moved and I could make out clearly a large dog sitting in the helmsman's chair.

It was a dangerous but common practice for fishermen to lash the wheel so they could do the work before they arrived in port when all they had to do was get the catch ashore. Then it was straight to the pub before it closed. I had no radio which would have been useless anyway with no-one in the other wheelhouse so we stood at the stern, waving a torch, jumping up and down, yelling abuse and beginning to feel terrified. Finally, someone saw us and ran to unlash the wheel. It was too late.

"Get down on the deck!" I shouted to Terry, "and hold on to something!"

The English Channel at that point is twenty-four miles wide, providing the trawler with plenty of room to avoid us but it hit the *Iolaire* exactly in the centre of the stern. Our boat slammed forward and Terry and I smashed into the wheelhouse. By the time the trawler was able to stop, she was quarter of a mile away. She didn't turn. The crew saw we were still afloat and carried on towards Folkestone, the dog barking loudly.

I was outraged. But we were lucky. If the *Iolaire* had been built of glass fibre, a common material for boats, we would have been food for the fishes we were trying to catch. Or if she'd hit us amidships we would probably have overturned. I felt luckier still when I saw that the big steel plate that protected the propeller had been bent upwards, so the bow of the trawler must have been rising as we collided. Had it been coming down, the plate would have buckled onto the prop. We had to get back to harbour quickly. It was impossible to see in the dark if the hull had been breached. I abandoned the long line and hoped we'd get it back but it had disappeared when we next went out to look.

Ashore, the trawler skipper flatly denied the wheel had been lashed and the crew claimed our navigation lights had been off. There was nothing I could do but tell them what I thought of them and leave it to the insurance companies to sort it out.

On shaking legs, we climbed the harbour wall and I said to Terry: "I'm going to make an exception and buy you a drink."

I had the boat taken out the water and the stern repaired, but the incident had removed much of the pleasure of owning her. Out in the narrowest part of the English Channel, running the gauntlet of super-tankers, bulk ore carriers, container ships, cross-Channel ferries and all manner of other shipping, I never felt really comfortable again. And it was the last time I went out in darkness.

The whole adventure ended weeks later when a drunken Terry took the boat under the railway bridge that crossed the harbour, an impossible passage at high tide. The top of the wheelhouse smashed into one of the arches and the poor old *Iolaire* looked a very sorry sight as a crane once again lifted her onto the repair yard's transporter. I sold her and never saw her again. Or Terry.

Angling boats in Folkestone Harbour.

– 12 –

Telegraph blues

MY FATHER, who could be a cruel man, used to scare me as a young child with threats that Peter the Painter would come and get me if I was naughty. That infamous figure from the early 20th century became my personal bogeyman, a grotesque monster who hid in dark corners and ate babies for breakfast.

I never thought about him again until after I'd joined the *Daily Telegraph* and was advised that Peter the managing editor was out for my blood. He was the same kind of terrifying individual although, to the best of my knowledge, had no appetite for infants. Tell most *Telegraph* journalists that Peter Eastwood was looking for them and they'd immediately pale. But to be fair to him, I had been very naughty. I had led a strike that cost the newspaper a full day's production.

The *Daily Express* and I had parted after five years when the management, panicked by falling profits, made an enormous error of judgment by offering exceedingly generous terms to any journalist who would volunteer for redundancy. In another moment of financial insanity, it even agreed that all applications would be granted. Those who knew they'd not dwell long on the job market took the money and ran, exiting by the dozen. It meant that, having given away one fortune, the *Express* had to spend another recruiting replacements.

I made my own error of judgment by opting go to the *Telegraph*, opening the door to the worst two years of my journalistic life. Actually, that's not entirely true. My first nine months there as a senior foreign news sub-editor were largely unproblematic and really quite easy, if not particularly enjoyable. The *Telegraph* didn't expect you to rewrite stories as thoroughly as the *Express* had and if a headline was okay and fit, only your own professionalism required you to try to come up with a better one.

It was changing a reporter's words that brought me the first difficult encounter with Eastwood who'd left a note on my desk to come and see him.

"You've been rewriting Clare Hollingworth," he said without a greeting and in a tone that suggested I had also been stealing office pens. Hollingworth was the *Telegraph*'s first staff correspondent in Beijing, a sensitive posting at a time when China was far less open than it is today.

"When her stuff needs turning into grammatical English, yes," I replied. "I've been very careful not to change what she's actually trying to say."

"Well, she's complained," he snapped.

"Are you saying her stuff is sacrosanct?" I asked. "Do you want me to just par mark it and let it go? "

"Don't argue with me," he said, dismissing me with a wave of the hand.

Clare Hollingworth was a Fleet Street institution and had been an exceptional war correspondent, credited with having scooped the start of the Second World War. In 1939 she was based in Eastern Europe and crossed into Germany where she observed squadrons of Nazi tanks lined up to enter Poland. Days later she broke the news of the actual invasion. She also reported on the desert campaign in North Africa and, after the war, covered the conflicts in Palestine, Algeria and Vietnam. On that basis alone, maybe her copy deserved to be left untouched. But while Clare, who died in 2017 at the age of 105, was a great news gatherer, her writing was fairly average.

The editor at the time was Bill Deedes, the former government minister and a very cheerful fellow; in the newspaper hierarchy, he was senior to the managing editor. At the *Telegraph* the situation was more complicated than usual: Deedes was in charge of the political direction of the newspaper, the leader writing and the features sections. Eastwood controlled the news pages. There was no love lost. One evening, Bill was in his office having a drink with his political writers when Eastwood knocked on the door and breezed in. "Bill…" he said.

"Peter," said Bill, "fuck off."

That's if you believe *Private Eye*, which I did because I was the one who sent it the story after hearing it from what we journalists describe as a reliable source. In this case Bill himself.

After the Hollingworth business, Eastwood and I continued to have little skirmishes, nothing too serious until an event that turned them into open warfare.

MOST EDITORIAL staff in Fleet Street were members to the National Union of Journalists. The NUJ leader within the office – the shop steward, in other words – was and still is known as the Father (or Mother) of the Chapel, a title going back to the times when print work was controlled by the Church. Norman, the FOC at the *Telegraph*, asked if I would join the NUJ committee as the sub-editors' representative.

"Sure," I said, knowing it would annoy Eastwood who hated all unions, particularly ours. But I had no idea what it involved. I had rarely attended union meetings at the *Express* and trusted the NUJ officials on the paper to look after my interests, which they certainly did in the case of the redundancy terms. If there was some effort required, it wouldn't be much, I thought.

A week or two later, a couple of elderly and distressed sub-editors asked to see me as their union rep. They worked on what was known as the Manchester desk. Basically, they sent London page layouts and stories to the office in Manchester which prepared and printed the editions for the North of England. It wasn't a taxing job.

We went next door to the King & Keys pub and took a booth at the rear. "What's the problem?" I asked after we settled down with our pints.

"It's these," said one of the grey-haired old fellows. I use the word 'old' reservedly, only because I was young and they were in their sixties, nearing retirement. I regret I don't remember their names. With shaking hands, they passed across a couple of identical letters terminating their employment and signed by Eastwood.

"I can't lose my job," one said. "I'll not get another at my age and I've still got a mortgage."

The letters gave no reason for dismissal, other than that the recipients would no longer be required. Every newspaper had a Manchester desk which was known to be a pasture for subs whose age may have robbed them of their edge. If there was any sentiment in Fleet Street, it was afforded to long-time servants of a paper who were a little past their prime. So getting rid of someone for the simple reason of reducing their pension entitlements was pretty shitty behaviour, but not untypical of the managing editor. There was nothing wrong with their work and it wasn't a case of redundancy. Eastwood would replace them with cheaper people.

Nowadays – in the age of wholesale reduncancies – such events are commonplace, unremarkable, and no-one would think to challenge them. It was quite different in the Seventies.

Back in the office, I phoned Norman at home. He agreed that I should raise it with all the sub-editors. Then I told Andrew Hutchinson, the night editor and my one great ally in my fight with Eastwood, although he couldn't be seen to show it. Andrew smiled and said: "Do what you have to do!"

"Okay, everyone," I shouted. "I need your attention. I'm calling a mandatory meeting of the subs. In the canteen in five minutes!"

Not everyone trooped upstairs. The *Telegraph* management knew they could stick two fingers up at the NUJ because there were just enough members of a rival union – the Institute of Journalists which had a no-strike policy – to bring out a paper. It had happened during industrial action in the past and while it wouldn't be much of a newspaper, precious advertising revenue would not be lost. This was the ace card the management used time and time again.

I explained the situation to the subs who showed concern and alarm but were doubtful we could do anything about it. "These IOJ bastards will bust their guts in the hope of a better deal in the next pay talks," said one.

"Maybe so," I replied, "but we can't just roll over. We have to make it as difficult for Eastwood as possible."

After passing a resolution condemning the management action and demanding the letters be rescinded, we went back to work determined to fight but without much hope of a positive solution. Norman and his deputy would take it up with Eastwood the following day and would report back to a 5pm mandatory meeting of all the NUJ members from the various departments.

At 5.30 they were still in talks and by 6pm it was clear the management had dug their heels in. At 6.15 Norman and Co walked into the room looking tired and defeated. I'll say this for the *Telegraph* journalists, while a few couldn't have cared less what happened to the old boys, the majority were outraged and wanted to strike immediately.

"What are we waiting for?" shouted one. "Let's hit them now!"

I had to shout above a great roar of approval. "They already have non-NUJ subs lined up for tonight and they'll use stories from the news agencies." The pubs were open and Norman suggested an hour's break. "We might have something for you when we get back, so be here at 7.30."

Four of us went off to see the FOC of the electricians' union who was wary of getting involved. "Why should we help you?" he asked. "What have you ever done for us?"

We pointed out that if the management got away with sacking older journalists to avoid giving them a full pension, they would do it to anyone. The FOC thought about it. "I'll talk to my committee and get back to you. Wait here."

We must have been quite convincing because he was back within twenty minutes. "Okay, we'll back you," he said. "We won't switch on the power. But you owe us big!" We certainly did because there was no other way we could have stopped the paper.

Eastwood smirked when we told him we were on strike until the letters were withdrawn. But by all accounts he went into an absolute rage when he discovered, after all his preparation to sideline us, that the presses wouldn't roll. He also had to face his own bosses after he'd assured them he would crush the rebellion.

The following morning, the letters of dismissal were rescinded and assurances given that no such action would be taken against any NUJ member without prior consultation with the union. Now that he knew we had friends in powerful places (if you'll pardon the pun), he would be less likely to try it on again.

Back at work that afternoon, having cost the company an entire day's edition, we were in a happy mood, particularly the two old fellows whose jobs we'd saved. But Andrew, my night editor friend, pulled me aside with a warning. "Eastwood is seething," he said, "and he blames you. So watch out. I'll keep you posted if I can."

Eastwood, said Andrew, had described me to the management as a dangerous Trotskyist troublemaker. I had to go to the library and look up what that meant and how I should correspondingly behave. Maybe I should grow my hair long, I thought. What the hell have I got myself into? was another thought. All I'd wanted to do was help a couple of old guys who'd been treated unfairly.

At the time, I was deputy chief foreign sub-editor. That meant that at least twice a week and during the chief sub's holidays, I was in charge of what news and pictures went into the foreign news pages and how they were presented.

When I was next due to lead the desk, I arrived in the office to find another sub in the chair. "Ah," said Andrew, rising quickly and shepherding me into the corridor. "The official line is that it's going to be a busy night and you're such a fast sub that we need you back downtable. The truth is that you can expect a lot more of this. Eastwood is not going to let it go. He'll start picking on your work next."

Andrew was a lovely man. Long and lithe, he often appeared in the corridor with his arm in the air, as if about to bowl a cricket ball. In truth, he'd suffered spinal problems from childhood and the bowling movement was intended to relieve the pain. He was also a gentleman drinker. He had a definite affection for alcohol but a slight glazing of the eyes was the only indication he might be in his cups.

It was unfortunate – or perhaps even fortunate – that in the midst of my problems, I was fighting a debilitating and very painful condition called cervical spondylosis, the wearing away of the vertebrae in the neck. I had to go to Guy's Hospital in London once a week where a harness was fitted around my head and weights added to the end of a pulley system. Literally, I was being hanged – for half an hour at a time. I never thought it was doing me much good and, after a few years, the medical profession decided it was a useless practice, of no benefit to the patient, and they abandoned it. Curiously, after having some teeth removed a year later, it disappeared never to trouble me again. A dentist has since told me the two were definitely connected.

But at the time I was not doing well physically or emotionally. With no likely solution to my neck problems and in the knowledge that Eastwood was out to get me, I was becoming quite depressed. Then I got a call from Andrew that helped to lift the gloom.

"You're not going to get anywhere on the *Telegraph* while Eastwood is there," he said as we sat with our pints at a pub table overlooking the Thames. "Have you thought about negotiating your way out with a disability benefit, maybe a year's money?"

"Are you trying to get me to leave?" I asked, amused.

"Not in the slightest. You're a friend of mine and I would hate to see you go," he replied. "But I'm thinking of what's in your interests."

"Well," I said, "as you know, I've been working on the *Observer* at weekends for the past five years and I know they would take me for longer. Plus my fishing column and other sports writing, I could recover what I'd lose from the *Telegraph*."

"Give it a thought, dear boy," he said.

I had little alternative. I could have got more than a year's money, but I just wanted to be away from the miserable place. I signed the papers, collected my stuff and went down to the King & Keys for a farewell pint. Some of the more militant members of the union were there.

"Can I buy you a drink?" I asked. How news gets around fast. As one, they turned their backs to me. As far as they were concerned, I had sold out.

– 13 –

All at sea

IT WAS THE *crack!* of a gunshot that turned my head towards the fishing boat approaching on the starboard side. A man was waving a rifle in my general direction and shouting liberal abuse across the few hundred yards that divided our vessels. I wasn't inclined to ask why he appeared to be shooting at me and ducked into the wheelhouse, looking around frantically but without success for anything I could use as a weapon if he tried to board. When I did venture a glimpse out the window, the boat was chugging past the stern and heading back the way it had come.

Shaken, I watched its wake in amazement. What on earth had just happened and how in hell did I get myself into this bizarre situation?

It began, I suppose, the previous night in the bar of the Celtic Hotel in Clifden, Connemara, on Ireland's wild west coast. Or... to give this peculiar event a little more foundation, I should retrace my steps to the invitation I received as fishing correspondent of the *Observer*, the national Sunday newspaper, from Bord Failte, the Irish tourism organisation.

My angling writing was incidental to my main job on the sports desk of the *Observer* but it provided me with some decent fishing along with perfectly adequate expenses. Ten pence a mile, a reasonable amount in those days, adds up when you drive from London to the north of Scotland for a few days of hopefully blissful salmon fishing. And there was a fee of around £40 per column.

When I was on the *Express* and later the *Telegraph*, I could work only on Saturdays for the *Observer*. But my departure from the

Telegraph freed me to work Thursdays and Fridays too if required, which was often enough. The rest of the week I was able to do more freelance work, including a little news reporting for the *Observer*. So leaving the *Telegraph* provided me not only with a better income but also time to accept invitations, such as the one to Ireland or from as far afield as Canada.

Brian Geraghty of Bord Failte was the stereotypical Irishman – affable, quick-witted and with more than a passing affection for the thunder of hooves on turf. A pretty good fisherman too, he picked me up at Dublin Airport and we drove to Lough Sheelin, a beautiful trout water then on the edge of ruin because of slurry seeping from pig farms on the surrounding land. The government has since taken greater steps to protect it.

"I just wanted to show you it's not as bad as some people say," said Brian, as we drifted in the twilight along the shoreline. We cast our flies ahead of the boat in the traditional lough-fishing fashion and while there was the occasional touch, it wasn't until the light had almost gone that the trout began to stir. We could see great clouds of hatching mayfly rising from the water and soon began to hear the slurp that signalled the trout were taking them from the surface. We caught a couple of decent fish each before the moonlight, which had become our only illumination, was snuffed out by cloud and we headed back to the inn for dinner and a couple of pints of the black stuff.

After a few days fishing the great loughs of western Ireland, Corrib and Mask, with fish, food and drink as plentiful as the contentment, Brian dropped me at Clifden and set off back to Dublin.

Connemara is one of the most beautiful places on earth, soft and gentle in many parts, wild and desolate in others and beneath the tranquility a darkness, a terrible sadness that's almost palpable. After repeated failures of the potato crop through blight, around one million people died of starvation in the whole of Ireland in the mid-1800s, leading to mass migration to America, Canada and elsewhere. A disproportionate number of these deaths took place in Connemara.

It was here that Alcock and Brown, the first men to fly the Atlantic non-stop, made an uncomfortable landing in a bog and where tourism was fast developing into a major industry through aid from Ireland's recent membership of the Common Market.

There is nothing unusual about the Celtic Hotel. It is, or it was at the time, a typical Irish hostelry, furnished in a fashion that would be copied and exported throughout the world. It was the clientele that was abnormal, at least on the evening of my arrival. Standing beside me at the bar was a very large Maori who looked as if he'd been left over from a rugby tour by the All Blacks. The question was unavoidable.

"What," I asked, "are you doing in this part of the world?"

"Well," he replied, "you might find it difficult to believe… but I'm building a Spanish galleon."

"I see," I said. It was a totally inadequate response.

"Yes," said the Maori. "Then I'm going to sink it in the bay and charge divers to have their pictures taken looting it."

"That's an original idea," I said, trying maintain a normal expression on my face. "Good luck with it." And with that I edged a little further way, turning to the barman to enquire if he knew of anyone who did sea fishing trips.

"I'll take you!" said a voice down the bar. This was Michael who owned a boat with his brother Joe. I asked if he ran fishing charters.

"Oh no," he said. "We have a boat and just do it for a bit of fun. We're going out tomorrow and you're welcome to come along."

I accepted with gratitude and we chatted for a while before I asked him what he did for a living.

"I blow myself up in coffins," he replied, and I thought: Oh God, not another one.

"Seriously," he said. "It's part of a stunt act. We've just come back from a tour of Australia."

He explained that he lined the inside of the coffin, really a not-too-solid wooden box, with explosives which, on detonation, blew out the sides in spectacular fashion while leaving him unharmed.

"I'm thinking of giving it up," Michael went on. "The last time my crash helmet got split right down the middle."

Michael and Joe's thirty-foot wooden-hulled fishing boat was typical of the small inshore craft that made a living from setting pots for lobsters and crayfish. Built to tolerate sudden changes in the weather, it was as safe a vessel as you would want and if it wasn't fast, it seemed reliable enough. In bright sunshine and conditions that could hardly have been improved, we headed around Slyne Head into the Atlantic Ocean, the town well behind us and only the gentle swell and America ahead. Joe cut the engine and we drifted with the current, catching pollack and the occasional flatfish on silvery lures.

After a couple of pleasant hours of this, Michael set the anchor and said he and Joe were going to do a little diving. Would I mind holding the safety rope and pulling them in if they gave two hard tugs? Not that they expected I'd need to. In wet suits and with masks and oxygen tanks, they rolled over the side and had been gone for maybe ten minutes when the shot rang out. I felt like hauling on the rope but waited until they surfaced, both of them giggling madly.

"It's just a little touch of the bends," said Michael. "They make you laugh if you come up a bit too quick."

"Do you know what just happened?" I asked in my best outraged voice as I explained the events of minutes earlier.

"Ah," said Michael, pulling himself over the side. "That would be old Pat. You shouldn't pay him any attention. He's a cantankerous old sod who drops his pots around here. He doesn't like us diving for crayfish."

"So it's okay if he shoots at you?" I asked, incredulous.

"Well, you see," he added, "there's a bit more too it. Diving for crayfish and lobsters is illegal in Ireland so he'll be away to tell the Garda. We'd best hurry up and be out of here, but first, give us a hand with the rope."

On the other end of the rope were three large sacks which Joe had attached, each full of crayfish. "There are plenty down there," said Michael, "enough for all the local fishermen, us included."

We pulled up the anchor and Michael pointed to a tiny island, no more than a collection of grass-topped rocks, a couple of miles away. "That's where we're headed."

I was still reeling from the realisation that I could be charged with aiding and abetting an illegal activity if the Garda came out to look for us or were waiting on the quay back in Clifden. What would the *Observer* have to say about its fishing correspondent being arrested for poaching? As if reading my thoughts, Michael said: "They've not caught us yet, so don't worry about it."

The approaching rocks guarded the entrance to a small bay in the middle of which were several large cages tethered to the bottom by metal weights. A tiny sandy beach gave way to grassy land on which stood a wooden hut.

When the cages were full, Michael explained, he would make a call to Paris and a French boat fishing in the vicinity would stop at the island and collect the catch. The money would be paid into an account in the Channel Islands. With the sacks emptied and the cages secured, we went ashore to the hut where Joe dug out a primus stove and a pan.

Among the crayfish was a sizeable lobster which he proceeded to cook while Michael retrieved from the boat a few bottles of beer, a loaf of bread and a jar of mayonnaise. In the afternoon sunshine, there was something unreal and exquisitely pleasurable about lying on the warm sand of an isolated island drinking beer and munching on a lobster sandwich dripping with butter and mayonnaise. It was, I felt then and still do, the best lunch I have ever had. Just a shame that I couldn't write about it.

WHEN MY first container load of antiques went up in smoke in a Brooklyn warehouse fire, I should have taken it as an omen and stopped then. Sadly, in those days I was rarely able to take hints, no matter how emphatically they were delivered.

With the insurance money but still tormented by the loss, I set about putting together another shipment for the store Terry and I were opening in Nyack up the Hudson River in New York state. The whole thing was pure foolishness. Terry was a London neighbour and a session musician and it was all his idea. It should have worried me that he drank as much as I did and that you couldn't depend on him to turn up for meetings. With similar flaws myself, I didn't see them as red flags.

This was in the mid-Seventies after I'd left the Telegraph *with a pay-off and had the time and money to go to auctions and search out dusty little antique shops in the south-east of England. I loved bidding for lots and haggling with dealers. I loved the look and feel of fine Regency tables, Chesterfield chairs, Victorian writing slopes, delicate pottery and all manner of objects. I loved the thought of all the people who'd handled them or sat at them or on them in the century and more since they'd been crafted. Maybe I'd been in the trade in another life.*

Terry, who had also filled a container, ran the store and I visited – usually to collect the proceeds of sales since he wasn't good at sending money back. In the months that followed, communications ceased and Terry eventually turned up in London claiming to be broke. It was fun while it lasted, albeit expensive fun. For a time before I left for the Middle East, I continued to buy in the UK for dealers in America and I've never lost that affection for beautiful items of age.

– 14 –

A man of fine words

HUGH McILVANNEY, my long-ago colleague, mentor and friend who retired in 2016 at the age of eighty-two after six decades in journalism, has been described as the greatest living sportswriter in the English-speaking world. He would be well placed if you included the dead ones too. The *Sunday Times*, where he had been chief sports columnist for many years, marked the occasion with a two-page spread and the kind of tributes you would frame.

Hugh and I worked together on the sports section of that other quality British Sunday newspaper, the *Observer*, back in the Seventies. From a journalistic perspective, it was like being around someone who could do magic. Ten years older than me, Hugh was – and clearly remains – an heroic figure.

By example and sometimes by comment and encouragement, Hugh, a fellow Scot, taught me there was more to writing than putting words together in an orderly fashion and to remain aware of my tendency towards linguistic laziness.

And what example! Of the ponderous British heavyweight Joe Bugner, a boxer remarkable for his lack of talent, Hugh wrote: "In his prime, Joe had the physique of a Greek statue, but he had fewer moves."

He wrote too that boxing had given the very shy Welsh champion Johnny Owen, who died following a brutal fight, his one positive means of self-expression. "It was his tragedy," wrote Hugh, "that he found himself articulate in such a dangerous language."

Boxing is Hugh's primary love and he has probably written more about Muhammad Ali than any other sports writer. His vivid descriptions of the Louisville legend include these lines on beating Joe Frazier after fourteen destructive rounds of the Thrilla in Manila: "His face had the greyness of terminal exhaustion and he moved as if the marrow of his bones had been replaced by mercury."

As well as working for the *Observer*, we both wrote for the now defunct magazine *Sports World* and, after reading an article of mine, Hugh reportedly told Alan Hubbard, the editor: "The big man can write a bit." It was just a passing comment, but one that Alan felt worth sharing. To me, who has always needed affirmation of my writing ability, it wasn't far removed from a pat on the head from God.

One thing he didn't need to teach me was how to drink to excess; we were both masters of that dark art.

On Saturday nights, after dictating his football match report for the first edition, he would come back to the office and rewrite it almost completely for the later ones. There was no such expression in Hugh's vocabulary as 'good enough.' Once, returning by train from a game in Liverpool, he realized he'd got the name of a scorer wrong in his match report. Knowing there would not be another train that night, he still got off at Crewe to phone through a correction.

With the sports pages finally put to bed, we would dwell long in the Cockpit pub next door, sometimes resulting in Hugh missing his last train home to rural Surrey. It became an occasional practice for me to put him up in my London flat where we'd do serious damage to my supply of malt whisky, and debate the finer points of Scottish self-destructiveness. That he would sometimes stay until Tuesday was a hardship only for the booze cupboard. Well, maybe for my first wife, Isobel, as well.

Towards the end of 2016, Hugh, who still lives in the south of England, embarked on a short tour of his home country with a treasure chest of memories and a small band of managers and minders, telling stories and signing books.

I joined the three hundred or so who were entertained at the Brunton Theatre in Musselburgh, near Edinburgh, by his compelling tales. It was a long evening, his third performance in as many nights, and by the time he sat at a table in the foyer to sign books, he was

Hugh McIlvanney (Photo Franscesco Guidicini/Sunday Times).

noticeably flagging. I had let it be known I was in the audience, yet as I joined the line I momentarily endured a notion that he might not remember me.

We had both left the *Observer* around the same time, Hugh to the *Sunday Times* and me to the Middle East where I lived for the rest of my working life and, for no particular reason other than distance, we hadn't connected again in the meanwhile.

When there was only me left in the line, Hugh looked up and said: "Mister Bain... how long has it been?"

"Thirty-eight years," I replied.

"My God," he said, "that long."

We went out to the street where he lit the remains of a Cuban cigar. I wished in the moment that I hadn't given them up. We had shared some remarkable times in the years when Fleet Street was still an enchanted place. There was so much to talk about but no time to do it.

"Do you fancy a drink?" I asked.

"I do," he replied, "but we have to get back to Glasgow tonight and I'm completely knackered."

We stood in silence for a moment or two, sharing the smoke from his Havana and a wealth of unspoken memories until the chill easterly wind began to reach into our elderly bones. Hugh tightened his scarf and discarded the butt of his cigar.

"Well, take care of yourself, Hugh," I said.

"You too, big man," he replied, gripping my arm with both hands.

When I reached home, I saw he had expressed on the inside page of his book the hope that I would remember the old days with warmth and affection. Oceans had flowed under the bridge since we'd last met and it was unlikely we'd see each other again.

The passage of the years weighed heavily and I felt a great sadness.

IT WAS a beautiful day; a little cold with the wind from the east. The November sun was low in the sky and I had to shield my eyes as I stepped from the main entrance of Roehampton Hospital in London. Late autumn leaves of various reds, browns and yellows had been swept by gusts into little piles, as if a workman had half-finished the job. Early afternoon traffic roared by on the ever-busy Roehampton Lane and on the golf course across the way, people hammered balls down the fairways. Nothing had changed yet everything was different.

Natalie Alexandra was born at one minute past one in the afternoon of the eleventh day of the eleventh month of 1977. The only other notable event of that Friday was the release of Mull of Kintyre by Paul McCartney's Wings.

Natalie took her time to come into this world. Her exhausted mother, Isobel, had been in labour for nearly twenty-four hours and, in the end, it had needed a pair of forceps to persuade her. I was in attendance when that wrinkle-faced infant announced her presence with resonating cries of outrage at being removed from her place of comfort and safety.

Until then she'd been a lump, a pretty big lump. A lovable lump too, but it took the transformation from lump to incredible little being for adoration to truly enter my emotional vocabulary. To my various self-descriptions I could now add father. I vowed I'd be a better one than mine.

Standing in that doorway, I wondered what kind of person Natalie would become. Would she be caring and compassionate, lively and funny, thoughtful, creative? Would she allow herself to love with all her heart and be loved in return? Would Punk, then all the rage, be gone by the time she reached adolescence?

Forty years on and all the prayers and hopes have long been fulfilled.

– 15 –

Hard times in the Gulf

TO REPORT on the Doha air crash, it really wasn't necessary to visit the impact site. I could have picked up enough information from the authorities and by interviewing some of the survivors. But when an opportunity presented itself for a close-up view of the wreckage only hours after the event, few reporters would have turned it down.

It was the morning after Royal Jordanian Airlines Flight RJ600 from Amman had ploughed into the runway while trying to land in a thunderstorm at Doha International Airport in the Gulf state of Qatar. Forty-five of the sixty-four passengers and crew on board the Boeing 727 died and eight were seriously injured. Some of the dead had been burned. I was hanging around the airport entrance when the air accident investigation team disembarked with government officials from a fleet of vehicles and marched into the building. I joined the end of the procession and was waved through.

No TV pictures, no disaster movie or vivid description, not even the cloak of professional hardness worn by many newsmen, could have prepared me for the scene of horror and devastation. It had been nearly midnight on 14 March 1979 when the aircraft hit the tarmac with considerable force, breaking into three parts as it careened more than 200 metres off the runway and smashed into the fire station. Baggage and debris were scattered over a wide area and white sheets or canvas had been laid on top of bodies recovered from the aircraft. Rescuers were trying to remove a body from a window of the plane. With no wind to speak of, the smell of burned flesh hung heavily and I was grateful to be handed a face mask.

I was walking around taking pictures and trying to stay out of people's way when a man in an airport uniform stopped me. The game's up, I thought, but he said: "Hey, can you give me a hand?" and gestured for me to pick up two corners of a tarpaulin on which lay the charred remains of a human being. The figure was completely blackened, even the teeth. It looked like a prop from a TV police forensics drama. There was little left of the flesh around the head and it was impossible to say if this had been a man or woman, or even a large child. The remains were not heavy and we carried them without effort to an ambulance. When I left the airport I threw up.

Later in the day, I met up at the British Embassy with a British businessman who had survived the crash almost unharmed by kicking out a damaged window to escape before the fire took hold. "There was another passenger behind me," he said, "but he was too big to get through. I tried to help him. It was impossible but I won't forget his cries."

So I wrote the story and spread it along with my pictures over four pages of the *Gulf Times* where I worked as deputy editor. I had been there for nearly a year after leaving Fleet Street and was wondering how mistaken a move it had been. Certainly, the sharp transition from the heart of quality journalism to launching a very minor newspaper in a hot and obscure country left me considering, not for the first time, my willingness to follow impulsive notions. I had answered the advertisement out of curiosity and was almost as surprised as Isobel when I accepted the job. Only years later did I realise the importance of that decision, one that set in motion dramatic changes to my life, personal and professional, some wonderful and some quite dreadful.

One element in leaving the UK was alcohol. Being a Scot, a Fleet Street journalist and the son of a drunk could appear as perfect pointers to a propensity towards alcohol abuse. I feared I was, as my mother might have said it, becoming just like my father. In any case, unlike such colleagues as Kelvin MacKenzie and Paul Dacre, I had probably got as far as I could in Fleet Street. Talent apart, there's nothing that slams the brakes on a career more rapidly than a reputation for heavy drinking and with it possible unreliability. Long-toothed reporters might have got away with it back then, but not those of us in editorial production where sharpness of mind was essential, not to speak of turning up for work.

I had read that alcohol availability in Qatar was limited. There was the thought somewhere in my head that a degree or two of difficulty might curb my enthusiasm for drinking. It was not a thought that lasted long. When I arrived in the country for the first time, I clinked my way off the plane, my pockets bulging with miniature bottles of Scotch. Isobel and six-month-old daughter Natalie would follow on after the fierce Arabian summer.

I was actually the first of any staff to arrive. The paper would be launched as a weekly, becoming a daily when a proper building had been constructed and new printing presses installed. The original editor, a pleasant old rogue called Charles Sharpe (I met up with him later in Dubai) resigned before he actually set foot in Doha, but not before he had taken the order for the presses and received a hefty commission from the manufacturer. That had been his intention all along. The replacement editor, Brian Nicholls, who had run an evening newspaper in Darlington, followed three months behind me.

I planned the launch from the kitchen table of my villa, at the beck and call of the likeable Qatari businessman Yousuf Darwish who headed the consortium of owners but hadn't a clue about newspaper production. Initially, very little of what I did was about journalism. I had to look for offices, set up lines of credit, organise supplies of furniture, equipment and all kinds of things.

Yousuf sent me to the bank with firm instructions: "Give the manager this cheque for one million rials but only after he's signed an overdraft facility for five million."

After I'd been sitting around the manager's outer office for fifteen minutes, his secretary told me: "Mr Abdullah will see you now."

I entered the room to find maybe a dozen Qataris and other Arab men lounging on sofas and in armchairs, chatting away happily and completely ignoring me. I hesitated, perplexed. This was not how you met your bank manager in the UK. Nowadays, of course, you are unlikely ever to meet him or her.

Mr Abdullah beckoned me forward, greeted me in reasonable English and bade me sit down. He snapped his fingers and someone poured me a small glass of sickly sweet tea. The noise around me lessened as I said who I was and what I wanted. It was a surprise when the manager appeared to repeat this in Arabic. A new hubbub of conversation sprang up among the assembled crowd. I was asked the odd question and my responses were duly translated and occasionally subjected to a comment that drew mild laughter. Then, with a flourish and a big smile, Mr Abdullah signed the overdraft letter, I gave him the cheque and we shook hands.

Outside the bank, one of the men caught up with me. "Good luck with the newspaper," he said.

"Thank you," I replied. "Er, who are all these people?" I asked.

"Oh, just businessmen and friends of Mr Abdullah. They come and sit around when they've nothing else to do. They all thought it was a good idea for Qatar to have an English newspaper and told him to give you the money."

SOON AFTER my arrival, Yousuf invited me to his home for Friday lunch (Friday being the holy day of the week). He welcomed me at the gate and led me to an open courtyard where thirty or more Arab men in traditional dress were seated cross-legged around a very large carpet on which lay great platters of whole sheep, rice and salads. A space had been left for me, in front of which was the only plate and knife and fork on the carpet. I pushed them aside and ate, as I already knew I should, with my right hand only. Yousuf, next to me, dug an arm into one of the roasted carcasses, wrestled with the innards and retrieved an enormous kidney which he held to my face.

"Er... not right now, thanks, Yousuf," I said, jerking my head back in surprise. I hoped I hadn't caused offence but he just shrugged, smiled and popped it whole into his mouth.

Some evenings I would drive a few kilometres into the desert where the Qatar Rugby Club headquarters stood as an isolated oasis for young Brits starved of company and alcohol. They played on a sand pitch and while I enjoyed the spectacle of rugby, the main attraction was the cheap beer. I later obtained what the expats called a booze licence, a small booklet with picture ID issued by the police. This allowed you to buy quite a substantial amount each month from designated alcohol outlets. So much for limited access.

I might occasionally be invited down to the Doha Club for dinner after shifting a few gins and tonic at home. This was an alcohol-free members-only establishment with sports facilities, a pool and an excellent restaurant. It was situated near the beach and, unfortunately, right at the end of the airport runway. From the glass-fronted restaurant, you would watch in increasing alarm as an approaching aircraft grew larger and larger until it seemed as if it was about to join you at the table. It certainly stopped all conversation as the aircraft roared overhead, metres above the single-storey building.

A couple of English pranksters had once, in the dead of night, hauled up an old truck tyre, applied black paint to its tread and rolled it on the roof, as if to represent the wheelmarks of a plane. They probably had not anticipated the frenzy of activity this created – or the extent of the inquiry – after a workman discovered the marks. The hoax should have been quickly obvious but procedures had to be followed. The subsequent hunt for the culprits was never going to succeed, especially since it was accompanied by the threat of long prison sentences.

It was mid-summer when editor Brian Nicholls arrived, ahead of either his family or mine. For the sake of convenience, he moved into my villa. In his forties, balding, affable enough and looking at the world through thick-lensed glasses, he was the right man for the job – meticulous, fastidious and, unlike me, very well organised. The moment I knew we wouldn't really hit it off was when I saw him ironing his underpants. That he was a moderate drinker wasn't a factor and it would be wrong of me to give the impression I wandered around half-pissed a lot of the time. I usually didn't drink until dusk had fallen. Well… maybe the odd G&T at lunchtime.

We had advertised for journalists, paste-up artists and administration staff in India and we would sit at the kitchen table sorting through thousands of applications. Ultimately, Brian went off to the

Meeting the Queen, 1979. Isobel is to the author's left.

sub-continent for what seemed like weeks of interviews and, slowly, the staff began to appear. Six months after my own arrival, the first edition of the *Gulf Times* hit the streets. I wrote a good part of it myself and, somewhere in old piles of papers, I still have a copy. It would not have stood comparison to any of my previous newspapers but it was nonetheless something to be proud of after all the time and effort spent on bringing it into being.

THE HIGHLIGHT of the year, or even the decade, for Doha's growing expat community was the visit of the Queen on board the Royal Yacht *Britannia*. It was part of her 1979 Gulf tour and the whole town was cleaned and dressed up for her arrival. The authorities made sure her route did not pass the army barracks where the firing squad carried out executions on the other side of the wire fence and where the wooden stake and single bracket of sand bags were visible to all. In those days, Doha wasn't really a hardship post (unless you were a murderer) but there were shortages. If, for example, you wanted fresh beef, rather than the frozen stuff, you would join the queue outside Ali Bin Ali supermarket on a Wednesday afternoon.

The British Bankers' Association was hosting a lunch for the Queen at the Gulf Hotel and asked me if I could write a story about it for the various inhouse publications of the member banks back in the UK. I would, of course, be invited to attend with my wife. At the last minute, probably to avoid infighting, they shoved us into the short line to meet Her Majesty.

I bowed, stuck my hand out and connected with the tips of her fingers. She winced. "And what do you do?" she asked.

"I'm a journalist, ma'am," I replied.

"How interesting," she said and moved on.

At the lunch, she ate sparingly and I wondered how she would react to the strawberries and cream since, as far as I knew, only synthetic cream was available in Doha. She touched the spoon to her mouth and put it down again without a grimace but gently pushed the plate aside.

AT THE end of my year, Brian called me into his office.

"We're not going to renew your contract, Ian," he said. "We don't really need a deputy editor." He was either too polite to mention my drinking or just didn't want to invite an argument. He wouldn't have got one since it came as no great surprise, but I was unsettled; I had a wife and child to support. Where would I go from here?

– 16 –

Drunk in Dubai

IT WASN'T the first time I had returned to my office at the *Khaleej Times* in Dubai after a lunchtime o' booze and slept through the afternoon, but it proved to be the last. When I woke up I found a hand-written note from the general manager saying: "See me in the morning."

I threw it in the bin and drove home to the apartment in the Maktoum Building on Zabeel Road, a large quadrilateral block with a central garden and play area. Most of the flats were empty when we moved in and it was perhaps a mistake to have chosen the top floor – the sixth. The flat roof wasn't thick enough and it heated up in the summer to the extent that the airconditioning couldn't really cope.

I told my long-suffering wife I might be fired.

"Not again," Isobel said with a sigh and a tear.

What a mess. I was editor of the daily newspaper's weekly magazine which I'd joined with such hopes after my sacking from the *Gulf Times* in Doha. With a family and no money, it had been an enormous relief to get the job. Now, less than a year later, I was about to pay the same price for the same old failing.

I liked the magazine. It was a long way from Fleet Street but it was mine. We were a small team. I commissioned a lot of the content, wrote some myself and bought in other material from showbiz and other agencies. I knew I couldn't drink every day because I wouldn't have been able to function at all, so I'd make sure each issue was complete before I embarked on a binge. Then I'd come off it in time to get the next issue under way. It was a delicate balance that was getting harder to maintain. There was no guarantee I could stop or that my staff, who must have been pretty sick of me, would save the day if I didn't. I usually stopped after the third day when I was too ill to drink any more, having eaten little or nothing in that time.

At home, I took a can of beer from the fridge and sat at the kitchen table, reflecting on my multiple stupidities, chances rejected and warnings ignored. On the fridge door were a couple of crayon drawings by my daughter, stick images of mummy and daddy, and photos of her playing on the beach. I felt a physical pain in my chest from all the grief I was causing. My father's son all right.

As much as I wanted to quit drinking, it seemed impossible. No matter how well-intentioned I might have been – and I'm not entirely sure that I was – there was always an inevitability about the next drink, the storm on the horizon edging relentlessly closer. It may have been the magnitude of my self-disgust and self-hatred that made alcohol so irresistible. Rather than face responsibilities and realities, I immersed myself in my wretchedness.

The worst was not the hangovers, the hour of retching into the bathroom sink or the shakes. Nor was it the snakes and demons that came through the walls and the windows whenever I tried to sleep, images so hideous that I had to open my eyes immediately or they would consume me.

What crippled me was the fear. It rolled over me in dark and terrible waves and I felt the terror of a cornered animal.

I had no illusions about the future I faced alone if I didn't stop. No job, no home, no family, no self-respect, treading in the footsteps of my father, a man lost in his craving and self-pity. So I swore to myself and to Isobel that I would stop, maybe tomorrow… or next week. Yes, next week. Definitely. I promise.

The next morning, trying to control my trembling hands, I presented myself at the general manager's office. Muzamil Ahmed was a seemingly unemotional man, feared as much as respected by the staff. He sat in his glass-walled office watching all our comings and goings. While the *Khaleej Times* was owned by the local Galadari Brothers, who also owned banks, hotels, car dealerships and much else, it was managed by Dawn Newspapers of Karachi. So the majority of its staff were Pakistani and Indian. Only a handful were British.

Waiting in his outer office for a meeting to finish, I thought of what situations he might bring up, like the time I was found face down in a flower bed at the British Embassy. Or the incident at Holy Trinity Church.

I had gone to the church for the midnight carol service on Christmas Eve, sober until I decided on a whim to drop in at a bar on the way. Having consumed several pints and a few Scotches, I should have gone home but persevered in reaching the church where I arrived in the middle of the outdoor candle-lit service. Pretty soon, I was desperate for a pee. I edged my way towards the fence where building materials had been stored and, in the darkness, started to relieve myself. I found I was urinating on a corrugated metal sheet. It sounded like a drumroll.

At that point, the carol ended, the lights came on and my bladder was not of a mind to immediately shut off the flow. I thought of Dennis on the *Kent Messenger*. At the time, I couldn't see the humour in it.

There had been numerous other occasions to which I'd been invited as editor of the magazine and where my misbehaviour must have been noted. Mr Muzamil, as he was known, could have loaded the gun with any or all of them.

A buzzer sounded and his formidable secretary invited me to enter. "Sit down," he instructed, leaning back in his chair while I sat on the edge of mine.

"You know that you cannot continue as editor of the magazine," he said. "This is a Muslim-owned organisation and you are an embarrassment to us."

I nodded. It was what I'd expected. I wondered how much time I had to look for another job before my visa was cancelled. If anyone would give me a job, that is. The practice with a dismissed employee was for the company to take his or her passport to the Labour Department for visa cancellation. At an arranged time, a representative of the company would then meet the employee at the airport where the passport would be returned with a one-way ticket to the country of origin. I hoped they would give me a week.

"You're a good writer," Muzamil went on. "It is shameful that you waste your talent and your life."

There was nothing I could say. He paused and looked at me. "If you wish to remain, we will employ you as a freelance. We will pay you per article and if you don't write, you won't get paid and then we'd have to look again at the arrangement. Would that be agreeable?"

I was stunned. This was not how the company worked. It was renowned for its ruthlessness. There were no second chances.

"It would," I said. "Thank you." I had to stop myself from blurting out extravagant expressions of gratitude.

"Don't waste this opportunity," he replied. "I will send you the details. And maybe you can help find us a new editor."

The terms, in the circumstances, were reasonable. Frankly, anything would have been acceptable. I would keep the visa, the company flat and the car. I would write 4,000 words a week for which I'd be paid 6,000 dirhams a month – about £1,200 – and I would have to originate my own material. I sorted out the next two issues of the magazine and arranged to take a couple of weeks of my holiday entitlement. Then I went out to celebrate.

Five days later I walked into the psychiatric unit of the Rashid Hospital in Dubai and asked to be let in. What took me there was the discovery that I could carry on drinking beyond the three-day barrier. The consultant psychiatrist studied me and asked: "Are you sure? We don't have an alcoholic ward. You'll be in with all the ordinary patients."

"I'm sure," I said, not really understanding what he meant by ordinary patients.

The first thing I noticed were the guards in police uniforms, not outside but inside the ward. They carried batons in their hands and reminded me of a conversation I'd had with a police lieutenant friend about allegations of police brutality. "Do you ever beat confessions out of prisoners?" I'd asked. "Of course not!" he retorted, then paused. "Only if we know they're really guilty."

The next assault on my senses was the combined smell of excrement, urine and disinfectant. I put my hand up to my face and the nurse leading me to my bed said: "You'll get used to it. It's not always as bad as this."

Then there was the noise – the shouts, cries, moans and groans. My bed was the usual public hospital variety in a ward of eleven others. I looked around me. Most of the patients were lying curled up or rocking back and forth, some in silence, others uttering weird sounds. Two were slumped by the far wall and it shocked me to see they were handcuffed to the water pipes.

There was no conversation among the patients, no games of cards or chess, no interaction whatsoever. They appeared all locked in their own little worlds until they sometimes exploded into the worlds of those around them. It appeared as if few had any sense of awareness of where they were or what was going on.

The nights were particularly bad. As I lay awake in the darkness, I wondered if I'd prefer the snakes and demons to the agonised, pitiful cries of men pleading for some once-beloved person in their lives to come and save them. Sometimes it was me crying out.

During the first couple of days and despite being pumped full of vitamin B12 and diazepam, I suffered physical pain and emotional agony. The shame and the guilt crucified me. The ache in my body began to ease on the third day but not the ache in my heart or the emotional turmoil. I drank because of existential pain, because the pain of living had become too intense. Alcohol brought me momentary relief. Of course, it came at a price. And I was paying it, not only in this bleak hospital ward.

There was little or no psychiatric treatment, other than the drugs. By the fifth day, I asked if I could leave. "Tomorrow," said the doctor. "After that, I don't ever want to see you again."

As far as the office was concerned, I'd been on holiday and the hospital had assured me my treatment would remain confidential. But I had to start producing articles. As editor, I had listed numerous ideas for future pieces and I'd taken the list when I left.

I attended regular meetings of the local branch of Alcoholics Anonymous and from those and my new sense of physical well-being, a hope began to emerge that, one day at a time, I could get my life back.

Writing 4,000 words a week was easier than I'd expected. My often acerbic television column, centred on the multiple blunders of the local English-language channel, Dubai 33, was popular and consumed at least 800 words. That plus a major feature and a shorter one made up the required number.

I unearthed all kinds of subjects. I found one of the heroes of the battle of Arnheim, the famous *A Bridge Too Far* over the Rhine, living and working in Dubai. I wrote a series of articles revealing all the under-the-counter air fares that broke joint airline agreements. I even wrote one on the work of AA which brought in a number of new members.

Mr Muzamil was happy I'd found him a new editor, one who could easily handle the job and, equally important, I could count on as an ally. I had called Charles Sharpe, the old rogue who had taken the contract for the printing press for the *Gulf Times* in Doha then pulled out of the job of editor before he'd even started. Charles was a jovial cove in his early sixties and he and his wife, Pat, were up for the adventure, especially since their daughter and son-in-law were living in Dubai.

I liked Dubai. In 1980, it was still a bit of a frontier town although it was far from the hardship posting that many multi-national companies – to the delight of their expatriate employees – considered it to be. As the months went by and my sobriety looked like holding, Isobel was happier and Natalie was discovering the pleasures of nursery school. The stories of my escapades were becoming yesterday's news as other hard core drinkers vied to replace me as the town drunk.

But there was something not quite right and it had nothing to do with booze. The comfortable life I was enjoying for the first time in years just didn't seem to be enough.

– 17 –

Abu Dhabi or bust

THE DESERT on either side of the road from Dubai to Abu Dhabi consisted not of rolling sand dunes but flat scrubland baked by the unrelenting sun. Stunted bushes and tufted grasses struggled to survive until the rains came briefly in December or January and the whole landscape rushed into colour.

Construction of the road, two strips of tarmac that stretched about 140 kilometres from the Trade Centre roundabout in Dubai to the UAE capital, had begun in 1971 and had only just been completed when I first began to travel it in the early Eighties.

It proved an irresistible test of speed and bravado for young men in high-powered cars until the authorities laid white-painted road humps – so high they could almost scrape the sumps of small trucks – at strategic points. These became deadly spots for unaware drivers when the paint wore off and the warning signs became obliterated.

The terrain was the domain of lizards and other reptiles, the occasional desert hare and the ubiquitous camel which, for those of us who frequently made the journey, was a very dangerous animal. If your car killed a camel you, your insurers or the executors of your will would have to pay the camel owner nearly 30,000 dirhams, about £6,000, in what they called blood money.

It came as no surprise, then, that the majority of the great beasts seen around the edges of the road were diseased, very old or lame. Who could blame the herdsmen for seeking to capitalise on the value of their rapidly declining assets? The problem was that such collisions were invariably fatal for all involved, the camel usually ending up in

Camels on the Abu Dhabi road, early 1980s (Photo Paul Woodlock).

the front seats. It took a few years of carnage before the authorities reversed the rule and made the camel owners liable for much greater compensation. After that, you couldn't see an animal for miles. Eventually they further enhanced safety by installing wire fences for the entire length of the highway.

In the interim period, however, you undertook the journey with considerable caution, especially at night when your senses had to be on full alert. For most of its length, the road was unlit and drivers coming from the other direction were, understandably, disinclined to dip their headlights. The trick was to watch carefully for any interruption to the glare of the oncoming lights which might indicate a bush in the barrier-free central reservation – or the movement of a camel or two. Or a whole herd.

They would appear as grey apparitions, crossing the road in ultra-slow motion or just standing in the middle of it in defiance of self-preservation. I once heard a terrible whack on the windscreen and realised with an enormous shock that I had just hit the tail of a camel. But my closest brush with death on that road came not with a beast of burden but a herd of cows and in a place where I'd have least expected it.

In the darkness of evening, I had just started out from Dubai and was passing the Trade Centre apartments when several cows broke through bushes in the central reservation right in front my Honda Prelude sports car. A taxi coming in the other direction had ploughed into the poor animals, sending them panicked into my path. I didn't even have time to hit the brakes. The Prelude, which was slung pretty low at the front, scooped up one cow which smashed against the windscreen, showering me with glass splinters. The windscreen bowed until it was just a centimetre or two from my face, and the animal rolled over the roof and spun down the road behind me. Miraculously, it got to its feet and ran off.

The car had stopped in the central reservation and I realised I was in even greater danger if I remained there. A great shriek of airbrakes heralded the approach of a jack-knifed articulated lorry so I followed the cow and took off across the sand as fast as my legs could carry me. I'm not sure what the offence was, but I was fined 300 dirhams and ordered to pay 6,000 dirhams into court in case the cow turned up dead. I'm pleased that it didn't and I eventually got my money back.

WHENEVER possible, I would avoid going to Abu Dhabi and, when I absolutely had to, I would try to get back before dusk. But nightfall comes early in that part of the world and it wasn't always possible. I just had to drive at no more than a hundred kilometres an hour or maybe slot in convoy-style behind a couple of other cars and take advantage of their headlights. But they were often too fast or too slow. Sometimes, with no other traffic, I would imagine I was driving down a English country lane with great trees overhanging both sides. In the absolute darkness there were times when I felt I could actually see them.

In the circumstances, it was with mixed feelings that I accepted one of my first contracts as a public relations consultant. The client was a government-owned oil company in Abu Dhabi and the connection came through an ex-journo friend who worked for the UAE Ministry of Information. The company wanted a monthly in-house newspaper in English and Arabic and it wanted me on hand to get it under way.

After leaving the editorship of the *Khaleej Times* magazine, I needed to make a decision about my future. Working as a freelance writer was a relatively easy but somewhat impoverished existence and not all ambition had been drained out of me by alcohol.

At the magazine, I had received dozens of what purported to be press releases from local advertising agencies. I recall one letter that said: 'Dear Sir' – they didn't even bother to personalise it – 'Enclosed is a photograph of our client opening his latest supermarket. As you know, our client is one of your biggest advertisers and we expect you to publish this in a prominent position.'

I remember throwing the picture in the bin, but the letter planted the thought that this town definitely needed proper public relations. The difficulties were that I had no PR agency experience, no trade licence, no money and only a shaky belief that it would work. Would companies that were still coming to terms with advertising be willing to pay separately for the less tangible benefits of public relations? All I had was an ability to write in a journalistic fashion and an understanding of what editors would publish.

What I needed to do, I thought, was to forget about UAE and Gulf companies, for the moment at least, and focus on multi-nationals seeking to create a greater awareness of their goods and services in the area. So it was back to the kitchen table, only this time it wasn't a newspaper I was planning.

After a few months of trying to work from home, I set up a one-room office in the bowels of the Dubai Metropolitan Hotel and was pretty pleased with myself when I stuck a brass plate that said Bain Communications on the door. It was expensive and I kept it well-polished.

Taking the oil company contract didn't exactly fit my intention to focus on multi-nationals but payment would be assured and, in any case, I was already in some financial trouble. Based only on the strength of my business plan, the most obliging of bank managers had allowed me a loan facility of up to 50,000 dirhams, about £10,000, entirely without collateral and I was running very close to the edge.

The person to whom I reported at the oil company was a very smart woman we'll call Maitha, a UAE national. The monthly newspaper had been her idea.

"I'm so pleased you're here," she said on my arrival in the office. "We've been trying for nearly a year to get this going and it simply hasn't happened."

It was a statement I didn't question at the time but wished later that I had. The department head was a wiry little man called Ali who, for reasons I could not understand at the time, took an instant dislike to me.

I tried for a few days to commute between the two cities but after three nights of driving back in the dark my nerves were frayed. Freshly sober, I needed to minimise stress and I was able to get a discounted rate at a reasonable hotel. It would take about a month to set it all up. After that I could visit as and when necessary.

The first issue looked good and received general applause except from Ali who picked at it like a scab. He didn't like the quality of the paper, the layout, the photography and the Arabic translations, even though they had been done by one of the best Arab journalists in the country – at some cost, I should add. And he particularly didn't like the praise I was receiving.

I'd made friends in the office with an Englishman called John who looked after the company's advertising and the two of us occasionally had a meal together. One night before midnight, as I was getting ready to go to bed, he knocked on my hotel room door.

"We have a problem," he said after I'd invited him in. "Ali wants you out."

"What's going on?" I asked. "He's been against me from the beginning."

"Well," said John. "You obviously don't know that Ali fought tooth and nail against your appointment because taking you on meant his whole team, which had failed miserably to get a publication together, would be displaced."

Ali's antagonism suddenly made sense. "So why are you telling me this at this time of night?"

John looked uncomfortable. "Ali has instructed me to give you a message. He says if you don't quit the contract he will arrange for you to be deported from the UAE."

I was stunned. "Can he do that?"

"For a long time he was personal tutor to a very important person in the ruling family," said John. "That's how he got this job. I wouldn't put it to the test."

After John left, I paced the room for a while. The mini-bar, which had been fairly easy to ignore, suddenly looked huge and inviting. It was a bad situation but I knew there was one way I could make it much worse.

In the morning, I went to see the general manager of the company, a European on secondment from a global oil giant. I explained the situation and finished by saying: "This is one of your employees."

It was clearly news the GM didn't want to hear. "I'm sorry you have a problem with Ali," he said, "but I don't see what I can do about it."

"You are kidding," I said, astonished.

He ignored me. "It's entirely up to you what you do. I don't think there's anything more I want to say," he said, rising from his chair to show me out.

Earlier I had called a contact, a long-time Abu Dhabi resident with good connections among those who matter. He thought it would be in my best interests to cut my losses and run. With a wife and child, I had no alternative. I told Maitha what had happened and that I had to leave. She was being moved to another department, she said. I went back to the hotel, typed out my invoice which was for a total of just over 100,000 dirhams, some £20,000, and included the hotel bill and other expenses. I drove back to the oil company and took it to the finance director's office. He told me to come back the next day. I was waiting for him when he arrived the following morning.

"I can't pay you all this," he said. "You've broken your contract."

I felt like hitting him. "Actually," I said, "your department manager broke the contract."

"That's not my concern," he said. "You'll have to leave this with me." I told him that in view of his company's deplorable behaviour, I wanted the money now.

I sat in his outer office, door-stepping him for half the day. I refused to leave because the reality was pretty drastic. I had little more than our emergency fund left – enough for one-way air tickets back to the UK – and that was untouchable. The electricity bill was due in a week and there was no flexibility. If you didn't pay within seven days they cut you off, high summer or not. But I hated the idea of doing a runner, of letting people down. Eventually, he called me back in and waved a piece of paper.

"I've spoken to the GM and this is a cheque for 56,000 dirhams," he said. "You can take it or leave it."

I took it. It meant I could repay most of the bank loan, cover the electricity charges, pay debts and have enough left to live on for a month or two. But it was close. At least, I wouldn't have to drive that bloody road again for as long as I could help it.

– 18 –

Roger and out

IT WOULD be easy to believe that Roger Sargent had emerged from the womb screaming with rage. I first met him on the *Khaleej Times* where he stood out as an exceptional writer, a decent sub-editor and a very angry man. Using his talent with words, Roger could paint a majestic landscape in broad brushstrokes or a penetrating portrait in fine detail, whichever was required. He was a good old-fashioned journalist who had also spent years writing books until he was defeated by the unwavering flow of rejection slips.

"The trouble," he once told me, "was that when life was good I could write like Hemingway. But when I desperately need money, it all came out like Harold Robbins."

Either style could have been financially rewarding but Roger would combine both in the same chapter. That was the problem with real life too – you never knew which person would be present on any particular day or when his mood might suddenly change.

He never told me what brought him to the *Khaleej Times* where I was editing the weekend magazine, but it soon became evident. We had both descended from greater heights – me due to an increasing fondness for the hostelries of Fleet Street and he because his growling sense of injustice, personal and in general, would too frequently roar into violent eruption.

A big man with a heavy *Magnum, PI* moustache, Roger could, on occasion, be charming and pleasant company. He was obliging whatever the newspaper assignment and meticulous in its execution. But then something would go wrong, a comment taken badly, a misfired joke and he could quickly ignite. Or he might simply read something in the newspaper that sparked outrage.

I've often wondered why anger so consumed him. He always seemed to be waiting for an excuse to express it. It was almost certainly related to physical and/or emotional trauma as a child or deprivation of some kind but it didn't give him much respite, not that he tried to curb it. If he'd attended an anger management course he might well have been expelled on the first day.

Roger didn't last long at the *Khaleej Times*, nor the *Gulf News* which he joined later and where – for one night only – he was put in charge of the sports pages. The editorial pages of English-language newspapers in the Gulf at that time were adequately produced but Roger despised what he regarded a second-best. On the night he was in charge, Roger took revenge on what he saw as uninspired layouts, average writing and dull headlines.

He produced a masterpiece of newspaper design, a Canaletto for modern times – bold and beautiful with big balanced photographs and headline sizes that might have been reserved for the announcement the Second Coming. The detail was precise and the overall effect stunning. But if Roger's back page might have been worthy of the walls of the Royal Academy or the Newspaper Publishers' Association, it was entirely wrong for the *Gulf News*.

This was a hand grenade hurled into the paper's quite conservative design, and the editor did not like it at all. The *Gulf News* management could not accommodate an unruly rebellious child no matter how gifted it might be, so Roger went back to the UK, freelancing for various magazines.

Soon after I set up Bain Communications in 1981, I required urgent help – even on a temporary basis. I thought of Roger who came willingly and gratefully. I sent him the air ticket and set aside my misgivings about his temperament.

For a time it worked well enough. But while he needed the money, it became clear that Roger couldn't deal with the work. He must have felt that writing press releases was below his dignity and that he was abandoning his journalistic integrity. When I produced a release, I did it as if I was writing a news story. And most of the stuff that came out of my office really were news stories. For example: 'Intel launches fast new chip' or 'Rothmans driver Al Hajri to compete in Egypt's Pharaohs' Rally' or 'Emirates to open five new routes this spring'.

That most of the Gulf newspapers published them without changing a word suggested the material was adequately written and worth using. Apart from that, editors in that part of the world didn't like having to rewrite. I felt I demonstrated some personal integrity by refusing to issue what I considered to be non-stories, even under pressure from clients. I had a reputation to build and it would not be helped if I deluged newspapers with duff stuff. Maybe I'm protesting too much.

While I could justify it to myself, I suppose Roger saw PR as a step too far down the ladder. At first, he did it well enough, if somewhat grudgingly. He let his feelings be known when he delivered his efforts, throwing them almost contemptuously onto my desk. But it soon became obvious he'd begun to sabotage the work by writing it badly which, for him, couldn't have been easy.

He stopped talking in the office, simply grunting when I asked him to do something. Tensions were building so I sent him to Bahrain for a fairly innocuous client event that he handled well enough before going AWOL. I liked this deeply troubled man and I worried about him. After a few days and a number of phone calls, I located him in the office of the *Gulf Mirror*, Bahrain's weekly paper where, the editor told me, he had just turned up and offered to do odd editorial jobs unpaid. When he returned to Dubai, I asked him as gently as possible what was going on, even when I knew that anything I said would light the blue touch paper.

"LOOK WHAT YOU'VE BECOME!" he screamed at me, his face purple and his mouth spraying saliva. "YOU'RE NOT A JOURNALIST ANY MORE! YOU'RE A PROSTITUTE!"

He may well have been addressing himself but Roger rarely took responsibility for his temper when there was someone he could blame. He was projecting his feelings about himself onto me.

He picked up my heavy desktop computer and raised it above his head – and above mine. I said nothing and didn't get up from my chair. He stood there trembling, a bead of sweat or snot dripping from his nose. I continued to look at him without, hopefully, showing any emotion. Somehow sense and maybe my bravado prevailed. He put it down and stormed out in a trail of abuse that echoed along the corridor. It was an experience that left me shaken and unsure of how close I had come to serious injury.

There had been stories, some from Roger's teenage son who came to visit him in Dubai, of explosive, violent acts that had left people physically hurt and vague references to domestic abuse. Roger's wife had divorced him a few years earlier.

"I thought," said Jyoti, my secretary, "he really was going to throw it at you. But that was stupid of you to just stare at him."

I never saw Roger again. He left the company car at the airport, its front bumper crumpled from being smashed deliberately into a pillar. I took the cost of repair from his outstanding wages and sent the balance to his UK address.

A couple of years later, I heard he had died from a heart attack. He was in his late forties. It wasn't a surprise. He must have been living with that risk for a number of years but it was such a waste of talent and possibility. I wonder how he might have fared as a writer and as a human being if his childhood had been kinder, if he had come to terms with his anger and if he'd found help.

I have to acknowledge that Roger did me one favour for which I remain enormously grateful. He found me Jyoti. They had met, as far as I can recall, in a hospital waiting room and in conversation she remarked she was looking for a job, her first after leaving school. She was seventeen or eighteen. Roger suggested she came to see me.

Jyoti became my girl Friday, general assistant, secretary, fixer, office manager – all those roles in one – and was the best thing that could have happened to Bain Communications in its fledgling years. Clever, organised, efficient, remarkably loyal and with wisdom far beyond her years, she took control of the administration as if born to it and in the five years she ran the office she saved me from many a foolish mistake in my dealings with clients, staff and media. It is no surprise that she now runs two hotels in Mumbai.

For some time after Roger left, I wondered if he had been right about me. There was a part of me that agreed with him. For practical and financial reasons – important ones that included the security of my own family – I had, as Roger would have put it, sold out. I was leaving journalism for commercial enterprise, the opportunity to make the kind of money most journalists never do. But for years I would continue to describe myself as a journalist when asked in casual conversation but definitely not on landing cards going into countries where it would have been reckless to do so.

For a while, I still kept my hand in, writing occasional pieces for the *Observer* and the *Economist*. An issue of the latter was banned in the UAE after it carried a front page headline 'Islamic Bomb in Dubai' and my full-page story inside on how a man with a Saudi passport had left three giant bars of Toblerone in his room in the Hyatt Regency Hotel when he checked out. The chocolate had been bound together by string or wire.

When three room cleaners going down in the service elevator decided to share it out, the large bomb within exploded, killing them and seriously damaging two floors of the hotel. The reason was fairly clear. Alcohol was freely available in hotels but an unwritten rule existed that Gulf nationals changed from their traditional long white *kandouras* into Western dress before they entered a bar. The Hyatt appeared not to enforce that rule. At the same time, the hotel's nightclub was known for its 'girlie' shows featuring scantily clad Eastern European dancers. It was relatively tame stuff but it attracted attention.

In my article – written under a From Our Correspondent byline – I added that the dress rule had been strictly enforced in all hotels immediately after the bomb and how girlie shows throughout the town had disappeared.

While I still got a buzz from these journalistic endeavours, they were risky. If the authorities had discovered I was the writer of the *Economist* article, I might have been in trouble for not registering as a foreign correspondent. I also had to consider my recent experience in Abu Dhabi.

So I reluctantly decided to let go of journalism completely and focus on the PR business. I had no doubt there would be many exciting times ahead but I felt sad, remembering all my dreams when I sat on that bus in Gravesend taking me to the *Kent Messenger* office and my first day in newspapers.

Dubai in the early 1980s (Photo Paul Woodlock).

IN MY EARLY years in Dubai, I produced and wrote a forty-minute documentary on the city using professional cameraman Mike Shepley and with Scottish actor Paul Young playing a visiting businessman and providing the voice-over. I called it Dubai Absolutely.

I didn't have a licence for that sort of thing so I used a video lab in Sharjah which did. In return, I paid it to copy, label and box the finished article. It had a whole bank of machines that could produce twenty or more at a time. Filming and editing costs were partly funded by clients and sponsors who in turn received subtle editorial coverage. Well, maybe some of it not so subtle.

I hadn't realised at that time how Wild West the Emirates were when it came to the copyright of intellectual property. Video stores would call me up.

"How many do you want?" I would ask. "Twenty? Thirty?"

"Oh no, just one. We'll copy it ourselves."

The video lab turned out to be run by a bunch of crooks. Its owners sold a considerable number through distribution but we never saw a dirham. I snatched back the master copy, but they simply copied from a copy and ordered more of our nicely designed covers from our supplier. Even Dubai Duty Free, a regular client, was selling pirated copies.

Those were the days.

– 19 –

Staying one jump ahead

I LOOKED up from the report I was writing in the coffee shop of the Dubai Metropolitan Hotel to find Princess Anne glaring at me from the next table. So I quickly looked down again. Was it a case of mistaken identity, I wondered. I was press officer for the international showjumping event in which she was competing but we had never spoken. Risking another glance, I was relieved to note that her eyes seemed fixed on my left ear or whatever lay beyond it.

I picked up a napkin, wiped my mouth in a casual sort of way and turned slowly to see where her attention might actually be focused. There, in the doorway, still in his riding gear, pint of beer in hand and laughing loudly with a female competitor was Captain Mark Phillips, Princess Anne's then-husband. It was clear from the way he propped himself up against the door frame, from the careless angle of his glass which was dripping beer on the floor, from the flush on his face and the distinct lack of clarity in his pronunciation that Capt Phillips was inebriated, much to the displeasure of his missus.

The princess gathered her things, gave him a final look of disgust, and marched out. The captain manoeuvred his way back to the adjoining Red Lion pub where, I understand, he was hassled by the other riders into buying a round of drinks – a rare event, according to them. I recalled a gossip column story in the British Press a little earlier on how his teammates grabbed Capt Phillips as he tried to leave a bar in Australia without putting his hand in his breeches. The brilliant headline read 'Almost a Clear Round for Mark'.

For Dubai to host a showjumping event with world-class competitors back in the 1980s was a remarkable achievement, especially on a make-shift soft-ball pitch. The man behind it was Majeed Khalil, the Palestine-born general manager of the hotel, a likeable little man with an adoration of all things British… well, most things, and an enormous pride in his own naturalised British citizenship.

I had done a deal with Majeed. In return the hotel's sponsorship of my work visa and for my one-room office, I would pay rent of 30,000 dirhams (£6,000) a year and carry out a small amount of public relations work. It was a foolish arrangement that provided me with little more than a lesson in better business practices. Our understandings of what constituted a small amount differed enormously and led to frequent fiery debate. Majeed's demands rose constantly and he met my attempts to secure some fees with vague promises that he would seek approval from the hotel's owner, Dubai businessman Khalfan al Habtoor. Of course, it never came.

Thankfully, my client in this instance was Dunhill, the sponsor of the event and sister company to Rothmans. Spectator seating consisted of scaffolding and wooden planks and we surrounded the course with Dunhill signage. The show was televised by the local channel, Dubai 33, and took place over several nights under powerful floodlights.

The venue was within the considerable grounds of the hotel, little of which had been beautified and consisted primarily of sand. It was what most of the local competitors – and horses – were used to. The British riders could not bring their own horses because of the slim possibility they might contract African horse disease, so they had to rely on a pool of locally-trained animals.

If the Brits didn't take it too seriously, the others certainly did. Equestrian sports were growing rapidly in the region and some very good teams came from Oman, Saudi Arabia, Kuwait and elsewhere, as well as a sizeable entry from the UAE.

The hotel sat on the edge of the Abu Dhabi road and was considered back then to be well out of town. Its construction followed the announcement of plans for a new airport in the same location but, while the hotel was built, the airport wasn't. That could have been a death blow but residential Dubai was beginning to sprawl out towards it and the hotel became a fairly popular venue for all sorts of things. And, much to my annoyance, the eager Majeed always had ideas to keep it in the news.

The British riders who, to the best of my recollection, included David Broom and Harvey Smith, plus Anne and Mark and a couple more, enjoyed coming to Dubai. It was a nice little holiday in the winter sun, a straight fee and some reasonable prize money. And just to keep it all nice and friendly, they agreed to pool their winnings.

The big winner that night had been Mark Phillips, hence perhaps his liquid celebration. Then I heard that Mark was not, after all, particularly keen on the idea of sharing his winnings, that he'd considered it a suggestion rather than an agreement and, thank you very much, he would take the risk and match his skills against anyone's.

This, as one might imagine, did not go down well with the rest of the British riders. While no comment was forthcoming from Princess Anne – or Mark for that matter – there were deep grumblings in the ranks. Majeed, who told me all about it, was anxious for the matter to go away and, particularly, for no word of it to escape into the Press, not that the local media, which did everything to avoid controversy, would have carried such a story.

On Sunday morning (Sunday being a normal working day in the Gulf), after the circus had left town, Majeed came rushing down to my office. His face was red and he was spluttering obscenities.

"Have you seen this? Have you seen this fucking story?" he yelled, handing me a piece of paper. "How the fuck did this get out?"

It was a fax of a story in the British newspaper the *Sunday People* all about Capt Phillips and the row that followed his decision not to share his significant winnings.

"Good Lord!" I said. "That's put the cat among the pigeons. One of the riders must have given them a call."

"This is despicable!" Majeed wailed. "Dreadful behaviour! How could someone do this?" I felt he wanted to add "to me."

I suspected the general manager's anguish was over the possibility that it might tarnish any hope of a small gong coming his way, not really for this event but for the establishment of the annual British

Week which showcased UK goods and services. Well, he didn't get a gong in the end, but he was still pretty pleased with being made a Freeman of the City of London, giving him, among other things, the right to drive sheep across London Bridge and to a silken rope if they ever found reason to hang him.

After he'd gone, I took a closer look at the fax. The *Sunday People* had certainly given the story a good show without, of course, a byline. It hadn't been cut by much and I knew there would be a cheque for £150 coming my way. I could have got more if I'd flogged it around the rest of the Sunday redtops but then, I didn't want to be greedy.

ALTHOUGH I had little interest in showjumping as a spectator, it seemed to follow me around professionally. On behalf of another client, I once handled the publicity for a smaller, national event in Dubai. That included, unusually, providing the bars over which the horses would leap. In a country with little in the way of trees, they were expensive items and I felt the organisers were trying to load the sponsor with extras.

Bars have to be of a certain weight, length and circumference and I gave the exact measurements to the firm that would prepare and paint them. Then I just got on with the part with which I was more familiar, providing information for the media and setting up a small press office.

I arrived on the morning of the show just as the suppliers were unloading the bars onto the ground. I stared at them in horror.

"These bars," I told the boss, "are square. They have to be round."

I didn't say it quite as calmly as that. There was a flourish of expletives and a great waving of arms and slappings of the brow. The bars were rapidly reloaded onto the lorry and came back in the correct shape just in time to prevent the horses and riders from having a very easy competition and the organisers from attacking me. I guessed they'd sort out their own bars after that.

– 20 –

The only game in town

SETTING UP Bain Communications was one of the smartest moves I made in a life littered with some very unsmart decisions. I didn't want to build an empire; I didn't have that kind of drive. I was looking for a creative, rewarding life without too many problems. I'd had enough of those. I would have been content with two or three well-paying clients, an efficient secretary and the freelance services of a skilled Arab journalist who could handle my translations.

That I resisted growth in a captive market indicated both a lack of ambition and the level of my business naivety, or even stupidity. Journalists do not generally make good businessmen but it wasn't quite as simple as that. There was something quite troubling in my neglect of opportunities.

In those early days Dubai was thriving but still a distance from the boom city it would become. Among the Brits, there were enthusiastic young entrepreneurs all over the place. Ian Fairservice, a slip of a lad back then, had leapt from the hotel business to launch *What's On* magazine, Quetin Cope set up Peel Middle East which became the Masteg Group, serving the oil and gas and other industries, and Brian Wilkie was starting Memo Express courier service. I was the only game in town for public relations and was in the enviable, and some might say ridiculous, position of being able to choose my clients. I did some work for Marlboro but then switched to Rothmans because I preferred their motor sports plans for the region – and they paid better. I signed with Airbus rather than McDonnell Douglas or Boeing because I've always supported the underdog.

If I had really exploited the situation, I'd have soaked up every non-competitive client I could find and then worried about how to service them. And maybe set up another company with different management and personnel to handle any conflicts of interest. As it was, most of my clients came to me.

It is much more difficult to teach journalism to publicists than to teach PR skills to journalists so I hired a couple of people with decent writing ability from the local English-language newspapers. And, of course, I was learning all the time. Our international clients didn't only want exposure in the UAE, they required it in all the Gulf states including Saudi Arabia and often as far as Lebanon, Jordan and Egypt. We needed to maintain contact with more than a hundred editors and writers. It also meant a lot of travel.

Even though I couldn't read or speak Arabic, I had to take a crash course in understanding the Arab media which included the national newspapers of ten countries, regional papers, the pan-Arab political and social magazines published out of Beirut, London and Paris, specialist press like motoring magazines and technology journals as well as TV and radio stations.

A number of the pan-Arab magazines – the equivalent of, say, *Time* and *Newsweek* – had transferred their operations from Beirut to London during the civil war in Lebanon and hadn't returned after it was over. I came up with the idea of getting clients to host irregular dinners and PR presentations for these London-based Arab editors. This also gave me the opportunity to have a few days at leisure in the UK. We would hire a private dining room in a top London hotel for a dozen people and it was always a jolly affair.

One client, British Aerospace (now BAE Systems), was keen to promote its new Eurofighter aircraft and I persuaded the managing director to host the group. His office provided a date he'd be available. To my dismay, it was right in the middle of a week's salmon fishing that I had already paid for. I went back saying that because of other commitments in that week, it would be difficult to get all the defence correspondents. The following week would be much better. The MD reluctantly agreed. When we eventually sat round the dining table, he told the guests: "I have such respect for your publications that I cut short a skiing holiday in Switzerland to be here tonight."

A country like Saudi Arabia might have four or five daily papers, Kuwait a similar number, so the regional list was extensive. We also needed to subscribe to all these publications so that we could provide evidence of publicity achieved.

Initially, I ran the business as a kind of newsroom, sending out lots of well-written press releases. If and when these were published, we would clip and photocopy them and compile a monthly cuttings book for the client. We also clipped anything that might be relevant to the client's interests, such as a new law or a competitor's activities. It was boring, painstaking work since we received up to forty newspapers a day. All of them had to be read and the staff be aware of what to look for. Sometimes we'd cut one of our stories only to find we'd slashed through another on the other side of the page.

Getting the material to the media wasn't straightforward. The first transmission machine I ever had was a telex which was a real pain to operate. Then we had basic fax machines. The problem was that some newspaper offices didn't have one, or if they did, it was often left unattended. And if we had pictures to send, they had to go by courier. Overall, that proved by far the best option; we could get the material directly into the hands of our contacts, and while the courier bills were enormous, the clients paid. For immediate events like motor rallies, we would hire a wire machine that would take half an hour to transmit a photo over the phone lines. But first you had to get your film developed and the picture printed…

FROM STARTING out, it would be a couple of years before Bain Communications evolved into a more sophisticated and complex operation, maintaining the bread-and-butter news service but producing strategies and initiating activities that would enhance client reputation, and much more.

Success, you might say, forced itself upon me. I twice had to move to bigger offices, hire more people, build an image for ourselves and do all the stuff that induces headaches and aggravation. One of the first hurdles was in registering the business and getting a trade licence of my own, an absolute requirement in that part of the world.

The authorities, however, had never heard of this kind of work. The common understanding in the Gulf of a public relations man was – and probably still is – a Mr Fixit who handles a company's dealings with officialdom, obtaining work permits and making visa applications and much more. Bureaucracy in Dubai was as stifling as in the UK, and all of it carried out in Arabic.

"We are not giving you a licence to trade in visas," I was told.

I explained what we did was promotion work for companies like Rothmans so they licensed us as a commission agency in tobacco, whatever that meant. On renewal a few years later, I was able to change the description to one more appropriate to our activities. Even the business's name was a problem. The Arabic word for communications is *etisalat* and, since that was the name of the UAE phone company, I was restricted in its use. We had to be called Bain Trading Communications. While I accepted that with the Arabic wording, I ignored the instruction to change the English name.

There was another issue. Foreigners were not allowed to set up a business without a local partner who would, on paper, own fifty-one per cent and bear legal responsibility. Since these partners didn't invest any money, the law was usually circumvented by the payment of a not-particularly-large annual fee in lieu of profits and an exchange of letters. I was fortunate in having a friend and a man of great integrity, Abdullah Omar, as my partner. He was very laid back and always made himself available when I needed him. Some UAE nationals made a great living from sponsoring dozens of businesses. In much later years, Dubai established free zones like Media City and Internet City where one hundred per cent foreign ownership was allowed.

SOMEWHAT TO my surprise, I generally enjoyed the work. To be more precise, I enjoyed dealing with clients, being out in the field, gathering information, writing releases and running press offices. There was also a buzz in handing over a monthly cuttings file several inches thick.

Rothmans had signed a potentially brilliant young rally driver,

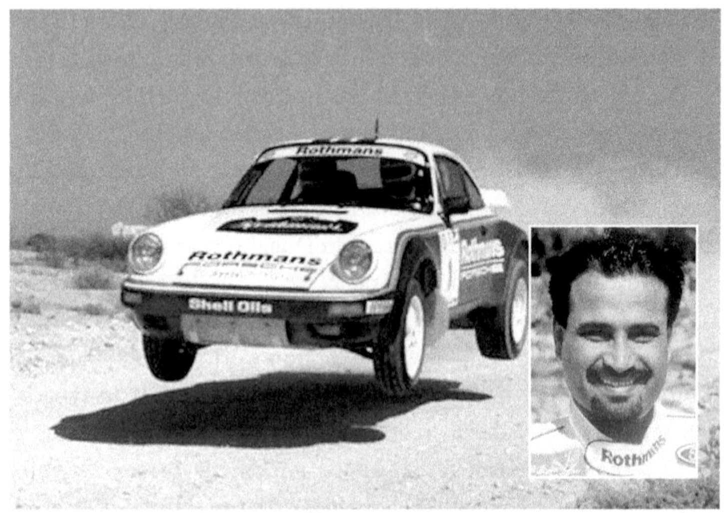

Saeed al Hajri, the champion Qatari rally driver.

Saeed al Hajri of Qatar, for the upcoming Middle East Rally Championship. With a decent car and a bit of honing from the rally team manager, former world champion co-driver David Richards, Saeed became a world-class competitor and I travelled with the team to events all over the Middle East, Europe and North Africa. His drive to fourth place in the World Championship Acropolis Rally in Greece, beating some of the great names in the sport, was exemplary. He also won the long-distance Pharaohs Rally in Egypt a couple of times and the Atlas Rally in Morocco, two arduous events across the toughest of terrain.

I would send daily reports on the rally back to our Dubai office where they were translated and immediately circulated to the media. Before the luxury of satellite communication, this often involved me driving at breakneck speed from somewhere out in the mountains or the desert to the rally headquarters to use a phone or fax. Since most newspapers didn't have specialist motor sports journalists, our well-written reports were generally published untouched.

My first portable computer was an Osborne. It was the size and weight of a small suitcase full of telephone directories and would have broken your knees if you'd put it on your lap. The screen, pre-

Windows, was two-and-a-half inches wide and there were brackets for a magnifying glass. It never left the office.

We took on a lot of sports teams and events, maybe just because there were a lot of them around as Dubai tried to establish itself on the map. One of my new recruits, Alan Ewens, travelled the world with the Dubai Victory powerboat race team. Emirates Airline, a very important client, was sometimes pushed into promoting powerboat races in Dubai and Mike Simon, the communications vice-president, once lamented to me that he had no budget for one event and could we do the PR for half the normal cost. He would make it up on other events which, of course, never happened. The following year, when I submitted a proposal for the same race, Mike was outraged. "What game do you think you're playing?" he spluttered. "This is double last year!"

We handled the press side of the Dubai Desert Classic golf tournament as well as the Dunhill showjumping and international cricket in Sharjah. That was where Ian Botham, fresh from a very late night party, dropped his bat on his way to the wicket but still hammered out fifty runs in half as many minutes.

We also ran the press office for the Dubai round of world snooker involving players like Stephen Hendry, Steve Davis and 'Hurricane' Higgins. Keeping Higgins from taking a swing at reporters from the UK was just in a night's work but the big story I kept out of the press was how I nearly killed world champion Hendry and his manager, Ian Doyle.

I was giving them a lift from the tournament venue back to their hotel. Driving towards the Garhoud Bridge at about eighty kilometres and hour in the centre lane of a three-lane highway with a large truck on either side, I watched helplessly as a black Range Rover swung out of a petrol station and into my path. It was doing thirty at most. I thought to myself: I'm completely snookered. Okay, no, I didn't. My thoughts and exclamations were much more alarmed and profane. Unable to switch lanes because of the lorries, I braked as hard as I could. I was actually out of my seat, standing on the brake. My old BMW 7 Series, bless it, screeched, smoked and shuddered as it laid a lot of rubber on the tarmac but it stayed straight and we just kissed the bumper of the offending Range Rover. A deviation out of the lane or poorer brakes and it could have been a wipe-out.

MY IMMERSION in events like these made the hassles of running the business worthwhile. But I was concerned by my lack of interest in the routine work or driving the company forward. Other firms sprang up, mainly from within advertising agencies, and some international PR networks opened branches, but we were well ahead, I believed, in expertise and ability. In any case, I thought there was plenty of work to go round. I actually liked the competition; it was always a great pleasure when we won a pitch for business against agencies like Hill & Knowlton, one of the global giants.

Latterly, the only company that scared me a bit was ASDA'A, started by another former journalist called Sunil John. I lost out to him too frequently in pitches for major clients. He was smart and ambitious and I admired him a lot. I consoled myself with the thought that he must be under-cutting me. Thankfully, he came into the market about twenty years after me.

I would get dreadfully behind with invoicing, to the extent that I sometimes had to draw money from my personal account to cover the pay cheques. Invoicing for PR work needed a little creativity and I felt that was beyond the capability of our part-time accountant. Usually, we were paid a monthly retainer, which was simple enough, with events billed separately. These would often take up more time than expected. For goodwill reasons, we might absorb the extra cost or spread some of it across other work. So I preferred to do these invoices myself because mistakes could be misunderstood.

I was largely unaware of it at the time, but this was an element of a self-destructive pattern that had originated in my early years and was taking greater form in my adult life. My fondness for tobacco, alcohol and sugar were all part of it.

The psycho-pharmacologist (a psychiatrist who specialises in medication management) in New York had told me that because my childhood had been a war zone, I'd found peacetime hard to deal with. She said I was suffering from adult attention deficit disorder and prescribed the anti-depressant drug Bupropion. It didn't make any noticeable difference.

However, certain things began to make sense. As a newspaper journalist working to absolute deadlines, it simply hadn't been possible to put anything off. So my largely unconscious desire to procrastinate never had an opportunity to flourish. Handling the publicity around sports events was of a similar urgent nature.

Given a crisis or an extremely time-conscious requirement, I was in my element. The other stuff was a yawn. Now and again, I would be forced into a massive catch-up, clearing my desk of huge piles of paperwork and producing dozens of invoices. Sometimes, when I was very late with an invoice – and you can only do this once – I would send the client a photocopy dated at the time of the event with a gentle reminder that we hadn't yet received payment.

In spite of all that, we not only survived as a business, we absolutely thrived.

"IF YOU don't pay Ahmed his money by the end of the week, you will regret it," said the menacing voice on the phone. "We know where your family are."

Ahmed ran the Cairo advertising agency used by my client. The money in question was in regard to expenses submitted fraudulently. I had asked Ahmed to take a number of Cairo journalists to a resort hotel in Alexandria for the weekend and familiarise them with our client's products.

But when I received the bills, there was something obviously wrong with the individual hotel charges. The original guests' names had been crossed out and the journalists' names overwritten. I rang the hotel which said all the guests had been employees of the agency on a weekend workshop. I wrote to Ahmed and the client, saying I wasn't paying up. Perhaps I should have gone to the police about the threat but I didn't take it particularly seriously and I didn't want all the hassle. I couldn't, however, just ignore it. Ahmed was a known fruitcake.

I happened to have on the staff at that time a translator whom we'll call Hani, a gentle bear of a man who was ranked high in the Dubai branch of the Palestine Liberation Organisation. Hani had spent seven years in an Israeli prison after trying to take on a gunboat in a rubber dinghy. He had since renounced violence and would later become under-secretary for housing in Gaza.

After prison, Hani had been provided with Egyptian travel documents and he had family there. I asked him if he fancied a trip to Cairo – in return for paying a quick visit to someone. I explained the situation.

"No violence," he said.

"Absolutely," I said. "I definitely don't want violence."

Hani had his chat with Ahmed and it must have been effective for I never heard from the agency boss or his cohorts again.

– 21 –

Salmon days

TO COMPARE one's first salmon to one's first love would be, in the eyes of those with a lesser obsession, to diminish rudely the value of romance. Yet to we who chase the increasingly elusive Atlantic salmon with an urgency that cannot ordinarily be explained, there is some similarity in the poignancy of two long ago but never forgotten episodes in our lives.

Her name was Judy. She was a student nurse and she taught me joy and sadness and how to squeeze pimples without ruining my face. That anxious and all too swift transition from boyhood to manhood was eased by her tenderness and a smile that contained its share of faint amusement. She was good with Lambretta engines too.

She once told me: "We'll know each other when we're both fifty," and the irregular exchange of Christmas cards across many thousands of miles gave the proof to the prophesy.

The first fish was equally wondrous and unhappily as brief. It happened on a small river on the west coast of Scotland a decade before any romantic encounter. I went back many years later and parked the car in the layby where I used to leave my old bicycle. A silver line still cascaded down the face of the mountain, as it always did in the summer rains, and white water tumbled through the rocks below my feet. It was here I captured the fish that was to add – unknowingly to me at the time – another dimension to my life. Not a salmon but a newly matured and equally innocent sea trout that had taken a worm on my hook. Its size was of no real consequence but oh!.. the wide-eyed wonder of it!

It was the kindling of a passion that burned fiercely for a while but then lay dormant for a couple of decades, the lure of running Highland water consoled by infrequent and inferior stillwater trout fishing in the south of England and sometimes nearly extinguished by career, family and social obligations. On rare occasions it sparked into life when fishing friends who had access to the best of rivers at the worst of times invited me to accompany them. I went with them to Iceland towards the end of a long summer drought and returned tanned and fishless… and to Norway where the river and the fields lay obliterated by the floods.

Whenever work took me back to the UK, I would try to sneak in a few days' salmon fishing. It wasn't always possible and clients weren't always as accommodating as British Aerospace had been. But I kept at it, even if it did take me forever to catch my first salmon.

I recall well enough a West Coast river in Scotland where the rising waters had reached the trees. After four fishless days I told my fishing friend Mike Shepley and his wife-to-be, Cheryl, I'd had enough and was heading home to London. "Probably the best thing you could do," muttered the water-logged ghille, wishing he could leave too. My friends remained and caught four salmon that afternoon and another four the next morning. Another time, I stopped to change flies and let an angler coming up behind me fish through. He took a thirteen-pounder from the spot below my feet. There was the occasion too when I handed the rod to my companion while I answered a call of nature. He immediately hooked a fish, the only one of the week.

That kind of misfortune went on for twenty years. Unwittingly, I became one of the best salmon fishermen who had never caught a salmon. I could cast a line like a magician, landing the fly softly and in exactly the right place. I could read a river like book, knowing where among the pools, streams and eddies the fish would lie.

I even wrote my *Observer* fishing column for eight years. But like the flying instructor who had never actually flown, I was a fraud. Not all tales, however, were tall ones. I figured that reporting the occasional capture of other species would save me from the attentions of the Serious Fraud Office.

With a track record remarkable for the absence of achievement, it was inevitable that I would lose the first salmon I ever hooked. And the second and the third. All three were on the River Eachaig in Argyll where I had been assured I would find success. The river was highish and a little muddy and I was fishing a large orange fly on a sinking line. With nearly a quarter century of non-catching to steer my thoughts in any direction but the right one, I was casting automatically to the far bank and letting the fly slowly sweep round before the retrieve. Two steps down river. Cast again. Easy. Textbook stuff. No-one could have done it better.

My mental composition of an excuse to the tax man was aborted by a force so strong and so sudden that the realisation of its cause came only with the mid-river leap of a salmon of about twelve pounds. There are few words that adequately capture the sensation of this ferocity and power when it's encountered for the first time. A couple of minor runs removed more breath from me than line from the reel before the fish settled in a deep pool, hugging the bottom on the edge of the faster water. My mind raced in circles and my legs and arms were shaking.

"A salmon! My God, I've hooked a salmon! This is it! This is wonderful! This is the day I've waited for! Where's the nearest smokery? No, I'll take it home fresh and gleaming and show them all! I've done it! My first salmon! I can't believe it!"

Calm down, calm down, I told myself. You're getting into heart attack country. The volumes of theory I'd absorbed over the years, the purity and extensiveness of knowledge that was permanently and neatly enfolded in my brain, chapter and verse, disappeared like the contents of a crashed hard disk. Dear God, it suddenly hit me, what do I do next?

Pressure, I thought, after holding the fish numbly for ten minutes. I'll give it some pressure. As I saw it, the fish had a choice: It could go up river or down. Naturally, it exercised an option I hadn't considered and propelled itself upwards through ten feet of water and four feet of air, dragging fifteen yards of sunken line behind it. At the crest of its jump, the fly came out.

Temporary insanity demanded that the fish re-attach itself immediately. It simply couldn't have come off. This was a cruel, stupid hoax and it wasn't funny. Any second now, the salmon would pick up the fly, pop its head out of the water and say: "Only kidding."

The rod, thankfully, was not an old favourite. I threw it on the shingle and with the frenzied animation of a cartoon character, jumped up and down in absolute disbelief and utter despair, near to tears as I screamed "Bastard! Bastard!" in an anguished voice that might have carried the length of the river.

On the next summer holiday, I didn't get out of the water in time. Immersed to the waist in a high coloured water, I stood watching the line strip from the reel until an enormous fish of around twenty pounds came to the surface about eighty yards away and rolled over the line, relieving itself of the fly. The twelve months had taught me to be more philosophical. Why, I asked myself dejectedly, could it not have been a fair bit smaller?

Two days later, I was easing a small five-pound fish to the net when it gave a final, token shake of the head and the line parted where the knot had been.

When the mood came, as it often did, to disregard forever the glorious moment of childhood and take up golf or womanising or any activity less unforgiving, the age-old passion would flare again, reminding me that all other attractions were of the lesser kind. It was, I convinced myself, better to have fished and lost than never to have fished at all.

IF I WAS ever to catch a salmon, I had to revise the whole process. The thought was there but the belief had gone, along with concentration, determination, expectation and even hope. Technique might have been near to perfect but the mechanical routine had to stop, the approach be reconsidered and each cast become the essence of anticipation, particularly if that vital ingredient – luck – continued its self-imposed exile. The change was more psychological than physical. And eventually it worked.

The Wall Pool on the River Eachaig shelves gently from mid-river to its maximum depth directly below the bank-supporting stonework on the far side. The water runs clear and fast and the salmon lie below the twin silver birches. The secret is to bounce the fly off the stones since the fish hold fast against the bank.

It was a cool August morning and the still air smelled acutely of that eager freshness that often follows rain. The intermittent angry buzz of a chainsaw echoed from the timber-clad hills, disturbing the rushing gurgle of the river while soft motionless clouds, like puffed-up feather pillows, obscured the sun. The gauge on the pool above had shown a decent height of water. Even the devil's advocate couldn't have argued the conditions.

Somehow, I knew the salmon was there and I knew I would catch it. I've had several hundred salmon since then, most of them released unharmed, but never since have I experienced that moment of certainty, that glimpse of fate. It was as if I was being made aware that twenty years of perseverance were about to be rewarded. I saw the flash of silver first and watched in fascination as the salmon rose in a gentle curve and took the fly firmly in its mouth. The line tightened without my assistance and not once in the next twelve minutes or so did I think the fish would escape. In spite of all my previous convictions, I was the epitome of calmness and I played the fish like a maestro.

To quantify the fullness of emotion as it lay glistening on the grass before I returned it to the river would be to risk an expedition into purple prose. But at last I felt complete as a fisherman. At the age of forty-three, I had finally come of age. And there would be something new to mention in my Christmas card that year.

– 22 –

In the fast lane

AFTER A VERY early morning flight from Dubai with a connection through London and a car drive from Brussels Airport to the far south of Holland, I was ready for my bed – if I could find it. I was booked into the Congress Hotel in a small town not far from Maastricht in the Duchy of Limburg, but after driving up the only street without a sight of it, I stopped at a small bar for directions.

"Oh, yes," said the smiling landlady, "you have found us. This is the Congress."

Not what I had imagined. It was a simple pub. A few locals sipping glasses of beer watched a football game on television. I must have looked as if I'd misheard her.

"You're in the right place," she assured me. "Come behind the bar and up the stairs."

She showed me into a tiny room with a print of the Madonna and Child on the wall and a bunch of dried flowers, dead and undusted, in a vase by the lace-curtained window. There was a single chair, a small wardrobe and a three-quarters bed, hardly bigger than a single.

She had just received a telephone call that my colleague, Bill Whiter of Rothmans, was unable to come and she appeared irritated by the short notice.

"So you will just have to sleep with someone else," she said.

My astonishment was obvious. "The rally is in town!" she exclaimed. "There is a big shortage of beds! I have a waiting list!"

I explained very clearly and perhaps a little too loudly that I would not be sharing a bed with anyone, even if Bill Whiter had come.

"Then I will have to find you something else," she said with a sigh of exasperation and showed me into what looked like storage space, with a camp bed up against the wall. I wondered where she had moved the mops and brushes. The only toilet in the place was right next door and seemed to be in constant use throughout the night. There would be no need to remind myself to speak to Bill's secretary who had made the hotel arrangements.

Lying there, trying not to listen to the noises that preceded the flushes, I recalled a recent similar event when I had set out with expectations of great comfort only to have them spectacularly denied. My client on both these occasions was the Rothmans Porsche Rally Team. I handled the PR for the team very much in a journalistic way, writing rally reports and feature articles for the Arabic and English media in the Middle East and organising picture and video coverage.

The earlier event I remembered was the Mille Pistes Rallye in the Var region of France. The route was entirely within the perimeters of an enormous French Foreign Legion camp and the event was to be used as a first European test for Saeed al Hajri who was not only exceptionally fast, but also managed, most times, to keep the car on the road. We were to be housed in a rather large and distinguished *château* only a few kilometres away.

The evening prior to the rally began in seriously grand style with a reception for the team thrown by Rothmans France on board a three-masted schooner in Cannes Harbour and to which all manner of dignitaries had been invited. I knew I had to leave in time to arrive at the *château*, some distance beyond Dragignan, by midnight when its doors, we had been forcefully informed, would be closed and would not under any circumstances be opened again until the morning.

Most of the team left early but I was enjoying myself. It's not often you get to pose on a magnificent yacht – the schooner was owned by Monsieur Bic of pen and razor fame – watched and resented by the crowds on the quayside.

Like Cinderella, I cut it too fine. I had reckoned I needed one-and-a-half hours to get to the *château*. I'd gone straight from the airport to the yacht in my rental car but my calculations hadn't made allowance for the tight and twisting country roads of Provence, particularly in darkness. By midnight, I was still at least twenty minutes short of my destination. I recognised the name of the next village as the main location of the rally office and for most of the teams taking part so I stopped in hope.

Even at that time of the night everything in the office was still buzzing. I introduced myself to the press officer and casually enquired if there might be a room somewhere for the night. He laughed and repeated my request in French to all the other rally officials who also laughed.

"Not a chance!" he said. "People are sleeping in their cars."

Mine was a tiny Renault and I didn't fancy the idea.

"Unless," he said with a smile, "you try that place across the road." He pointed to a dilapidated four-storey terraced house with lights ablaze and with people, mainly women, hanging around its door. "They normally rent rooms by the hour but you never know…"

They did have a ground-floor room for the night, said the landlady – or maybe she was the madame. It cost a fortune but it was, probably, fractionally better than the Renault. The toilet, she said, was on the top floor and no visitors were permitted without her approval. But if I needed company…

No thanks, I said, looking around the room illuminated by a single unshaded light bulb. It might have been wiser to have avoided close inspection of the bed, but it looked as if the sheets hadn't been changed for some time and I quickly replaced the bedcover in case something jumped out. I laid some of my clothes on the bed and formed a pillow from a sweater. With a coat to cover me, I was all set, except… I needed a pee. Four storeys up and God knows what the toilet would look like. I'm sure it wasn't the first time the room's cracked and spotted hand basin had served a secondary purpose. How the mighty had fallen, I mused. But I knew a bit about that anyway.

BACK IN Holland, after a fairly sleepless night, I resolved to find new accommodation but needed first to catch up with the team. I found them in a hotel much nicer than mine, and yes, it did have a room I could have, thank God. Something else to talk to Bill's secretary about.

"We have a problem," said the team manager. "The rally starts in a couple of days and we don't have a driver."

It transpired that Saeed had been checking out of his hotel in Frankfurt on his way to Holland when his briefcase containing his passport and money had been stolen from beside his feet. The Qatari embassy would issue a temporary passport that would get him back to Qatar and nowhere else.

A rally team in a major event is quite a sizeable ensemble consisting of a number of service vehicles and their drivers plus several mechanics, a manager, the rally driver's navigator, the sponsor's representative and someone like me. It is also a very expensive operation and such a debacle as this might be catastrophic for the team's whole rally programme. All kinds of pleadings had gone on in Doha, London and Germany but an exception to the passport rule could not be made. The gloom deepened as we sat around the breakfast table.

"I have a thought," said one team member. "What if we smuggle Saeed into Holland and smuggle him back out again afterwards?" Someone laughed and others shook their heads as if to say "what an idiot."

The idea was quite preposterous. These were the days long before the Schengen Agreement and Convention which abolished borders within mainland Europe. It was also the time when the Red Army Faction, a third-generation Baader-Meinhof terror group, was pretty active. Borders were strictly enforced and control points actively manned.

"So let's do it," said the team manager. "It's either that or go home."

"What about all the practical problems?" asked John Spiller, Saeed's long-time co-driver and navigator. "Apart from getting him here, he'll have had no opportunity to practice the route."

Before a rally, drivers are allowed to spend a few days driving the route which can be one or two thousand kilometres in length. They shout comments to the navigator who writes them down, such as "hairpin right thirty" which describes the current part of the route and the speed at which to take it. In the actual rally, the navigator reads these back to the driver. For each rally, there can be several hundred notes.

Spiller and a mechanic would go out the next day and put together whatever practice notes they could manage while plans were laid to bring Saeed over the German border. A meeting point in Germany was arranged. Three or four of the team in a Range Rover would pick up Saeed that evening.

It was real cloak and dagger stuff and it's unlikely the volunteers considered how many years they – and particularly Saeed – would spend in a German prison if they were caught. Smuggling anyone across borders was pretty heavy duty in terms of criminal activities but the involvement of an Arab would raise the penalties to different levels.

Those of us waiting anxiously at the hotel wondered who would arrive first – the team or the police. We could all be arrested for conspiracy. It was a country hotel so we hung around outside, smoking and watching the road. When a set of headlights appeared there was a collective holding of breath. Then a sign of relief. It was the Range Rover, thank God.

"It went like a dream," said the team leader. "Saeed lay on the floor behind the front seat and the border control people didn't bother to shine their torches in the back. They saw a bunch of Brits coming back from an evening out in Germany and didn't look any further. That's not to say we weren't crapping ourselves."

Even without decent pace notes, Saeed completed the rally in a commendable third place. His appearance on the podium was noted by newspapers and television throughout Holland. And yet he simply hadn't been there. Well, not officially. The team smuggled him back across the border at nightfall, only this time they managed to find an unmanned crossing.

DRIVING BACK into Helsinki after testing the Rothmans Porsche rally car in the forests of Finland with former world champion Ari Vatanen and Saeed al Hajri, the road in front of me was empty. Across the central reservation, all three lanes coming out of the city were solid with traffic. It was midsummer eve and the next day would be a national holiday and a big festival. The nose-to-tail exodus went on for kilometre after kilometre, as if the entire population was rushing to escape some terrible calamity.

As I entered the city, the atmosphere became increasingly spooky. The streets were deserted and I half-expected balls of tumbleweed to come rolling round the corner.

It was a beautiful June evening without a cloud in sight and the sun still high in the sky as I went in search of a restaurant or café with some life in it. But most of them were closed and the odd one that was open was empty. I began to feel very alone.

Then I came across a rather large place with half-a-dozen diners sitting by the window. With some relief, I went in. I chose a table near the back and just as I settled in, the other people got to their feet.

Only they didn't leave. To my consternation, they got on the stage. One of them said something, presumably in Finnish. In the fear that he might have been addressing me, I kept my focus on the tablecloth. He spoke again in what I suspect was another Scandinavian language. Then I heard the words: "Excuse me… is there anything you'd like us to play?"

"No, no," I said, mortified. "Please carry on."

This was infinitely worse than eating alone. They played a couple of numbers, after which the band leader left the stage and headed over to my table. Oh God, I thought, what now?

"Er… would you mind if we packed up and went home?"

– 23 –

My friend James

JAMES OSBORNE was fourteen when he left school and was on his way to becoming an Amateur Boxing Association champion. He was also illiterate. Twenty years later he was ranked among the top heavyweights in the country, not as a fighter but as a sculptor in bronze.

The hands that scored points in the ring went on to turn out powerful, evocative studies of humans, horses and hounds that convey the essence of animal vitality, and while he might have had difficulty spelling the names of the tools of his craft, he had no problem with their application.

We met during an exhibition of his work at the Dubai Metropolitan Hotel where my newly-formed PR consultancy had its first office. In quiet times, we would sit in the coffee shop and he would talk about his art and inspirations and his humble beginnings. I was struck by his integrity and his understanding of – and affection for – the animals he sculpted.

Five years later, in 1986, we went into partnership and set up the Osborne Studios in London's Covent Garden. It was opened by Prince Edward in a summer night celebration attended by artists, critics and friends and marked the beginning of a succession of high-level commissions, including one of the Queen's horse Burmese which was destined for display at Windsor Castle.

His two-thirds life-size bronze of Eclipse, the greatest racehorse of all time, stands at the entrance to the members' enclosure at Newmarket Racetrack in Suffolk. A life-size Boy on a Rocking Horse sits in one of London's Royal parks and the final major piece before

James's death, the Dolphin Fountain, was unveiled in a Brighton square by Princess Alexandria.

With his barrow-boy Cockney accent and a face damaged by ABA-approved leather and repaired twice by surgeons, James appeared as the least likely member of the artistic elite. Nor could one really imagine him hanging out in Tangiers with the notorious gun-runner and cigarette smuggler 'Dandy' Kim Waterfield and the Woolworth heiress Barbara Hutton.

"It was like something out of an Errol Flynn movie," James once told me. "Kim was an amazing guy. He was married to one of the Warner Brothers' daughters. I heard later he was jailed in France for robbing her father's safe."

James was still a teenager when he bought a one-way ticket to Morocco to broaden his experience. "I set up my easel on the quayside and I sold everything I painted so I never really went through the struggling artist bit. Kim took a liking to me. He once asked me out on his boat but I didn't go when I saw it was full of bullet holes and half the stern had been blown away by a shell."

James extracted himself from the *dolce vita* and moved on to Spain, then South Africa, New York and France. His literacy improved but he still had to ask fellow passengers to fill in his landing cards. In Paris he got caught up in the student riots of 1968 and witnessed extreme violence as the police tried to crush the protests. What he saw on the infamous 'Night of the Barricades' shocked him so much that, for reasons he never explained, he turned away completely from painting.

"I think eight people died that day. Illiteracy had protected me from the world. I didn't read newspapers so I had no idea what was going on. I left Paris the next day and never picked up a brush again."

Sculpture always attracted him, even as a young child when he used to carve shapes from lumps of chalk. When the family moved from London to Brighton he was refused a place in art school because he couldn't read or write, but his innate talent helped him find employment in the restoration of the ceilings at the Royal Pavilion.

After Paris, he took an unpaid job as a journeyman in a bronze foundry in London just to learn the skills.

"It was run by an Italian family and they cast a pair of Irish wolfhounds for me. One day Henry Moore walked in and bought one of them. Unfortunately, I didn't recognise him."

I never quite understood my relationship with James. I greatly admired his talent and we shared a passion for creativity. While he might have wished for a better knowledge of words, he was articulate in the physical expression of his art.

"When I was in the foundry, people would come in and say what a buzz they got out of watching the metal being poured and I would tell them that was because they instinctively recognised the elements of fire, earth and water. That's what they were made from."

We also shared difficult beginnings to our lives and a love of animals. James once told me of seeing a horse die on the racecourse: "This one came down and broke its neck. I couldn't get it out of my mind so I made a series of three bronzes showing the animal taking the fence, then clipping it and falling.

"I just made them as a statement, a protest against the steeple chasing. Horses get killed all the time in racing and that's too high a price to pay for people's enjoyment."

James died suddenly in 1992. He was fifty-two. Shortly before his death, we had talked about hard times as children and he said: "It doesn't really matter where you start. It's where you end that counts. I want to walk away from this life knowing that it's been worthwhile."

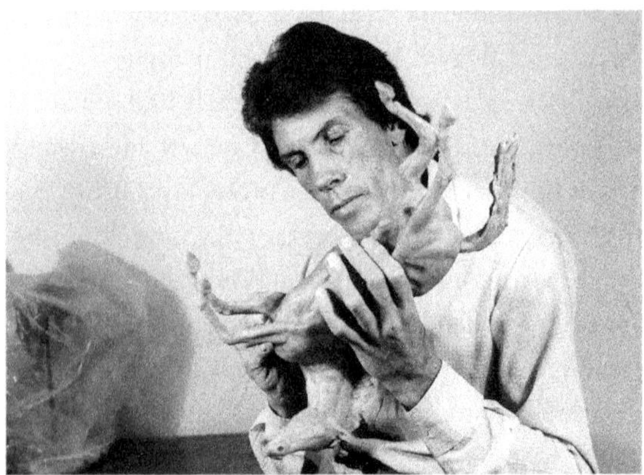

James Osborne working on clay models for a pair of bronzes.

– 24 –

A passage to India

THE DOCKS of Dubai in the mid-day summer sun were no place to begin an adventure with any degree of enthusiasm. It was drained from you with the sweat that ran into the eyes, matted the hair and acted as an adhesive between your back and the plastic seat of the bus taking passengers across a blinding white acreage of concrete to the gangway of the MV *Dwarka.*

Most of those boarding had already gone aboard and the crew viewed the stragglers with the same irritation with which a stadium of spectators, waiting for the next event, silently embarrasses the last runners in the marathon.

Being late and last created an unspoken bond between the few of us clambering from the bus with canvas bags, bright tartan-clad suitcases, large cardboard cartons, television sets and a number of electric fans, their shining blades regrettably stilled. The man getting off behind me, a red-bearded Pakistani deck passenger, carried a huge box of washing powder and for the next few days I never saw him without it.

The previous time I had set foot on the gangway of a ship was a little more than fifteen years earlier, a ship much younger than the *Dwarka.* It was my last day of three years in the British Merchant Navy. The two stripes of gold on my uniform, the second one glued on because it came as a surprise and I didn't have a needle and thread, had probably turned green in some forgotten trunk in an attic more distant than the memories.

This, then, was to be a voyage of nostalgia and also one of curiosity.

Some months earlier I had researched the sinking of the *Dara*, an almost identical sister ship to the *Dwarka* that went down off Dubai in 1961 with the loss of 238 lives, victims of a massive explosive device hidden on board by Omani rebels. I had studied the layouts of the *Dara* and I wanted to see how they compared.

The last sling of passenger belongings – multi-coloured trunks, refrigerators, washing machines, bundles and boxes – swung inwards amid the clatter of the steam winches, the oaths of the handlers and the alarmed cries of the owners who could see the loss of an awful lot of savings if the protrusions from the net tipped against their favour.

It hit the bottom of the forward hold with a gentle thump and the contents cascaded as the net was whipped from under them. Karachi or Bombay, it didn't matter, said a deck officer. Once the ship was under way the crew would go below and sort out the destination. In that heat I felt some pity for them which I should have reserved for myself, Isobel and our three-year-old daughter, Natalie. There was, I soon found, no airconditioning in the passenger cabins.

"You're one voyage too early," the purser said jovially. "We're putting it in next trip."

To residents of the Gulf, airconditioning in summer was as vital as breathing. It was in our homes, our offices, our cars and we would never have thought of going without it. To be deprived of it was to go naked through the streets. The disbelief gave way to mild shock. The dining saloon, at least, was cooled by two massive units of considerable antiquity.

"We've been expecting you," boomed a voice across a couple of tables as we sat down to a late lunch. "You're the reporter." Its owner got up and limped out. "See you later," he said. That wasn't the captain in civilian clothes, surely?

He turned out to be a very pleasant old fellow who sounded very English but always wore a kilt for dinner. Retired from the British Council in Bahrain, he and his wife were going home the long way, taking in a couple of voyages before their journey ended at Heathrow.

Going the hard way and in another direction were the only other European passengers on board, a young English couple with the look

The MV Dwarka *in Muscat, 1981.*

of newly-weds who were heading overland to find a better life in Australia. They had joined the *Dwarka* in Kuwait, enticed on board by a BBC documentary on the ship.

"It does feel rather hot," remarked the husband who always seemed to be about to say "I say" but never did. His wife, fresh-faced (until we hit the monsoon) and English rose-ish, recalled their train journey through Turkey. "The toilets were so awful I didn't go for twenty-four hours," she said.

If you can think of a ship as a living thing – and it's not too difficult – you can tell a lot about her character, her heart and soul, from the dining saloon. If you can draw relaxation from her mahogany-panelled walls, take comfort in the conversations that reverberate around them and feel no need to rush your meal, then you're absorbing a bit of the essence of that ship. And the atmosphere in the *Dwarka*'s saloon was a good one. Matured with age, like a decent port.

A very young Queen Elizabeth smiled down on the balding pate of Captain Grenville Hankin who, with his senior officers, occupied the centre table of three. And on the opposite bulkhead, a clock that looked more art deco than 1940s ticked quietly on towards a time when it would be permanently stopped.

On the forward and after decks, the hatch covers were put back in place, the derricks lowered and secured and an explosion of colour appeared within minutes. Families of Indian and Pakistani deck passengers spread themselves wherever they could, staking out boundaries. They hung up saris and tablecloths of red, yellow and blue for privacy and for shelter from the fierce Arabian sun. So the *Dwarka* left Dubai as if dressed overall.

Once settled, the passengers considered themselves to have territorial rights over their own couple of square metres until they left the ship. There they sat, ate and slept. Dormitory-style accommodation was available within the ship but the people preferred the stars at night and the fresh smell of the sea.

The *Dwarka* was, relatively speaking, a small ship, less than five thousand tons, yet in fair weather she was licensed to carry more than a thousand passengers but only half that number in the monsoon season. Most were heading for Karachi, going home from their labours in Kuwait, Bahrain and Dubai with up to twenty pieces of baggage.

"It's not fair," complained an Indian accountant on leave from Bahrain and going back to Bombay. "The Pakistanis only have to pay one-fifth of the customs duties imposed on us."

Built in 1947 by Swan Hunter on the Tyne, the *Dwarka* was unique in that she was the last British passenger ship on a regular route, other than ferries and cruise liners. A heavy mantle and a sad distinction. Her sister ships had gone before her – the *Dara* to the ocean floor, the *Daressa* sold and the *Dumra* scrapped.

In the dead of night, above the solid thud of her ancient diesel engine, the whir of fans and the rush of air past the cabin window, you could hear the creaks of her stretched woodwork, like cries of lament. Almost as if she knew what fate awaited her.

Perhaps not surprisingly, many of the younger officers did not regard the *Dwarka* with much sympathy. More familiar with the modern vessels of the P&O fleet, a voyage on the *Dwarka* was a time machine trip to the Dark Ages, a punishment perhaps for some past misdeed. I recall in my own sailing days how my response to the arrogance of a senior officer sent me up the Gulf in high summer on a ship with no airconditioning. I used to sleep on the boatdeck until they 'blew tubes' one night to clear the funnel and I awoke under a blanket of soot. At least the *Dwarka*'s officers had ACs in their cabins, a discovery that left me smarting with envy.

Only days from the end of their five-month tour of duty, they were demob happy. "When I get back to Hartlepool, I'm going straight round to the girlfriend and…" The bar talk was effusive and full of home, the *Dwarka* forgotten. But not by Capt Hankin. A small bearded man, he had previously fought for and won a stay of execution for the vessel, although he accepted the reality of his position. When the time came he would, metaphorically speaking, go down with his ship. Early retirement at the age of fifty-four.

"My hobby is electronics and I might start a small business along those lines."

He pointed to the ship-to-shore radio which sat in his cabin behind the bridge. "I built that from junk that I found in a barge in Karachi. There was a rat's nest in it."

The *Dwarka* flew the flag of the British India Steam Navigation Company, although that line had long been absorbed into P&O. From a fleet that at one time numbered more than one hundred, there were only the *Dwarka* and the educational cruise ship *Uganda* remaining at the time of my voyage. Even in the early Seventies there had been forty.

Out of Muscat, the final stop before the sub-continent, the *Dwarka* rode the swell of the Arabian Sea with the ease of a young filly rather than the old mare she was. The first of the monsoon clouds hung low on the horizon and the breeze was filled with the smell of rain.

On the bridge the third mate, who made pin money from printing souvenir *Dwarka* T-shirts, eyed the glass and confirmed the likelihood of stormy weather. Below him on the forward deck, a cacophony of noise rose from the multitude of tape-players and radios.

"Even with all those passengers, there is very rarely any trouble," said Hankin. "We have security men on board but they are hardly ever needed." The proximity to their destination took the heat out of any disagreements.

They were going home. Tomorrow Karachi. There was a palpable force field of excitement around the decks. What time are the trains to Lahore, to Rawalpindi, Islamabad and Peshawar? Many of the men had been away for years. Babies some had never seen had grown into toddlers, toddlers into bright-eyed youngsters and they into teenagers with all the problems that age brings.

"If your father was here…." Tomorrow, or the next day, he would be.

Some passed around photographs, dog-eared and faded from constant handling and exposure; others kept their pictures to themselves, studying them in quiet contemplation. But the joy, the sense of occasion, was contagious. It swept the ship like a bristling wave of electricity and few on board could have stayed unaffected.

The export of labour, of human life, may not be the most lucrative trade in which Pakistan and India participate but it is certainly the most precious.

When the rain did come in a torrent they sat in it, looking to the heavens as it ran through their hair and down their faces, soaking shirts and saris and gurgling away into the scuppers. If baggage and belongings hadn't had to be stowed, they might have stayed there.

The *Dwarka* arrived in Karachi in the greyness of the monsoon. Leaden grey skies, battleship-grey destroyers in the naval port and along the wharves grey-painted cranes bowed like praying mantises. Karachi didn't appear all that different to the port I'd sailed into seventeen years earlier. A slightly taller skyline and an element of orderliness among the porters, kept in line by an officer who wielded his swagger stick like a conductor's baton, were subtleties of change.

The migrant workers poured ashore, rehearsing what they'd tell the customs officials who were bracing themselves for the onslaught behind a barricade of tables, the way London shop girls do behind counters as the doors open on the January sales.

"They'll get through all these passengers in four hours," said the purser. "Before, it used to take a day or more."

The hold baggage followed, dumped unceremoniously on the quay and an Indian lady, bound for Bombay, felt the panic of the helpless as she identified her roll of gaily-coloured mattresses among it.

When it was all over, the *Dwarka* slipped her mooring springs and a heavy smoker of a tug pulled us into open water. The pilot, as familiar with the ship as he was with Karachi navigation, ordered half-ahead from the small bridge that dominated the superstructure and gave the helmsman his course.

She ploughed her way out of the mouth of the creek through an armada of fishing boats, some with their nets bulging astern. The pilot jumped from the rope ladder, waved a farewell, and there was nothing between the *Dwarka* and Bombay but an angry sea.

The equine comparison may have been a bit unfair; a grand old lady of the sea would be a better description. And like the elderly who know the years grow shorter, she seemed to relish the day, the moment. A bit rheumatic, she groaned in the heavy weather of the monsoon but she entered Bombay on schedule and a homing instinct nosed her into the pier.

The *Dwarka* was a relic of another era, an age when the red ensign ruled the waves. Captain Hankin had hoped for another three or four years before economics decided her only value lay in salvage. But the end came sooner, not twelve months after my voyage. On full power, she was run up the beach at the Karachi breaker's yard. And when the giant metal cutters and oxyacetylene torches were done, all that remained for Grenville Hankin and those who had sailed on her were the memories.

– 25 –

The last old lady of the Raj

HERMIONE MONTAGU would probably have been a little offended at being described as the last old lady of the Raj. As if one had finally put a name to the Unknown Warrior. But she carried that same air of ancient glory, an enchantment of times when the Empire's sun was at its zenith and those who ruled it were the chosen people.

And if that sense of superiority was not her personal feeling, it was one wished on her and her kind by breeding and the possession of old wealth. In India, that world of attitudes had virtually disappeared, even among the maharajahs, but she lived in the last remaining corner of it simply because she had never known any other and, at her age, she was much, much too old to change.

Her home was Northwood, an old, very British cottage in Shimla, the summer capital of the Raj, and she lived surrounded by the verdant magnificence of the Himalayan foothills and the relics of society balls at Viceregal Lodge, theatre at the Gaiety, croquet, Kipling and afternoon tea at Davico's.

She had seen most of her contemporaries, those who had stayed on after Indian independence in 1947, pass away, but she spoke with that natural disregard for death that only the elderly possess. She was not eighty-eight, she told me, but eight-nine next birthday. "Make sure you get that right."

I met her at her house which lay on one side of the sharp ridge on which Shimla is constructed, down a steep road which taxi drivers, who know nothing of caution, took with reckless abandon. Time (and my driver on the first attempt) had passed it by.

Hermione Montagu in Shimla, 1981.

Its inner walls were lined with portraits of stern Victorian men gripped by tight collars and the sense of occasion and of beautiful women in extravagant finery affording that wistful expression that was as near to a smile as their images were socially allowed. Watercolours of near and distant landscapes adorned the halls and reception rooms along with rosewood tables, mahogany cabinets, regency settees and the bric-a-brac that nobody collected but simply came together.

She sat in her bedroom, relaxed in a long low chair, wrapped against the approaching chill of early evening and not at all puzzled by my wish to meet her. The BBC had been to see her "on their way back from China," she said, but couldn't remember how long ago.

The shadows of age and the depths of time had played tricks with her memory and although a minority of her recollections did not stand immediate enlargement or later examination, the generalities of her early years, of a strange marriage and her life in Shimla were reasonably acute. Her voice, with just the normal quaver of the vale of years, carried strongly and emphatically across the room. "I have to speak loudly," she said, "because one of the servants is getting old and deaf."

Despite the colour of her skin and the social status that embraced her, Mrs Montagu claimed to be as Indian as anyone native to the country. She was born Hermione Cunningham Mitchell in 1892 near Lahore and her father, Sidney, had been born in Rawalpindi in 1863 of British parents. Her mother, Eliza Catherine Chadwick, had entered the world in Sutton Coldfield, England, in 1864. "We called her Bunny."

"She was related to the Chadwick millions and first came out to India to stay with the family of Sam Gold. Then unfortunately, or some people might say fortunately, she met my father. He had quite an important position in the Punjab Police. I think it was superintendent general. That's his portrait over there.

"I went to school in England, a school for young ladies near Dover, I think, but I wanted to get back to India," she told me. Her parents were in Britain at the time, but it was difficult to demand too many details since interruptions tended to change her flow of thought. The year was 1909 and she was seventeen at the time but what follows may not be in precise chronological order.

"I told my father I had three very fine proposals of marriage. There was the young Sugden who was heir to a baronetcy; Douglas Hall, the son of a very influential banker, and… did I say young Sugden? Well, there was one more.

"The trouble was that I wanted to marry my first cousin. But on his mother's deathbed he had given her his word that he would never marry me. She had some old-fashioned ideas about first cousins being married. He said: 'If I can't marry the girl I want, then I won't marry at all.' So he became a homosexual. Do you know what that means?

"Out of spite, I married Gerald Montagu. He was a lieutenant in the Royal Fusiliers. I spent only one night with him, then he went off to America to make his fortune. But he came back with a mistress, a Red Indian squaw."

Mrs Montagu pressed her parents into letting her return to India alone. "I told them I was only in love with my country, India." She went to live in Chapslee, the home of her aunt, Lady Constance Ker, who was married to Sir Arthur Milford Ker, manager of the Alliance Bank in Shimla.

I never learned what happened to the rogue husband, if there had been a divorce, why she retained the Montagu name or why she didn't marry again, but in the stillness of that darkening room lit by a single lamp that cast the shadows of a remote past, I felt it wasn't too important.

"Did you take a job?" I asked. "Oh no," she replied and looked at me with the tolerance that a village affords its idiot. "I didn't have to work. I did odds and ends at Chapslee."

If Mrs Montagu was recovering from matrimonial misery, the Kers were in the throes of it. "After Arthur gave Constance the news of their son's death, she looked at him and said: 'The first thing you have to do is get out of my rooms and stay in your own. The less I see of you the better. I was always in love with your cousin Malcolm but he seemed more interested in Eileen Meakin.'

"Arthur used to beg: 'Connie, can't you spare me a little of your time?' but she would reply that she couldn't loiter with him. I thought it was most unkind myself. He stayed in his rooms and he died there of a broken heart because his son had gone and his wife had never loved him."

If you think all this might have been taken from the writings of Barbara Cartland or Denise Robbins, bear with me. This was real-life Shimla and real Shimla people and their intrigues were typical of Raj society of that time. On the top of the Mall where the road forks is Scandal Point, a spot that got its name for better reasons than normal chit-chat.

At the turn of the century, one writer commented: "Nowhere possibly in the world are the passions of human nature laid so open for dissection as they are in the remote hill stations."

Another correspondent, the artist Val Prinsep, wrote: "Shimla is an English watering hole gone mad. Real sociability does not exist. There arises the most terrible squabbles, especially among the fair sex, and it is difficult to find two of the fair creatures who are on friendly terms."

Class distinctions among the British were rigidly upheld and at one time an order of precedence was published with government or military officials towering over lawyers, bankers or merchants, regardless of their wealth. The *Times* reported: 'The public service is the aristocracy and those who do not belong to it are out of the pale.'

One place where rank or status had little influence was the Gaiety Theatre, modelled on London's Garrick, but on such a compact scale that the roof caved in when an entertainer removed two pillars to create more stage space. Generals and lieutenants played opposite each other in T*he Rivals*, *She Stoops to Conquer* and *The Mikado*, and it is recorded that Lady Teazle was particularly good in *School for Scandal.*

The theatre still stood in the Mall and you could almost hear the laughter, the applause and the rustle of crinolines and smell the gentlemen's pungent cheroots. The presentations continued to be well attended and if the culture had changed, the atmosphere had not and the Gaiety remained a relic of the British presence on which the curtain had not come down.

"I never played there," said Mrs Montagu, "but of course I used to go very often. I would travel in my rickshaw pulled by five coolies to get us along very quickly."

Naively but quite innocently, she went on: "All the men were dressed in the colours of their employers. My coolies wore white in the summer and the rest of the year dark green and yellow. We also used them to go to the grand balls at Viceregal Lodge. These were lovely affairs with everyone in their best uniforms and gowns. I was a very good dancer. We would dance into the early hours. It was a very good life."

There was more to do in Shimla, she said, than some historians suggest. Cricket at Allendale, 'fancy fairs' and gymkhanas while the English adoration for horse-racing manifested itself twice-weekly on the track where ability in the stirrups competed with performances on the Gaiety stage for the glittering prizes of social favour.

"I played tennis and badminton, and croquet on the lawn at Chapslee. I can still hear the sound of the mallets." Her eyes broke through the dimness of retrospection and she smiled quietly at the memory.

"I also had my horses, six of them, very big and very beautiful. We couldn't take them onto the Mall, it just wouldn't have done, so we would race them along a stretch known as Ladies' Mile. I had a very light touch and would leave everyone behind."

The ban on Mall traffic extended not only to horses and cars – but also to Indians, except those of aristocratic birth, the ruthless apartheid of empire.

The Mall wound along the crest of the ridge where the British *memsahibs* strolled in their hundreds, window shopping in the Shimla branches of London stores – Hamiltons, Richards, Whiteaway and Laidlaws, Rankins, the Army and Navy store. They had gone with the last of the British baggage that piled aboard the coaches of the small-gauge mountain train that took six hours to complete its spectacular ninety-kilometre journey from Kalka.

Davico's restaurant, which echoed to the clink of crockery in the afternoons and the tinkle of glasses and refined laughter in the evenings, was still in business. The modern clientele came from the two thousand or more Indian and foreign tourists who arrived in Shimla every day through the summer and who might have wondered at the spring in floorboards designed to ease the weariness in the feet of the Raj's dancing gentlefolk.

The big shops were divided into two or three to accommodate the needs of the tourist trade and on the fierce gradients of the ridge's slopes, hotels thin as elevator shafts have removed much of the forestry. But the Mall continued to thrive in its renewed importance, decaying a little with its unrepaired windows above the shops and missing brickwork like gaps in a beggar's teeth.

I watched Tibetan porters carry loads their own weight on tarmac where the wheels of the Viceroy's carriage once clattered unobstructed to the great Anglican Cathedral of Christchurch, a Victorian pseudo-Gothic inspiration that dominates the town and where 1,850 people crowded in to celebrate the coronation of Edward VII in 1902. When I took communion there one Sunday the congregation numbered fourteen. A tarnished brass plate on the front pew tells you it is reserved for the Viceroy and, even after so many years, it still intimidated me into sitting one row behind.

"I don't think about the changes," said Mrs Montagu. "I am really happy here. I don't read because my eyes are not good and I don't listen to the radio because I don't care for the news. I have a small record player and I like musicals like *My Fair Lady*. And I have my friends."

Before I left, we had talked about London. She had not visited the city since 1930. Were the lobsters still as good at Green's Restaurant and did Gunter's still sell the best ice cream? Then she asked: "What would I think of England now?" She was tired by then and didn't really seem to want an answer. I was glad I didn't need to give one.

In the hallway, near the front door, I stopped to look at a painting of a very beautiful young woman with waist-length blonde hair hanging off a bare shoulder, soft blue eyes, high cheekbones and wearing a gentle smile. "Yes," said her companion who saw me out, "that's Hermione."

In 1985 Mrs Montagu died in her home in Shimla at the age of ninety-three. Northwood, and Chapslee where she first lived, are now hotels.

– 26 –

Flying into trouble

FROM THE days of my childhood when we moved home with depressing regularity, through my years… wonderful, exciting years… on the high seas and later as a journalist and PR consultant, I always seemed to be going somewhere. For a decade or more I averaged about a hundred flights a year, most of them across continents. When retirement reduced the travelling dramatically, I suffered withdrawals – feeling hemmed in and irritable. Without fully realising it, I had become so addicted to travel that the craziness of airports, the dreadful lines at immigration and security, the flight delays and missing baggage, were prices willingly paid.

But there was an age before all that got too awful, when flying was still adventurous and hair-raising incidents were almost expected. We frequently took to the skies in aircraft so old and decrepit that any inquiry into their safety records might have prevented us ever getting on board. Would I, in 1962, still have crossed the Atlantic in an old DC-6 had I known that, up to that point, its type had recorded thirty-five fatal crashes in which more than twelve hundred people died? Probably.

I once flew from Marseille to Toulouse in a bag of mechanical bones called the Nord 262 – an aircraft, I discovered later, that had suffered seventeen losses from the 110 that had been built. The metal seats were welded to the floor and the stewardess served coffee from a small vacuum flask.

On another occasion, I was flying over Canada's northern wilderness in what was described as a Second World War interceptor fighter-bomber converted into a float plane when I asked the pilot why we were following the river instead of taking a more direct route.

"Well," he said, "I blew a piston through the side of the engine last week and was stuck down there for three days so I'm not taking any chances."

I was on board the Pan-Am Boeing 747 *Clipper Maid of the Seas* a few years before it was blown up over Lockerbie. An engine failed as it took off from Dubai and we spent the next three hours dumping fuel over the Gulf before we could land there again. My greatest concern was that we weren't allowed to smoke. Initially, immigration officials in Dubai refused to let us back in. "You haven't been anywhere," they protested.

There's a belief among some frequent flyers that the odds against crashing must reduce with the increasing number of uneventful flights. It's actually something of a myth because these days the chance of your plane going down is so remote that it really doesn't matter how often you're airborne. Someone worked out that if you're flying on a Boeing 777 Cathay Pacific flight from Hong Kong to Los Angeles on any given day, there's a one in 4,068,434 chance that your aircraft will crash.

That, of course, is the logical view, one that generally goes out the window each time we're pinned back in our seats as the engines thrust us down the runway. And how often does it seem, as the tyres continue to go thump, thump, thump, that this must be the longest damned take-off in the world?

That we rarely, if ever, think the odds against dying in a car accident – a much more likely possibility – must shorten each time we get behind the wheel suggests we worry less about situations in which we have a measure of control. Yet, regardless of the statistics, people who fly a lot still have experiences that send the heart lurching – perhaps heavy turbulence with the aircraft suddenly dropping a hundred feet or more, or the loss of air pressure or the need to go around again for another attempt to land in bad weather.

"Let's try that once more," the Gulf Air pilot told us after aborting the Doha landing from a wheels-down position, "and hope that the baggage train doesn't cross the runway again."

Another time, flying into Amsterdam, the passenger next to me was in close conversation with a member of the cabin crew. He then turned to me and said: "That's my girlfriend. She suggests a move to seats nearer an emergency exist. The hydraulics have failed on the landing gear." We moved and, thankfully, the only indication of a crisis were the ambulances and fire engines chasing us down the runway as we landed safely.

Such incidents are not exactly close encounters considering today's safety standards, but are alarming nonetheless. Even with the exceptionally high quality of aircraft design and maintenance, and the professionalism of air crew, there will always be problems when we require many tons of heavy metal to defy gravity for long periods of time.

Gravity came pretty close to winning on an occasion when I was handling the public relations for Airbus in the Middle East. We were running demonstration flights of the then-new A320, the first fly-by-wire civilian aircraft, for Press and airline pilots and executives. We carried out nineteen flights in three days.

For these flights, we allowed a guest pilot to fly the plane, including take-offs and landings. There was always a senior Airbus pilot in the second seat in case anything went wrong – which it did one hot summer's day in the Gulf.

At the time of its introduction, the A320 was unusual in that, instead of the traditional yoke in the cockpit, it had a sidestick, not unlike the joystick of computer games, that the pilot used to control it. On this flight, with the airline's board of directors, a dozen journalists, government VIPs and Airbus personnel down the back, the guest pilot pulled back on the stick to lift the wheels off the ground and, inexplicably and simultaneously, bent the control to the right. I was sitting towards the rear and I watched aghast as the wing tip was about to smash into the ground. We were centimeters from disaster.

In that vital split second, the Airbus pilot seized control and from then on guest pilots were only allowed to fly the aircraft once it was in the air. But few of the passengers that day had any idea how close they had come to a fiery death.

My most bizarre aviation experience began with my missing a BA flight from Heathrow to Cairo for the most careless and amateurish of reasons. The departure time had been 1600 hrs and, without checking, my mind had taken on the foolish idea it was 6pm. It happens to the best of us. I needed to be in Cairo for a meeting at nine in the morning. There was, said the ticket desk, a connection through Budapest on a Hungarian airline in an hour. I took it. The first leg on a Tupolev something-or-other passed without incident and so did most of the second one on a Boeing 737 until we had begun the descent into Cairo.

The captain came on the air to announce that due to unforeseen circumstances we were returning to Budapest. He apologised and said there would be another aircraft waiting on the tarmac to take us to Cairo. We had already flown nearly three hours and it would be the same time back to the Hungarian capital. I was the only passenger in first class and, perhaps a little too shrilly, demanded to know from the purser what the hell was going on. He went into the cockpit and came out with the captain who told me: "I'm sorry, but a windscreen has shattered. It's intact but it's full of cracks. Come and have a look."

I followed him onto the flight deck. The screen on the left, his side, was starred and impossible to see through. To my mind, the danger was that it might give at any moment.

"Wait a minute," I said. "We have to get on the ground. Look, you can see the lights of Cairo from here." I pointed through the co-pilot's window.

"It's not likely to break," said the captain. "Aircraft windscreens are layered and these cracks are probably in just one layer."

"But we can land now, in twenty minutes or less!" I exclaimed.

He shrugged. "It's not as simple as that. Head office instructions are to return to Budapest."

It seemed to me the airline knew the plane would be grounded and there might not have been the funds in Cairo to buy a new windscreen – if one existed – and have it installed by Boeing engineers. But there was nothing I could do. The normal procedure in such circumstances, I read later, would have been to declare an emergency, release the oxygen masks and drop to 10,000 feet before landing at the nearest airport. Some airlines, said the advice, had their own rules…

It wasn't the best time to recall an incident a few years earlier when a windscreen of a British aircraft completely shattered and the captain was sucked half-way out. The co-pilot managed to land the plane while the cabin crew held onto the captain's legs. Thankfully, that didn't happen on the long nervous journey back to Budapest where we were herded towards the arrivals hall.

"Everyone please make their way to the bus," said an airline official. "We are taking you to a hotel for the night."

"No you're not!" I yelled. "What about the aircraft that's waiting for us?"

"That flight is cancelled," said the official, turning his back on me.

I refused to board the bus. "I need to be in Cairo in the morning," I said, becoming increasingly agitated. "Otherwise, there's no point in my going."

"You can't stay here," said the official. "They're closing the airport for the night."

I decided I had endured altogether too much nonsense. "I'm not going anywhere until you sort me out another flight," I said.

He and another member of the ground staff were about to put up an argument but took another look at me and huddled over a computer. "We can get you on a flight leaving here in five hours for Rome where you can connect to an Al Italia flight to Cairo," said the official. There was nothing to do but agree and he reissued my ticket. Then security locked me out of the airport. I sat on a bench outside and between short snoozes smoked endless cigarettes until the airport reopened.

Rome was the tightest of connections and, already in a state of exhaustion, I had to run the length of Leonardo da Vinci Airport to arrive at the gate just before it closed.

Cairo traffic was in its usual state of chaos, even in the early afternoon. It's the only city I know where six lanes of vehicles can fit into four lanes of highway.

I eventually got to my meeting, dishevelled and weary beyond caring. All the heads at the conference table looked up.

"Ah, Ian, you're here," said my client. "We wondered where you'd got to. Everything's gone remarkably well and we're just wrapping up."

MY FRIEND and Rothmans PR colleague Bill Whiter was deep in the heart of the Great Pyramid when the earthquake struck. He was terrified and wondered if he'd accidentally touched a secret trigger because part of an enormous stone freed itself and nearly crushed him. Or so he claimed.

I was in my room at the Mena House Hotel, a former palace in beautiful grounds and very close to the Pyramids. Bill and I were in Cairo for the Pharoahs Rally, a tough endurance test of man and machine in which Rothmans driver Saeed al Hajri and a couple of hundred others were competing over three thousand kilometres of desert tracks.

The first I knew of the 'quake was the noise. A prolonged roar drew me to the window and I expected to see a number of large trucks or even tanks approaching along the main road. But the only signs of abnormal activity were in the courtyard of the stables where the camels and horses were kept for tourists. The animals were clearly very agitated, rearing and trying to pull away from their handlers.

Then the shaking began and I had to sit on the bed to stop myself falling over. It was pretty obvious what was happening. Pieces of masonry from the roof passed my window.

I thought I would climb into the wardrobe but it wasn't full length so I decided to get under the bed but found there was no space. It came down to protecting the most important part of me so I lay on the floor and stuck my head under the sturdy bedside table.

It was over in forty seconds and I made my way into the corridor. Some people were screaming in their rooms, trapped by jammed doors. I managed to free a couple.

The earthquake measured 5.8 but in a city not built for major seismic events 545 people died and 6,500 were injured with hundreds of buildings destroyed and 9,000 seriously damaged.

– 27 –

Riders of the storm

SOMETIMES heroes just don't get the recognition they deserve. Admittedly, I hadn't rescued someone from a swollen river or pulled a child from under a bus. What I had done was save my client, Emirates, from an acute embarrassment and all the airline wanted to do was forget it. I wasn't overly bothered; I just added a bit more to the bill.

Michael Fish also hated to be reminded of a blunder, one that never escaped him for the rest of his career as a BBC weatherman. Michael had scoffed on air about the possibility of Britain's being hit by a hurricane. Then it happened with a vengeance – leaving eighteen people dead and a £1.5 billion trail of destruction.

It was 1987 and the two events are connected. The Dubai Champion Stakes, a prestigious Group 1 race, was to be run at Newmarket on Saturday, 17 October. It was sponsored by the Dubai Government which gave it to Emirates to exploit, if it wished, in terms of publicity and entertainment. So the London office invited a hundred important travel agents for a grand lunch and a day at the races. A very large marquee containing twenty circular tables would be erected alongside the winning post. London-based guests would be brought by coach.

My job wasn't too difficult. I would work alongside the airline's promotions manager, Najah Hussein, to make it all run smoothly, particularly since Najah at times had a way of creating complications. I needed to confirm staffing and service with the caterers, organise delivery of the floral arrangements for the tables, make sure guests and Emirates personnel had badges for access to the paddock and members' enclosure, make sure there was a bookie in close proximity, look after the travel trade media, and lots of other, little, things. We also had half a dozen uniformed Emirates air hostesses who would mingle with the guests and later accompany the triumphant horse and jockey into the winner's enclosure. They needed to be in the right place at the right time.

It would have been no hardship if everything had gone to plan. I had done it before at Newmarket and at Longchamps in Paris, that graceful racecourse set in the heart of the Bois de Boulogne where Dubai sponsored two major races each spring. The airline was eager to promote its new Dubai-London route and flew British travel agents across the Channel for both events. One of the lessons I learned there was never to put lamb cutlets on the menu in France. Though they were done to a perfect pink, almost the entire British contingent sent them back as undercooked. The travel agents might have been well-travelled but their tastes remained firmly at home. The chefs sighed, shook their heads and cooked them to a crisp.

I had arrived from Dubai ahead of the Champion Stakes to spend a few days at our Warwickshire home with Isobel and Natalie. They had moved back from the Gulf largely for Natalie's schooling and because our ancient farmhouse, with bits of it dating to the 14th century, really needed to be lived in; a wonderful house but not a particularly sensible buy. Although I was in the UK more or less every month because of Emirates and my UK clients, the separation put more strain on a marriage that had already suffered badly from my drinking days and my constant travelling. It would be a few more years before it came to breaking point.

The hurricane had swept along the south coast in the early hours and up across the counties of the south-east. The West Midlands were on the far edge of its path and experienced little of its rage. As I set out for Newmarket on the Friday morning the air was breathless, the clouds gentle and there was little evidence of the storm's passing. But from all the news bulletins, it had been extraordinarily brutal and the nation was stunned. We were, thanks to Mr Fish and colleagues, completely unprepared. A storm like that hadn't happened in Britain in nearly three hundred years.

In normal circumstances, it would have been about a two-hour journey but it took me nearly five. It wasn't until I was approaching Milton Keynes that the massive damage began to present itself. The further I drove, the more the landscape looked like the battleground of the gods. Great trees had been ripped from the earth, their branches broken and hurled distances. Farm buildings lay flattened, hedgerows had been stripped and power lines hung loose from uprooted poles. It was breath-taking in its enormity. I could feel that something of terrifying power had passed this way only hours before.

The authorities had acted quickly and on the major roads most of the fallen trees had been dragged to the side. Some roads were flooded and impassible but such is the great web of English country lanes that it wasn't too difficult to find alternative routes, even in those days before satellite navigation. Occasionally, I had to join a queue of traffic behind tractors as they went about their business of clearing debris.

From a distance, Newmarket looked relatively unscathed. But as I drew nearer the tragedy began to unfold. The great avenue of trees that lined the town's western approach had disappeared, their once towering trunks now stacked unceremoniously by the roadside or dragged into fields. Not a single tree remained standing. The buzz of multiple chain saws rent the air. Further on, branches had crashed through the roofs of several houses and bricks were scattered where garden walls had come down. A few cars lay flattened and I prayed they were empty at the time.

I headed directly for Newmarket Racecourse. Completely open to the elements, the Force 12 winds had gusted here at up to a hundred miles an hour and the damage was frightening. The track's white-painted railings had been ripped from the ground and lay flat of the grass, many of them broken. Workmen were hurrying to repair and dig them back in. Great marquees of canvas and steel, intended for the entertainment of guests, had been plucked from their bases and tossed almost carelessly along the track.

The Emirates marquee right by the winning post was a sorry sight of twisted metal and torn canvas, yet it remained standing in a crippled sort of way. There were workmen all around it.

Someone pointed out the foreman and I asked him: "How long will it take to put it back together?"

"We're taking it down," he replied. "Our boss says it's too dangerous."

"Just stop everything for the moment," I told him. "I'm going to find the clerk of the course. And give me the number of your boss."

On my way to the main building, I passed James Osborne's statue of Eclipse, rubbed its bronze nose and thought of my friend. He would have found this all quite amusing. The clerk of the course, whose name escapes me, did not but he was remarkably calm amid the chaos.

"I've got a hundred guests arriving in less than twenty hours and I need another venue, maybe somewhere in the main building," I said.

"Not a chance," he replied. "We're overcrowded as it is."

"Have you seen anyone from Emirates?"

"No, and I've not been able to reach them either."

I used his office phone to call the Emirates office in London again but none of the management was there. I couldn't get through to Najah's somewhat primitive mobile phone and I didn't have one myself. These early versions cost well over £2,000. She was not at her hotel. I called the boss of the marquee company who repeated that it had to come down.

"Absolutely not!" I said with some vigour. "You have to fix it. We have one hundred guests arriving by 11 am tomorrow and there's no way of cancelling them. So I need it up and finished by that time."

"It's impossible," he protested. "We'd have to helicopter in a new kitchen. The existing one is lying somewhere out on the track."

"Do it," I said, only a little concerned that I had no authority whatsoever to give such instructions or even have that conversation. Everything concerning arrangements with contractors was handled by the UK office of HH Sheikh Mohammed bin Rashid al Maktoum, now the Ruler of Dubai.

The boss continued to demur. Time, as they say, was of the essence. I thought to myself that I would either save the day or hang myself in the trying so I took the plunge: "Have you done much work for Sheikh Mohammed's office?"

"Yes, quite a lot."

"So how do you think he's going to feel about this?"

The boss hesitated. "Okay, okay," he said. "I'm on my way over. It'll take me an hour or two to get there."

I walked back across the track. "It's going back up," I told the foreman. "Your boss is coming but you might as well start."

In the hotel that night there was a message from Najah saying she'd be along with the main Emirates group in the morning. I sat at dinner on my own and it crossed my mind that a very large glass of red wine would be very nice and much deserved. But it was only a fleeting thought.

I thought longer about my relationship with Isobel. While it had worked for some time, it wasn't working now and I had become complacent, even unkind. I should have tried harder to repair the marriage and it may well be my guilt that claims I didn't know how. Isobel remains a lovely lady and lives happily with her partner only a mile of two from me in Edinburgh. We get on well.

I WAS AT the racecourse early the next morning. The weather was overcast but it was dry and again the air was still and crisp. I could hear birds singing. Our red and white marquee looked good although its reconstruction was still unfinished. I don't know if they'd worked through the night but they'd done a great job. If it looked just a tiny bit squint, that was a minor concern.

The crew had just fixed the final bolt and secured the last of the supports when the coaches from London arrived at 11 am and with them the Emirates entourage. I started to tell Najah what had happened. I'd hardly got into the story when she interrupted me.

"Excuse me, Ian, I've got to check something with the florist," she said, disappearing. I could understand why she didn't want to know.

As the guests sat for lunch, Sheikh Mohammed walked in with Sheikh Ahmed bin Saeed, the head of Emirates, and looked around. I heard someone say to them: "This is the only marquee left standing. It's amazing." The sheikhs nodded and said nothing. They didn't know and I wasn't going to tell them.

ON THE Swissair night flight out of Dubai, I asked the purser about the flying time to Geneva. "About four hours after Kuwait," he replied. Kuwait? I had no idea the flight stopped in Kuwait. But other than an interrupted sleep, I guessed it didn't matter too much.

We landed in Kuwait just before midnight on 1 August 1990, boarded a number of passengers and took off again about an hour later, a perfectly normal stopover. It was only when I checked into the Noga Hilton in Geneva and turned on CNN did I realise with a shock that we were probably the last flight out of Kuwait before the invading forces of Saddam Hussein captured the airport.

One of the next flights to land was not so fortunate. A British Airways jumbo on route to Madras was seized, the passengers detained and the aircraft eventually set on fire.

I had several acquaintances in the city at that time. Some were captured and used as human shields, others were taken across the border to Saudi Arabia by smugglers who knew the desert trails and a number holed up together in villas, hiding out while friendly Kuwaitis brought them food.

After the war, one of the latter – I think it was Fraser Martin – told me how they must have been betrayed by neighbours, for a couple of weeks later the Iraqis rolled up in an army truck.

"Where you from?" an Iraqi captain demanded of the first man.

"Britain."

"Get in the truck," ordered the officer, giving him a shove. "And you?" he said to the next.

"Scotland."

"Okay, you can stay."

All of those taken were eventually released or freed by the allied forces while I understand the 'neutrals' who remained in the villas were helped by Kuwaitis across the border to Saudi Arabia.

– 28 –

The eyes have it

PROFESSOR Svyatoslav Nikolayevich Fyodorov, member of the Congress of People's Deputies, member of the Russian Academy of Sciences, candidate for the Presidency of Russia and the man who introduced laser eye surgery to the world, sat on the other side of my office desk drinking coffee from one of the nice cups we kept for special visitors.

"Mr Bain," he said, "I am bringing my eye hospital ship to Dubai and I'd like your company to find us patients."

I sat back. This seemed to be an enormous task. First, there was the far from small matter of getting official permission. The professor's surgical techniques were virtually unknown to the public outside Russia, and the Dubai Department of Health and the UAE Health Ministry were pretty conservative in their attitudes. The approval or rejection of such methods was not, however, entirely their decision. The final word would come from Sheikh Mohammed bin Rashid al Maktoum, then Crown Prince of Dubai and Deputy Prime Minister of the UAE.

"You'll have to tell me more," I said.

The professor, a thickset figure in his early sixties with an overgrown crew-cut and a cheerful smile, was a hero in his homeland, having overcome massive official and professional resistance as he pioneered techniques that would later be adopted globally as standard practice. Although his eye hospital outside Moscow, the largest in the world, had an enormous turnover of patients, he wanted to introduce his revolutionary surgery to wider audiences. As well as setting up satellite clinics within Russia, he had hired and converted a small cruise liner, the *Peter I*, with which he had successfully toured ports in the Black Sea. Now he wanted to take it further afield and test international demand. Dubai would be its first stop.

"You will understand how important this is," Prof Fyodorov said. "After Dubai, we are planning to take the ship to Cyprus and maybe Gibraltar but if we don't get the patients here, we may have to turn around and go home. Not only will that be a financial disaster for us, but a lot of people will be left without the treatments we can offer."

Then he warned me: "There are special interest groups, authorities and institutions who will fight to stop us because we have revolutionised eye surgery. Opticians hate us because we enable myopic people to throw away their glasses. You will have to deal with major resistance… and it could get nasty."

I'd never known a situation where the success of a venture might depend so heavily on public relations. It was a little scary. Advertising could alert potential patients to the ship's presence and process. But it would be the image we created and the generation of positive media exposure that would help people decide whether to trust a bunch of Russian doctors with the most precious of their senses. I knew there wasn't another PR firm that could handle it better, but it worried me that we'd be putting our reputation very visibly on the line. More important than that, what if patients were left worse off? There were multiple opportunities for it all to go horribly wrong.

We also had to believe that the immediate item on the agenda – obtaining permission – would be achieved.

I told Prof Fyodorov I'd have a talk with colleagues and get back to him the following day. I spoke at length to account directors Barbara Saunders and Boutros Boutros and we agreed we had to do it. Risky or not, it was a challenge we could not turn down.

The initial announcement and early advertising brought an abundance of interest and a sandstorm of protest. Anyone whose business might be damaged by the presence of the vessel howled loudly and the Arabic and English newspapers were full of letters, some quite libelous, attacking the professor's skills and ethics and questioning the necessity for what they called potentially dangerous procedures. Reporters followed up with interviews of the outraged self-interest groups and there were times when I thought we might be doomed before we'd really begun.

Tempting as it was, we refrained from rushing to defend. That might only have served to extend the controversy. So unless the media asked us for comments – which they seldom did in the beginning – we tended to ignore the attacks to focus on positive news. In those days the Press in the Gulf didn't generally write balanced stories. It was usually one way or the other but we had few complaints because they also soaked up virtually every release we sent out.

We started the campaign about a month ahead of the ship's arrival, producing stories of the operations and their expected outcome, the unique way the operating theatres within the ship actually worked, profiles of Prof Fyodorov, the number and expertise of the medical staff involved, the success rate of the various procedures and glowing comments from Western patients who had undergone surgery in Moscow. It was very largely an educational process aimed at potential patients. The opposition continued but the public interest was overwhelmingly in our favour.

It was also vital to win over ophthalmic surgeons, consultants, general practitioners and health officials from throughout the UAE. Getting their support would be half the battle. So we organised a series of weekly lectures by the professor and his leading surgeons who had arrived before the vessel. Many medical people knew Fyodorov by reputation and demand forced us to raise the frequency of lectures to three times a week.

While we could always rely on him to turn up on time, sometimes the hard part was rounding up his team who had discovered the Aladdin's caves that were Dubai's shopping malls. At that time in the late Eighties, goods in Russian stores were much less plentiful.

That said, Fyodorov had picked them well. They were professional to the core and their friendly attitudes and cheerfulness belied the Western image of dour, unsympathetic Russians not long rid of the shackles of oppression. Not all the ship's crew, however, were so enlightened.

The shipping agent, Ibrahim al Sharaf, worked on procuring the required licences. The *Peter I* would dock at Jebel Ali, the largest man-made port in the world. The Sharaf agency, which represented many shipping companies that used the port, had influence in the right places but that alone would not be enough. Those at the highest level would have to be satisfied that this was in the best interests of the people.

We eventually got the nod that permission would not be refused and we got on with stretching the reach of our news and information coverage to countries across the Middle East, from Iraq to Egypt and North Africa with the primary focus on the Gulf states.

The immediate response would have been considered exceptional by most standards. Bookings poured in. But the ship had a huge capacity for patients. It could handle nearly five hundred a week whether for examinations or surgery. My concern was how to maintain the momentum for the four months or so from the initial announcement to the departure of the ship.

The best PR is word of mouth and that would happen. But in a situation like this it would be a slow process and we didn't have a lot of time. We also had to consider the possibility of any disgruntled patients going to the Press with tales of horror or simply neglect.

I worried that the flow of patients might tail off. The ship was such a hungry mouth to feed. Then I had a brainwave. With the professor's agreement, I invited every short-sighted journalist we knew throughout the Gulf to have free corrective surgery. I didn't want to press them for fear of something going wrong but simply referred them to the information we were putting out and let them make up their own minds.

I can't remember the exact figures, but I recall that about fifteen or twenty accepted. That was the turning point. After their operations, all successful, they wrote in lavish praise of the procedures. One journalist filled two pages of his newspaper with pictures, information and boundless accolades.

A great rush of calls swamped the switchboard of the booking centre at the Al Sharaf agency and it became clear the people there simply couldn't handle the volume. Nor did they really know what to say to callers or how to manage the flow. We provided emergency training while Al Sharaf installed more lines and more staff.

The interest was now enormous and our office was even getting calls. Barbara Saunders received a telex from a member of the Bahrain Royal family who began: "I understand you are in possession of a Russian eye hospital..."

I went down to Jebel Ali port with my team the morning after the ship's arrival. It looked every millimetre a Soviet-era cruise liner built to an unfashionable off-the-shelf design. There was little that was graceful or majestic about the *Peter I*. The ship had been intended to reward the efforts of Communist Party managers rather than give a dangerous glimpse of leisure and luxury to the proletariat. But with its refit and its mission in mind, I could see it in a softer light.

The medical team consisted of fourteen doctors, sixteen nurses and eight technical specialists. The futuristic-style operating theatres had been designed for speed and throughput. There was a kind of conveyor belt system that sounds quite awful but was actually safe and efficient. It meant that different surgeons completed different aspects of an operation as the patients passed from one to another. It was less of a factory-style belt and more of a 'daisy wheel' multi-station configuration.

The majority of patients were myopic and their surgery was often done in minutes, but more complex issues such as glaucoma, retinal detachment and astigmatism took more time. However, there were limitations to the treatments on the ship and some patients were referred to Fyodorov's hospital near Moscow. Others were told that, sadly, nothing could be done for them.

That produced the next wave of negative media coverage. All patients paid a non-refundable examination fee whether or not they went on to have surgery. Many of the rejected patients demanded their money back and complained to the newspapers when they were refused. For us, it was more of an irritation than a crisis.

If the call centre couldn't handle the demand, neither could the non-medical crew on the ship who were more used to dealing with Black Sea peasants than relatively wealthy Arabs. They left patients waiting for ages when they tried to book in, and the reception staff were often unhelpful and sometimes downright rude. As we watched a Saudi prince arrive on the dock with an enormous entourage, I could see disaster walking up the gangway. Thankfully, the prince chose to stay at the nearby Jebel Ali Hotel resort as, in fact, did many others.

After discussions with the professor and the project director, they decided to send many of the front-line staff home and bring in hospitality-trained personnel from local hotels.

There was a similar issue with the onboard meals. Residents of the Gulf are used to lavish spreads and great choices so the offerings of the *Peter I*'s galleys were meagre and often, to my taste at least, unpalatable. The solution was to bring in the food and catering staff from the Jebel Ali Hotel which must have made an absolute fortune from all the business it was receiving.

"Except in the operating theatres, it's all a big learning process," said Prof Fyodorov with a sigh – and a smile too, for the project was succeeding well beyond even the most optimistic expectations.

In the end, we never seemed to run out of patients and the ship remained in Jebel Ali for six months, double the intended period. Those of us at Bain Communications put in a lot more time than we were paid for but it didn't matter. The professor and his team had seen more than 12,500 patients before the ship sailed for Cyprus. It was a remarkable result.

Public relations work in general can be interesting and rewarding, but we had experienced nothing like this. In the immediate aftermath, there was a gentle euphoria that gave way to a sense of deep satisfaction. PR isn't always about selling computer chips or cars or airline seats. Just sometimes it does things that lift the human spirit and are of real benefit to people.

Our team didn't stay together. Barbara went off to start her own PR company and Boutros, who took the plunge and had the surgery himself, joined Emirates Airline where he is now senior vice-president corporate communications. Everyone moves on and I brought in more people and more clients but I can look back now and say to myself: "Ah, those were among the best of times."

THERE WAS little love lost between Lord King, chairman of British Airways, and Jean Pierson, president of Airbus, and even less after my small intervention. Until it took over British Caledonian and inherited ten A320s, BA had never operated an Airbus. It didn't help King's mood when his passengers voted it the most popular aircraft. He continued to denigrate it in a way that puzzled the industry.

"The A320," Lord King announced, "does not keep its promises. It is not meeting the performance levels that Airbus claims it would."

I was handling the Airbus public relations in the Middle East and King's remarks were an irritant. We were in the middle of a campaign to sell the A320 to airlines in the region.

So when the chairman of Lufthansa, prompted or not, told the European Press that Lord King should learn his business instead of making a fool of himself, it was too good to ignore.

"No brand new aircraft keeps its promises," said the Lufthansa chief, "and everyone knows that, apart, it seems, from Lord King. As more aircraft come off the production line and refinements are made, the figures will meet the projections." Because of that, the first models are sold at discounted prices.

So I wrote a little story around this and sent it on unheaded paper to my editor friends.

I really had no idea the airline was holding its global annual conference in Bahrain. When his lordship opened the Gulf Daily News, *he may have choked on his breakfast* croissant. *'Lord King is a fool – Lufthansa boss', said a headline.*

Sir Colin Marshall, the CEO, was dispatched to the newspaper offices to determine the source, following which a serious complaint was made to Airbus. I heard of it from the head of corporate communications and, glumly, offered to resign the account.

"No need for that," I was told. "Monsieur Pierson is highly amused."

– 29 –

Going to blazes with GM

IT TOOK two hundred firefighters, and helicopters with water bombs to bring the blaze at Fess Parker's vast California ranch under control. We were present, sure, but we didn't start it. Our chaps from the Middle East were completely innocent. Well, this time anyway.

We were in the parched hills above Santa Barbara taking part in what General Motors call a 'Ride and Drive' in which international journalists get to try out the coming year's Chevrolet, Cadillac and GMC models.

Okay, so we'd been in trouble in previous years, once when a tearaway reporter from Kuwait drove an oncoming pick-up off the road in Montana and was chased into our hotel by a gun-waving cowboy screaming "I'll kill the bastard!" and another time when six police cars chased a Middle Eastern miscreant through the streets of genteel Palm Springs at seventy miles an hour.

General Motors was my client and for a number of years I led a group of regional motoring writers on this much anticipated jolly. They were actually a pretty solid bunch, responsible and respectable. I considered most of them good friends. The very occasional chancer didn't get invited back.

This time, thankfully, others were to blame. Two young Taiwanese journalists, in fact. While the rest of the international Press corps and our hosts were having a pleasant lunch at the ranch of the actor who played Davy Crockett in the TV series, they decided to go for an unauthorised spin in a Chevrolet Corvette, the legendary sports car.

And spin they did. Driving far too quickly over the blind crest of a hill, they couldn't make the sharp bend immediately ahead and may have tried a hand-brake turn for the car shot backwards off the road and onto rocks that punctured the petrol tank.

The men clambered out unscathed and made off back up the road while the Corvette went up in flames with a great whoosh! As did the dried out eucalyptus trees. They actually exploded with a bang, one after another, as the blaze spread like, well… wildfire.

The Corvette has a plastic body and in this instance it just melted. That was the picture that made the papers and TV stations across the States, the worst kind of publicity and lots of it. The American Press was intrigued by the circumstances and some reporters also liked to stick it to the car companies when they got the opportunity.

It would have been worse if the Taiwan pair had been sent home in coffins instead of just in disgrace and the phone lines from Detroit must have burned as explanations were demanded of the Ride and Drive organisers. Months later, GM got a bill from the fire department for half a million dollars.

MY JOB at these events was to make sure our journalists were in the right places at the right times and that they got enough hours in the different vehicles and with the GM officials they wanted to interview. For the most part, it was easy, relaxed work. It took me to many parts of the US, through a lot of Europe and even to Australia.

The Chevrolet Caprice was the biggest-selling American car in the Middle East but something of a gas-guzzling dinosaur in the US where latterly only the police and taxi fleets bought them. When GM stopped producing them, the region needed to source an acceptable replacement which they believed they'd found in the top-of-the-range Holden made by GM Australia. They just took the left-hand-drive version, put a Chevrolet badge on it and renamed it Caprice.

The concern was that traditional buyers would not consider them genuine Caprices if they came from anywhere other than America. We undertook a major campaign of persuasion that included taking the Middle East motoring media to a Ride and Drive event near Melbourne. The Press loved the car – and so did the public.

No vehicles were manufactured in the Gulf region; the population base simply wasn't big enough. This gave rise to fairly valid criticism that the car giants were taking a lot of money out and putting nothing back in. Not just the Americans, but the Japanese who controlled by far the major share of the market.

I was always on the lookout for something that would benefit the community and I almost dismissed it when it came along. Peter Hellyer, a friend who worked for the Ministry of Information in Abu Dhabi, told me of an Australian archaelogical team led by an American professor which was about to excavate an ancient site on the border of Sharjah and Umm al Quwain, two of the seven emirates that make up the UAE. It was looking for a little help with expenses.

There was never any question that it would produce Egyptian-style treasures so, being quite ignorant of these things, I wasn't really interested in anything less. But I met up anyway with Dr Dan Potts, professor of archaeology for the Near East at the University of Sydney.

I had imagined some old-fashioned middle-aged character with both feet in the past and quite unworldy in other ways. Perhaps I'd watched too many movies. Dan couldn't have been more present and switched on. He was charming, funny, in his thirties and able to articulate the ancient world in modern language. I warmed to him immediately.

He told me the site at Tell Abraq was believed to be the first bronze age settlement in the lower Arabian peninsula. Until then, the inhabitants of the region had led nomadic lives. There was evidence of the kind of people they were, how they lived, what their health was like, that they traded with Bahrain and Mesopotamia. As he spoke, they began to come alive. I was hooked.

"How much would you need from GM?" I asked. I was expecting a hefty sum.

"Well," said Dan, "if we could have a little help with air fares and some living expenses… about $10,000 US?"

I just stopped myself from asking: Is that all?

"You'll have to come over and take a look," said Dan. "Then you can decide." So I went.

I began to see the potential. This was quite a discovery. There had

Interviewing Dr Dan Potts for the schools video on the Tell Abraq Bronze Age township, about 1996.

been some earlier digging at the site but nothing of great consequence. From five thousand years ago, Tell Abraq had grown into a town of several hundred people around the raised fortress which had its own water well. There was evidence of fishing and farming. Wheat and barley grains and fish and animal bones were found along with tools, stone vessels and ornaments. Once on the shoreline, it now lay seven kilometres inland and alongside the main highway.

Excavations of a tomb revealed bones from around 150 men, women and children. From these, the archaeologists could tell that men had been short but powerfully built, clearly used to hard labour.

All this provided information from which a picture of the people and their town emerged. Dan's wife, Hildreth, produced drawings which formed the basis of detailed colour images of life in the town in these early days of permanent settlement. It was fascinating stuff.

Gary Rowley, GM's managing director in the Middle East, loved the whole thing. So did Detroit. When executives from motor city flew in for meetings with regional dealers, they spent hours at Tell Abraq where Dan was the perfect host, showing them various artifacts discovered at the site and leading them through the town's development over the millenniums until the well ran dry and the people moved on.

I wrote several major features with photographs and drawings for magazines and newspapers throughout the Middle East, along with video releases for TV stations. We invited journalists to the site to interview Dan and his team. The exposure was tremendous.

We also developed, in cooperation with the UAE Ministry of Education, a programme for schools that included attractive booklets in Arabic and English and a fifteen-minute video documentary, coupled with school visits to the site. For the next couple of seasons, Gary upped the sponsorship fee substantially and we got further mileage from subsequent discoveries. It turned out to be exactly the kind of community project we'd been hoping for.

IT WAS GM's policy to replace its Middle East management every two or three years and I was sad to see Gary go. We had become good friends and, at the same time, I knew that with him our contract was secure. He warned me that his replacement, Jim Steinhagen, might be more difficult to deal with. And he was right.

Jim disliked me before we'd even met. I called him to arrange a meeting to discuss the PR plan for the coming year.

"How do you know I'm not going to cut off your legs?" he asked.

"I hope you're speaking metaphorically," I replied rather weakly. I couldn't think of a better response.

The relationship did not improve. It actually worsened considerably. Jim knew I had been very friendly with Gary. There were stories in the GM office that the two of them had a history going back to their days together in Detroit. I found it hard to believe that could be the reason for Jim's hostility towards me but I could not think of another. We were producing great work.

Gary used to brief me regularly on new developments, even with confidential internal information that gave me a better idea of how to frame future PR efforts. Jim stopped doing that and I had to scramble for bits and pieces from the brand managers.

He also gave the Press information about which I knew nothing. So when reporters called me for further details, I had to tell them I'd get back to them. It was incredibly frustrating and fast becoming intolerable. Yet I had to allow it to happen while I tried to repair whatever was wrong between us. Nothing seemed to work.

One day he told me he was allocating a quarter of a million dollars to a golf day that was a spin-off from the Dubai Desert Classic. I argued strongly that I could not see the benefit in this because the vast majority of GM buyers were Arabs who did not play or like golf.

What Jim didn't tell me was that he'd been pressured by GM's sponsor, a senior Dubai official who was in charge of the government's involvement in the main tournament, and that it was a political decision that had nothing to do with value for money. Every GM supplier except me was invited. I asked him about my omission.

"I didn't think you were interested in golf," he replied.

The time, I felt, had come to take an enormous gamble. I had been thinking about it for a while. This was a million-dollar-a-year account that I desperately did not want to lose but the situation could not continue.

Bain Communications had not been hired locally. I had been called to Detroit where we were appointed by executives who were a couple of steps higher on the corporate ladder than Gary or Jim. With my heart in my mouth, I faxed them a six-page letter of resignation, detailing all the difficulties and copied it to Jim who happened to be in Detroit at the time. I received a short response rejecting my resignation and telling me to have a conversation with Jim when he returned to Dubai.

He had apparently been told that even if only half these reported incidents were true, there was a serious problem and he was instructed to get it sorted.

Jim summoned me to the GM office in Dubai's World Trade Centre.

"Why didn't you talk to me about this?" he asked, pointing to my letter.

"How many times did I try, Jim?" I replied. "You didn't leave me with any alternative."

I would like to say things improved, but Jim had been wounded and while we managed to get along, there was always an edge. About a year later, Jim was assigned a new role in Detroit and his replacement was an ever-cheerful down-to-earth Englishman named Alan Batey, now President of GM North America. Happy days were here again.

Wedding day, 1998.

SHE WAS in business class on the Emirates flight, a petite and attractive young woman in her early twenties. I took the empty seat beside her and we introduced ourselves. Her name was Sharadha Balasubramanian, a reporter from the Gulf News *in Dubai.*

"Let me give you a Press pack," I said, handing over a wadge of material about Emirates' inaugural flight to Hong Kong. I was leading the Press group on the trip, as I had done on the many occasions my client Emirates had opened a new international route.

"I'm only here because my boss was too busy," said Sharadha.

"Well, I hope you enjoy the trip. There's a pretty full schedule of events."

One free evening, when most of the other journalists were out on the town, I noticed her alone in the coffee shop of our hotel and we talked long about life in Dubai, her home in India and mine in Scotland, our careers and our various travels. When the group returned to Dubai, I stayed on in Hong Kong to resolve some issues with the local PR agency and it was some time before we encountered each other again.

I had not thought about a romantic relationship. Although my marriage to Isobel was heading rapidly towards divorce, I was more than twenty years older than Sharadha. But it just seemed to happen. Her father and step-mother's understandably stiff opposition eventually turned to liking and mutual respect.

Sharadha and I were married in 1998 and it's a little bit of a conversation piece when people today ask us how we met. She didn't stay in journalism and is now a psychoanalytical psychotherapist in Edinburgh where we live happily with our delightful dog, Leela.

– 30 –

Fire and ice

WHEN I first flew into Iceland many years ago, I looked down from about three thousand feet and marvelled to the passenger beside me at the size of the sheep. They clearly bred them big up here. Further into the descent, I realised they were actually bales of hay wrapped in white plastic and left dotted around the fields. I felt a little foolish.

I learned later that farmers sometimes get three cuts of hay as nature adapts itself to the four short months of relatively warm weather. Not what I'd expected this close to the Arctic Circle. But then, Iceland is a land of surprises – even if what seems like half the world has discovered them.

It was all very different a few decades ago when Icelandair had a monopoly on flights and most visitors were intrepid explorers or anglers like me who came for the salmon and Arctic char in the wild rivers and mountain streams.

One of the first rivers I fished was the Svalbardsa in the north-east, reached after two domestic flights in light aircraft. On the edge of the dirt runway at Porshofn, the shell of a crashed plane served as a reminder that flying in these wind-torn northern parts can be hazardous.

The airport building was a small portacabin and the air traffic controller also served as ticket salesman and baggage handler. On busy flights someone – usually a little old lady – got to sit next to the pilot who would ask her politely not to touch the controls.

I stayed an hour's drive away in a schoolhouse converted during the summer holidays into accommodation for travellers. The restaurant area was the assembly room and, to get back to my room from the showers, I remember having to weave my way through the diners dressed only in a wet towel. The schoolmaster, who also served as manager and chef, would sometimes arrive up-river to ask if we would catch him a salmon for dinner that night.

Some of the best pools on the river were in a canyon a difficult seven-kilometre trek across bogland and rough terrain from where the track ran out. When I got there I couldn't see an easy descent from the higher ground so I tried edging my way down a steep slope on my back. Unfortunately, the ground under my feet gave way and I began a rapid slide, thinking in that moment that it would be a miracle if I got out of there with less than a broken leg. Then my heels hit a ledge a metre or so above the rocks and I came to a jarring halt – torn, bloodied and bruised. I fished on, of course, but it took me a very long time to get back to my vehicle.

It was on the Svalbardsa, renowned for large fish, where I hooked and eventually lost the biggest salmon that has ever graced my fly. At that point, the river ran through an area of sandstone and, over the centuries, the force of the sapphire-blue stream had carved out a deep channel by the far bank where the fish would lie. The difficulty was in wading out far enough through the treacherously honeycombed riverbed to cast a fly that would drift across the channel.

The salmon actually chased the fly downstream, took it in a great splash and made off towards the sea, stripping most of the line from my reel. Then it turned and sped back towards me as I tried desperately to reel in the slack line. It jumped very close to me, an enormous silver and black fish more than a metre long and probably weighing around thirteen kilos.

Trying to edge my way back to the bank in order to run with it downstream if I had to, I kept tripping over the water-carved lumps of sandstone so I had to stand there and play it as best I could. The fish made several more leaps and, on the last one, shed the fly. I didn't begrudge that king of the river its freedom. I would have released it anyway.

Sitting on the bank in the warm evening sunshine with the smoke from my cigar curling slowly in the still air, I watched Icelandic ponies run in their unique gait on the other side of the river and sheep defy gravity on the steep sides of the nearby mountain. With just the sounds of the river and the plaintive cries of the whimbrels, it was pretty close to my vision of paradise. Arctic terns, these amazing little birds that migrate each year to the other end of the world, darted along the river picking up flies. Step near a nest and they'll draw blood from your head. Later, in an astonishing sight around midnight, I watched the sun touch the ocean and rise again. A shiver ran up my spine.

It's what we call the fishing, rather than just the fish, that has taken me back to Iceland every summer for the past twenty years or more. The 'fishing' encompasses these magnificent wild places, the bird life, the camaraderie in the lodges, the greeting of old friends and, of course, the captivating sight of salmon breaching the surface as they run upstream, back to their beginnings after a year or more feeding far out in the North Atlantic.

The rivers are owned by the farmers through whose land they run and the fishing is tightly controlled. By government rule and depending on the size the river, sometimes only two or three anglers at any one time are allowed to fish a whole river. On the really big waters, like the East Ranga where I am to be found at the end of each July, the river is divided into 'beats' of three to five kilometres each with two rods (fishermen) per beat. It all comes at enormous cost and I've sometimes wondered about all the really useful ways I could have spent that money. Then again, nurturing the soul must be pretty high up that list.

Sometimes you have no idea who your companion on that beat will be. A few seasons ago, I waited patiently by the riverbank for the appearance of the other rod. Eventually, three black Range Rovers rolled up and disgorged a dozen people, among them two exceptionally beautiful young women in full make-up.

It was all quite unreal but explained by the fact that the entourage was part of the cast and crew shooting the film *Prometheus*. My fellow rod that morning was the director Ridley Scott. I guess the rest were there to cheer him on. We didn't speak, only exchanged nods in the way that experienced fishermen do, and my guide Skuli and I moved to a quieter stretch.

They are definitely not mean people, but Icelanders don't leave gratuities. They may do when they travel abroad but it must go against the grain. Many believe it to be a dreadful practice. I occasionally entertain or annoy my Icelandic friends (the division is about fifty-fifty) with a fantasy of how I was the one who introduced tipping to Iceland in the early eighties. The tale itself is true enough.

When I got up from my meal in a burger-and-fries cafeteria on the edge of Akureyri I left a few coins on the table. "Excuse me," said the young waitress as she cleared the plates, "you've forgotten your change." I smiled at her in the way that seasoned travellers do. "Oh, that's just a small tip," I said a little smugly. Of course, I didn't realise that she'd never heard of a tip.

She frowned. "I don't understand."

"A gratuity…" I said with a measure of patronising pomposity, "…a small token of my appreciation of a meal well served."

She still didn't understand and certainly didn't appear to enjoy my humour. "You want to pay more than the meal cost?" she asked.

"No, no. It's for you." I was growing uncomfortable.

"You want to give me money?" She pointed somewhat disdainfully at the meagre collection of coins. "Why? What do you want from me?"

She was no more than seventeen, blonde and attractive. Quite late at night, we were the only people left in the place. She looked anxious. Clearly, she thought I was up to no good and began to back away towards the kitchen door. "I don't want your money. I already get paid."

I thought it best I depart, which I did, promptly, blustering my way out the door.

The fantasy suggests that she must have spoken to her waitress friends about her weird encounter and at some point they would have come to the conclusion that although this was a strange thing for people to do, it didn't require anything on their part – not even a smile, thank God – and was therefore pretty neat since there was money in it. And these folk were foreigners after all.

The idea possibly spread from that small café across the country and it's true enough that in the years that followed I began to notice little white bowls partly filled with coins appear beside cash registers in cafés and bars. And now it's endemic. You couldn't stamp it out if you tried.

My Icelandic friends would never dream of tipping after a meal, no matter how good it was or how convivial the atmosphere or how friendly and accommodating the restaurant staff. Mind you, one look at Reykjavik prices and you can understand why.

"I'm totally against it," said Skuli, my guiding friend of many years who would be mightily pissed off if his client didn't slip him a decent fold of notes at the end of the week.

"Ah, that's different," he said. "I'm totally against *giving* tips."

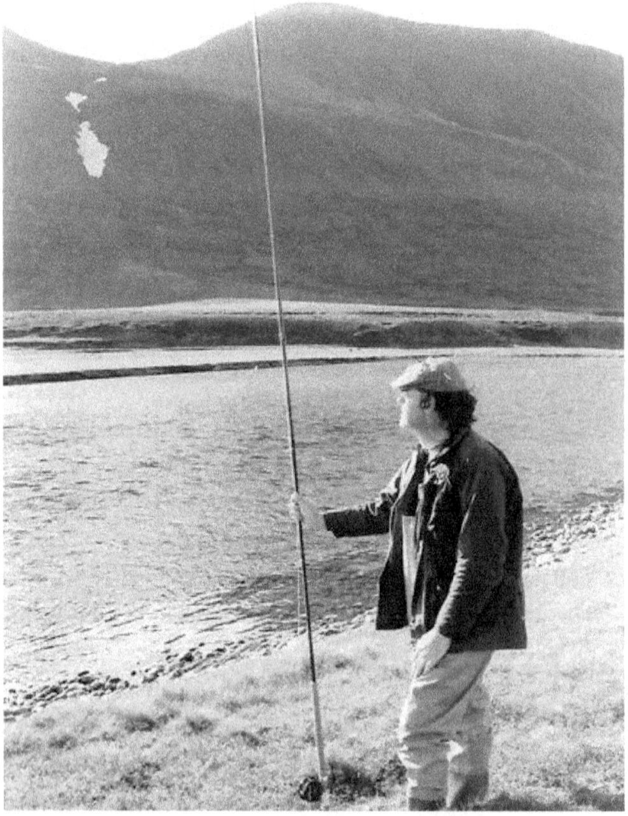

On the Svalbardsa River in north-east Iceland, 1994.

– 31 –

A fool and his money

I USED to wonder at pop stars who'd reached the top of the pile and found that it just wasn't enough. Why, when they'd achieved the fame and fortune they'd longed for, had so many turned to drugs and booze? Was it to soften the disappointment that lay within their enormous success? Or perhaps they were seeking an echo of that original, almost innocent, buzz.

It may sound ridiculously grandiose to compare myself to a disillusioned Elvis – even on a minuscule scale – but there was a kind of similarity. On the surface, everything was going well. Business was good and growing. I was making excellent tax-free money and had interesting and prestigious clients, most of them household names. I had just entered into a loving relationship that would lead to marriage so I was very happy in my personal life. I had friends, a beautiful daughter and yet… there was something wrong and I didn't know what. It was nothing definable, just what might be called a general dissatisfaction.

I couldn't put it down entirely to the procrastination that plagued me through much of my life. That was certainly part of it but I was equally concerned (and paradoxically unconcerned) about my overall disregard of my own well-being. I'd been happily off the booze for years but I was smoking an evil number of cigars a day, devouring what dietitians call the wrong things (I'm a connoisseur of club sandwiches dripping with mayonnaise or Thousand Island dressing) and avoiding any form of exercise. I once tried to sign up at the Hilton gym but the trainer rejected me on the basis I was too old and unfit. Of course, being old in Dubai is very different to being old anywhere else. In Dubai you're old at forty. I did buy a treadmill but after a couple of runs it sat unused in the spare room – as I imagine many treadmills do.

The procrastination served to illustrate how I was sabotaging myself and my business. It was serious but it wasn't deadly serious and I could live with it. I figured that the cause had to be seated deep in the unconscious, undoubtedly with its origins in the various traumas of my childhood. The inner child, the little boy whose needs had not been met, was acting out his anger and grief in a very self-destructive way. I wanted to resolve it because it's a hell of a scary notion that part of you is out to get you. Like something from a Stephen King story.

I didn't think I had a mental health issue. I wasn't depressed or borderline or suffering from any major psychological disorder even if I was, unconsciously and indirectly, trying to kill myself. I didn't need a psychiatrist but I thought it might be worth having a few sessions with a psychotherapist. Except in those days in Dubai they were in pretty short supply. I found an American whom I immediately disliked when he started talking about himself rather than listening to me. He'd once been a Hell's Angel in LA and he showed me his tattoos.

"Tell me," I asked him, just to get his reaction, "do you believe in God?"

"Well, Ian," he drawled. He seemed to insert my name into every other sentence. I found it horribly patronising. "Ah believe that you believe!" he said, grinning smugly at his crass cliche.

"I didn't say that I did." He ignored me.

Later I asked around and learned that his licence in California had been withdrawn after he allegedly assaulted a female patient. He probably needed help more than I did. So I crossed psychotherapy off my list.

But the more I learned about the unconscious mind, the more I understood – or at least recognised – my behavioural patterns. For example, over the years I gave away an enormous amount of money. This was due partly to my inherent generosity but also to the powerful unconscious belief that I didn't deserve to have it. To members of my family, I gave with genuine love and the desire to help them, but my largesse extended to friends, acquaintances and even people I hardly knew, some of whom hadn't even asked for financial help. With only a couple of exceptions, I do not begrudge a penny of it.

As a businessman, I was unbelievably foolish in multiple ways. I used to joke that if I had a boss, he should fire me. Some joke. I failed to collect monies owed and, as I've previously mentioned, sometimes didn't invoice for work already done. One beneficiary of my unintended philanthropy was someone who could most have afforded to pay – Sheikh Mohammed bin Rashid.

Sheikh Mohammed was behind a three-day international camel symposium on the health and care of these great and sometimes ill-tempered beasts of the desert. Experts and delegates came from around the world and I was asked to run the media side. The whole thing tickled the international Press. I put out a lot of stories and set up a media office within the conference centre. I just never got around to invoicing for the work.

You might wonder what kind of accountant my company had. It's a good question. I had the accountant I deserved – a part-timer who came in once or twice a week, prepared all the outgoing payments, wrote out the cheques and presented them to me for signing. To be fair to him, he would sometimes raise concerns but I tended to brush them aside. I was always busy with more interesting and creative things and I resented the time I had to spend with him.

If I'd had a full-time financial controller back then, the debacle that was Bain Design – in itself a good idea – would probably never have happened. I set up the unit as an offshoot of Bain Communications with an excellent young designer, Nick Adams, in charge. We entered into a partnership agreement; I provided the equipment and office space and we agreed to split the profits fifty-fifty. The big Apple Macintosh computers we needed were outrageously expensive and set me back the equivalent of £12,000 each. I bought four of them.

The new unit had five staff and all went swimmingly in the first year when we showed a gain of 250,000 dirhams, about £50,000. The difficulty came a while later, after I agreed that Nick, who had his own financial weaknesses, could draw advances against future profits. Nick loved to travel, mostly to Bangkok with its multiple attractions, and he was gone a lot. He once went around the world first class.

I think he lost interest and wanted out when he realised how long it would take before actual profits caught up with his advances. And without him putting much effort into winning new business or doing his share of the work, there weren't going to be many more profits. I have to admit, with a great degree of shame, that Nick didn't have unfettered access to the unit's funds. I signed every one of his advances.

Nick loved computer games. I would often go down to his office and find him playing one called *Railroad Tycoon* or shooting down enemy aircraft in *War in the Pacific*.

"How long," I asked him, "has it been since you did any work?"

"About a couple of months," he replied disarmingly.

Only a few weeks after coming back from one holiday, he told me he was going off on another, to Bangkok yet again. I told him he had to stay and sort out the business, but he went anyway and it was obvious he was seeking to engineer his dismissal. I had no alternative but to sack him.

Nick's debts to the business were substantial and I didn't like the idea of him just walking away from them – even though I'd allowed them to happen. So I sued him for 400,000 dirhams (£80,000). Nick counter-sued for the same amount, claiming that in the four years he'd worked for Bain Design he'd never once had a holiday. The court asked to see his passport. Unfortunately, said Nick, he'd just lost it. The court appointed an expert to examine the accounts. When the expert offered to find in my favour for a consideration of 25,000 dirhams, I abandoned the claim.

The design unit continued without Nick. It ticked over and did some excellent work and I'm grateful to the staff who persevered through those difficult times. And Bain Communications, the parent company, was doing very well.

I have to make clear that Nick didn't set out to take advantage of me. I created the situation which played to his weakness for the good life and provided him with the funds to support it, funds he would not otherwise have had at his immediate disposal. A few years later, I met him in the street and we went for a coffee. He felt badly about the way it had turned out and offered me a cheque, as a small token of redress, for 10,000 dirhams. I took the cheque but forgot to bank it.

ALL DRESSED up in my Highland finery, I was attending a Burns' supper at the Sheraton Hotel in Dubai where I delivered the Immortal Memory, a fifteen-minute tribute to the great poet. It had taken me an age to research and write (long before Google) and I was pretty pleased with the reception it received.

After the various toasts, I noticed an accordion leaning against a wall in the corner of the room. I turned to Hamish, my immediate neighbour, and said: "Oh God… somebody's going to be playing a bloody accordion. I can't stand that thing."

Hamish, who worked for Dubai TV, nodded and I went on at length about my dislike for that wheezing instrument and how it played a great disservice to Scottish music. Hamish's disinclination to offer a thought brought about a slow realisation that was immediately confirmed by an announcement from the floor: "And now, ladies and gentlemen, please welcome Hamish on the accordion!"

– 32 –

The strange stuff starts here

THE IDEA of asking a spiritual healer to help resolve my chronic procrastination seemed like a forlorn clutching of straws, and a potentially embarrassing one at that. From any perspective, I couldn't think of it as more than a foolish notion, a last gasp and probably hopeless attempt to curb my self-destructiveness. Yet I went. But I didn't tell any friends.

The introduction came through Sharadha. She was attending meditation classes with a German lady who had a reputation for doing good work with physical and psychological problems.

"Do you think she could help me?" I asked her.

"You should ask her yourself," Sharadha replied, not unkindly.

The catalyst that took me to the doorstep of Karin Meyer-Reumann was another piece of self-inflicted damage, an episode that brought about the realisation that, regardless of protests otherwise, my behaviour must be bordering on some kind of insanity. And after my experience with the psychotherapist, I didn't know where to turn. I was in despair, a state that only served to add conviction to my self-disgust.

I had lost a cheque for £6,000 from a British client. Actually, I knew roughly where it was but did nothing to retrieve it. When papers on my desk accumulated, I used to move them onto a knee-high shelf that ran along a glass-fronted wall of my corner office overlooking Sheikh Zayed Road so that, after a while, it held a series of not very neat piles, each about a foot high.

Buried among them was the cheque. I argued to myself that it wasn't going anywhere, that I'd eventually dig it out before it became invalid. Which, of course, I never did. When we moved to bigger premises, I just dumped the papers. This was just before the appointment of a full-time accountant who took control of the finances even if I sometimes thwarted him with incomplete invoices and expense claims. As for the cheque, I had intended to ask the client for a replacement but somehow never got round to doing so.

It was familiar territory. What was new here – and this is significant – was the acknowledgement that it simply couldn't go on. But how do you change a mind entrenched in a belief in your contemptibility? How do you convince it that these ridiculous actions were all part of a terrible misunderstanding, an erroneous perception founded in traumatic childhood experiences?

The most I hoped for was to be a little kinder to myself, a little less self-punishing. That would be enough. But I definitely needed help in achieving it.

Karin was a delightful, attractive lady of early middle age. She and her family lived not far from Sharadha and me in Jumeirah, one of the leafier suburbs of Dubai with individual houses rather than apartments. It was home to large numbers of European expats, primarily British. Flame trees lined many of the streets and multi-coloured bougainvillea festooned garden walls. At a time before foreigners could buy property, our rented house was a large modern Arab-style villa with a five-metre tree in the atrium and a garden that stretched from one street to the next. Exotic birds like hoopoes and parakeets were common visitors.

"What can I do for you?" Karin asked after introductions at the door of her own not insubstantial home.

"I'd like to become a healer," I replied without hesitation. I still have no idea how I came to say that. Even more than twenty years on, I sometimes wonder if I actually did or if it was just an unspoken thought. Then again, if an unconscious part of my personality could seek to cripple me in one way, could not another part give voice to a genuine desire?

Certainly, Karin reacted to it. "Well you'd better come in," she said and led me to a large sitting room where she served tea. I've never felt particularly comfortable in other people's houses, but there was a genuine welcome here and a warmth and, despite my misgivings about going, I felt at ease. She never asked me to explain myself other than to describe briefly why I'd sought her out.

Karin invited me to join her meditation group and, if I wished, to have individual sessions. These were, by any measure, inexpensive – about twenty-five dirhams for the class and eighty dirhams for the sessions. We left the money in a mug on the shelf. I attended every week I was in town. It was a beginning of a relationship that helped to change my life.

There were never any flamboyant demonstrations of whatever psychic abilities Karin possessed. She never made any claims or performed what might be thought of as party tricks. She didn't read palms or tea leaves. Yet they were revealed in subtle and not so subtle ways.

In one guided visualisation, Karin led the class of about a dozen up an imaginary hillside trail with obstacles along the way. She asked us to focus on the journey and keep moving onwards. At one point, I saw in my mind's eye a small path to the side and went off to explore it. After a few moments, Karin paused the meditation and said: "Ian, please get back on the main track."

Her large meditation and healing room was on the first floor. In Dubai's perpetual sunshine, it was bathed in soft light that filtered through net curtains and in soulful, atmospheric music, both of which suggested another reality. Karin herself dressed mainly in white and once, as she sat cross-legged on the floor, I saw a flash of white underwear. I was momentarily mortified. 'My God!' I thought, 'she'll know I looked at her knickers!'

There was no wave of a wand, no road to Damascus enlightenment that snuffed out my procrastination. I continued to undo office manager Nirmala's attempts to file the papers on my desk and it was the unrelenting efforts of new finance manager Sankar, rather than any meditation practices, that prevented me from failing to collect monies owed. But I also continued to visit Karin whenever possible.

I was unable to define the attraction. A sense of peacefulness might be a good description but it was more than that. Maybe a sense of belonging, of being in the presence of a deeper knowledge.

If you're a complete sceptic who thinks all this is utter tosh, I'm afraid it gets worse so maybe you should jump this chapter and the next couple or toss the book. But I understand your misgivings. I had serious doubts myself (in spite of my strange doorstep utterance). But the more I learned and experienced, the more able I was to keep an open mind.

In the individual sessions, Karin would take me on visualised journeys through forests and fields and across rivers with coloured stepping stones – red, orange, yellow, green, light blue, purple and white. Each colour represented the major *chakras* of the body. Healers ancient and modern believed that these energy centres could become blocked or distorted by emotional issues and lead to illness. Focusing on the colours helped to re-energise the *chakras* and therefore the physical body. Looking back on it, it was elemental stuff but vital in the beginning.

We would sit on cushions facing each other across the room, cross-legged and backs against the wall. Sometimes, when I had a lot going on at work, I found it hard to concentrate. Karin gently chided me into making more effort. There was, however, one much-repeated exercise that I didn't understand and that was becoming a bore.

"Imagine," Karin would say, "your higher self, that enlightened part of you, is motionless about six metres directly above your head. Invite it to come to you. Bring it down slowly. Visualise it coming closer and closer as your crown *chakra* opens to take it in. Very slowly and gently. And when it touches the top of your head, bring it slowly into your body, centimetres at a time and let it fill your entire being."

The problem was that I felt nothing at all. We did it week after week after week. Karin never questioned what – or what not – was going on with me and we simply moved onto another exercise. But we always came back to that one. Like bathing in the colours of the *chakras*, it became part of the routine.

At the same time, I never once felt like giving up. I liked Karin and my meditation classmates who came from a great mix of backgrounds but all with an almost identical goal: To learn more about themselves and how to resolve their issues. It was great that Sharadha was in the same class although she seemed to be leaps and bounds ahead of me.

Many months passed before something different happened in the higher self exercise. One afternoon, as I visualised that superior aspect of myself nearing the crown of my head, I began to feel a tingling. It was mild at first, like pleasant pins and needles. As I continued with the visualisation, it grew and changed into powerful sensations of joy and I could physically feel my whole body filling up with a wonderful energy. Water streamed from the outer corners of eyes, wetting my shirt, as I sat in what I can only describe as pure bliss.

"My God," I said, looking at Karin who was wiping her own tears. "What happened?"

"You've just experienced your higher self," she replied.

I had also crossed through a barrier into… well, it sounds overly dramatic and perhaps a little self-aggrandising to say… into another dimension. There will always be arguments for and against the existence of senses beyond the physical ones of sight, hearing, taste, smell and touch. Maybe it takes a personal experience to believe that clairvoyance, intuition and such are real.

John, a friend and neighbour in Dubai, had uncanny intuition without ever having tried to cultivate it. Driving down the highway with his family, he once shocked himself by slamming on the brakes. As he came to a halt, several cars ahead collided.

On another occasion, he had serious doubts about boarding an aircraft at Muscat. But it was the last flight of the day and he wanted to get home to his family in Dubai before the weekend, so he pushed them aside. When he took his seat near the rear of the plane his anxiety intensified but the press of boarding passengers prevented him from getting off.

The aircraft lost an engine on take-off and struggled into the air, then spent ages dumping fuel before it made a hard landing back in Muscat with a number of passengers suffering minor injuries. "The captain's hands were shaking when he left the cockpit and his face was white," John told me.

My new-found intuition was not of that calibre but it was strong enough and it had its uses. Just holding a book, for example, I would know if it was worth reading. I experimented in bookshops by picking up a trash novel – which left me with a dull ache – and a book like Eckhart Tolle's classic *The Power of Now* which was like touching a live wire.

A YEAR or two into studies with Karin, she told me she was going to teach me how to die. She often made such blunt statements without any explanation that might add a degree of comfort to the upcoming exercise. But I was used to her by then and lay unconcerned on the treatment table. She sat with her back against the wall. This is a much-abbreviated version of her words:

"You are in the black void. Lie down and sink into its velvet smoothness. Notice that you can breathe without difficulty. Now the flesh and the organs are beginning to melt away. See all the muscles and sinews fall from the bones. And the bones themselves are disintegrating, the small ones first, then the large ones until there is nothing left."

I sat up abruptly. "I'm free!" I yelled. "I'm free! Look at me! I can fly!" I was ecstatic.

Karin permitted me this 'freedom' for a little while and then said: "Now we are going to build you a new body."

"No!" I screamed. "No! I don't want one! Don't do this!" I cried tears and for a minute or two was inconsolable.

Later, Karin told me that when it came to dying I would not have a problem. Then she added: "But promise me you will look both ways when you cross the road." I smiled but the look on her face was deadly serious.

TO SCEPTICS who have read on, I did warn it would get weirder. Ah, says one, you were hypnotised. I suppose it's an outside possibility but, as I understand it, responses under hypnosis have to be suggested before the subject acts them out. And what I'm about to describe now is even more peculiar.

There's much in print and celluloid about people being possessed, even by the devil himself. Where would the cinema be without these gory tales? The church takes the possibility seriously enough to carry out exorcisms but I've never been fully convinced of the existence of demons and such. Evil, to me, has a man-made quality. Some spiritual friends disagree.

But I do believe in attachments, figures that are more of a nuisance than anything else. For a number of years I had seen in my head the face of a Norman soldier wearing a pointed helmet with a noseguard. I never thought of him as an attachment until later and hindsight suggests I may have collected him during my days of heavy drinking when my energy field (aura) was severely depleted. I never mentioned him to Karin, perhaps because I wasn't certain if it was just my imagination.

Karin had invited a visiting British healer, Lorna Todd, to lead a meditation for the group. With my eyes closed, I was following Lorna's direction well enough until the soldier kept appearing right in front of my face.

Against a purple background, the face drifted in and out. He wouldn't look me directly in the eye, just over my shoulder or at my chin or forehead. At the same time, my breathing became laboured. I had a sudden image of me soaring into the universe, hand in hand with my higher self. Out in space, I slowed and stopped. At the same time, the purple background overwhelmed the face and I slumped forward, gasping for breath. Karin came to my side and laid one hand on my diaphragm and the other on my back.

"It's okay now," she said. "He's gone."

"Who's gone?" I asked.

"The soldier, of course."

"Did you ask him if he wanted to move into the light?" I asked somewhat naively.

"I did."

"And what did he say?"

"He said 'fuck off.'"

– 33 –

A most unusual school

IT WAS a situation I knew well. I'd experienced it nine times before in towns like Oban and Auchtermuchty and Glenrothes: getting ready to enter assembly on my first day at a new school, adrift in a sea of unfamiliar faces and on the edge of anxiety; not hearing what the teacher just said but, from the hushing of the hubbub, assuming it was a request to file in quietly.

The last time I had been in this position was more than forty years earlier. Although this occasion ploughed up the old feelings of unease and trepidation, there was excitement too. This was quite a different kind of educational establishment. For a start, unlike my other schools, I had come willingly. And through the open doors at the back of the building, I could hear the gentle Atlantic surf break over the sands of Miami Beach. There was nothing like that near the Gordon School for Boys in Gravesend.

But as nine o'clock approached on that warm September morning of 2000, the question remained: What was I doing here? I had a business to run and clients to service. Was this another of my foolish misadventures? My uncertainty, perched stubbornly on my shoulder like Long John Silver's parrot, squawked incessantly in my ear. Too late now, I thought as the double doors opened into a large ballroom with rows of several hundred metal and canvas chairs. On the left side of the stage, a harpist played.

I had signed up for a four-year course in Brennan Healing Science at the Barbara Brennan School for Healing, the largest and most highly regarded of its kind in the world. Its founder was a former NASA physicist who had turned from assessing the energy field around the earth to exploring the one around the human body with its similar nuances and fluctuations.

One initial snag had been my lack of any acceptable proof of education, something required by the Florida Board of Education, which licensed BBSH. As I've mentioned, I had to sit a GED – the equivalent of a high school diploma – at the age of fifty-six. I deliberately chose not to study for it so that I would have an excuse if I failed.

I can't say that I came to the school completely unaware. It was Karin who first mentioned Barbara's intriguing – and initially quite bewildering – book, *Hands of Light*. On the strength of reading that, Sharadha and I had travelled to the US to attend an introductory workshop. So fascinating were the events and teachings of that weekend that Sharadha enrolled immediately. Resistance, as much as the pressure of business, held me back. But, three years later, there I was embarking on what I hoped would be some kind of life transformation, just as it had said on the packet. If the work here would put even a small dent in my chronic procrastination and my belief in non-deserving, then the time, the effort and the not-insubstantial costs of travel from Dubai, hotel and school fees would be more than worthwhile.

But my presence wasn't only about my issues. I suppose that at some point in our lives, most of us ask the question: "Is this it?" From my experiences with Karin, it was clear to me there were realms beyond the physical but my understanding of them was vague and confused.

A much smaller number of people go on to ask "Who am I?" with all the follow-up questions that arise from there. How much of who I believe myself to be is determined by my negative life experiences, particularly from childhood? How much of me is authentic? How much is hidden behind a mask? How much is coated in the layers of fear and anxiety that come disguised as bravado or confidence? And what can I do about it? Google is never going to provide much in the way of answers.

The Barbara Brennan School of Healing met five times a year for nearly a week at a time and by the end of that first week I was reeling.

With Barbara Brennan – happy times at healing school, 2004.

I was pleased and relieved that Sharadha was with me. As I started my first year, she began her fourth and final one. I wanted to hang out with her and her friends during leisure time but she cast me off in a kind way. "You need to be with your own classmates," she said and she was, of course, quite right.

The 150 or so first-year students were divided into seven small classes in which we practised basic healing techniques and learned about the different levels of the human energy field, focusing on the first three that related mainly to the physical body.

One of our class teachers in that first year was a down-to-earth Southern lady called Laurie Thorp who would label us "the fucking awesome class". It was an accolade we wore like a badge but I suspect she told that to every class she led.

The small classes combined twice a day for healings or lectures by senior members of the faculty including Barbara who always seemed to exude a goddess-like quality. Her abilities were extraordinary and she could read you like a book. At least twice in the week the whole school would gather with her for meditation and talks.

In the healing skills aspect of the training, we learned about states of being, the four dimensions of humankind, astral healing, spine cleaning, time capsule healing and if I've lost you already, you can imagine what it was like for us bewildered students who not only had to understand what they meant but how to apply these healings and in what circumstances.

The other side of the training centred on what the school called awakening skills. This was based on the understandable principle that healers need to be healed themselves, at least to a reasonable degree, before they can attempt to heal others. We would have to gain and demonstrate an understanding of the life pulse, listening and contact skills, the wound, the higher self, lower self, mask and shadow. There's more – defence, intentionality, transference, boundaries, ego and superego, witnessing, asking and experiencing, and surrender. My first-year student workbook contained 350 pages and was more than an inch thick.

That might give you an indication of the effort required and the discipline and thoroughness that prevailed. While the teachers were dedicated, compassionate and highly skilled, they cut through bullshit like sharks after a seal. If they seemed to call you out for the smallest misdemeanor, it was to make you aware of whatever defence mechanism you were employing at the time. "Good morning, dear one," I said to one teacher. "You're being seductive, Ian. Don't do it," she replied and swept on.

It was a whole new world – confusing, baffling and absolutely amazing. I had viewed the vast landscapes of spirit and self as an overwhelming and impenetrable fog. Now, even if I didn't understand most of it, here it was being sliced up into just about manageable portions.

The essence of this kind of healing work is that problems in the body show up first in the human energy field. If there is a distortion around, say, the heart *chakra* this may manifest in the physical even years later. We learned, with much trial and error, to discern the problem in the field using what Barbara called Higher Sensory Perception and repair whatever was out of alignment.

I can see sceptical readers shaking their heads. That's okay. I'm not out to convince anyone.

But the remarkable thing is that you actually learn to understand what is going on. There are different ways of perceiving. Some people see the field visibly, others with inner sight, some feel their way through a healing and some, like me, use what is known as direct knowing. There's often a bit of a mix.

It amuses me when some writer from the *Daily Mail* or a similar tabloid undergoes brief psychic-type experiences and then reports how nothing happened for them. It's even more unfortunate when they choose healers whose egos may be a little on the unhealthy side.

Like my higher-self experience with Karin, these things don't come immediately or easily. You have to be open enough to receive them. And being open means a willingness to suspend your defences and allow yourself to be vulnerable. That can be very painful.

The teachers at BBSH were clever, even cunning. As the large class – the students from the whole year – made their way into a particular lesson, they would play some jaunty, cheerful music. Then, into the middle of that, they would sometimes drop an Italian tenor's lament. They caught me every time with Puccini's *O mio Babbino Caro – Oh my Beloved Father*. Softened up by an embracing sense of safety, my readiness to learn and my willingness to be open, it went straight to my heart and I began to bubble, as did others. My tears were not for the loss of my father, but for the one I never had. Regardless, they brought me towards that place of surrender required for the exercise we were about to undertake.

They formed us into an inner and an outer circle so that each student faced another.

"Now try to read the field of the person opposite you and share with each other what you notice or receive," they instructed. Oh God, I thought, this is impossible. And it was. The first time I got nothing. I was anxious and far too subscribed to the belief that I would fail.

The inner circle moved around one and I was facing a red-haired lady whom I didn't recall meeting before. Try, I told myself, to relax and open up. So I did my best to surrender and just see what emerged. I had to accept that if nothing happened, that would be okay too. Suddenly, I knew that this lady had a major issue with a sister. Then I saw in my mind's eye a field of cows.

It came as quite a shock: was it simply my imagination. When it was time to share, I asked her tentatively: "Do you have a sister?"

She almost exploded. "Do I have a sister! She is the meanest bitch you could ever meet!"

Gosh, I thought. But what about the farm?

"You know something?" she went on, "she even named one of her cows after me!"

Wow.

The next student was a woman in her mid-thirties. Encouraged by the accuracy of my previous perception, I was gaining confidence and I thought I'd try to focus on any medical issue. So I stood with my eyes closed and my hands at my side, palms open.

This woman, I realised very quickly, could not have children. But how could I even suggest that?

"Er," I said. "I'm drawn to your abdominal area and I could be entirely wrong but I wondered if there might have been a problem there."

She nodded and said rather sadly: "I know what you're getting. My tubes are blocked and I can't have children."

This was amazing stuff. Sceptics may suggest I must have picked up conversations involving these people and that, consciously or not, I retained the information. That might be fair conjecture were it not for the many similar experiences during my years at the school. To be truthful, they unnerved me a little and I've never made a casual habit of reading other folks' fields. In any case, a genuine healer would never do that without permission.

Barbara told us: "In the past, clairvoyance, clairaudience and clairsentience – in other words, psychic abilities – were considered only as gifts for the few. I learned how to teach them and that's why I called it Higher Sensory Perception because it's simply expanding our normal senses to broader ranges."

Subjecting us to the anguish of an Italian tenor as we filed into class was only a minor way of penetrating our defences. The biggest and certainly the most successful was what they called process work. These were special straight-to-the-point classes that might have won the approval of the Inquisition.

Actually, the torture was internal – as a volunteer struggled to allow his or her vulnerability to be exposed under the sometimes less-than-gentle coaxing of a teacher. It usually involved the breaking down of a negative belief about the self – I am not enough, for example – and ended in an emotional and even physical collapse. It was all about accessing previous no-go areas.

I was normally a willing subject, probably because of the work I'd done with Karin. Sometimes I would come out in sympathy with the volunteer and slip into my emotional wounds, wailing away in unison. It was a pretty good bonding experience for the class.

But the teachers didn't just drop you in an ocean of shit and leave you to swim for the shore. They employed what was known as the healing response which brought you out of the mire in a very positive way and left you feeling good about yourself for having had the courage to go there. It's a lovely thought that one immersion in all that emotional pain would be enough. Sadly, it never is because those beliefs are deeply ingrained and take a lot of shifting.

If this all sounds too miserable, forgive me. Overall, my years at the school were absolutely joyful and I learned an enormous amount about myself and about being authentic and considerate in contact with others. But the work was always tough and demanding.

Each term we had to pass a large number of skills. When it was obvious we were having difficulty we were sent to tutorials at seven in the morning. I was a regular attendee, so accustomed to going that I sometimes mistakenly turned up when I hadn't been asked. Some students, usually only a small number, had to take the whole year again.

Although I felt bad for them, I liked that kind of integrity. The school lost a lot of students for a variety of reasons, often financial, but some dropped out because they just couldn't face their deepest feelings and the depth of the work. They received all the help possible but there was never a question of easing standards to let them through. We also had to bring evidence of at least eighteen sessions a year with a psychotherapist to illustrate that we weren't irredeemably nuts, and we were required to complete some pretty tough (for me anyway) homework assignments.

I don't want to suggest that BBSH was or is a kind of Hogwarts although there always seemed to be something magical going on.

But after a while, what at first appeared to be quite miraculous or in the mystically extreme became perfectly normal. It was as if we were living in two worlds.

I began to love the work and the people. There was a deepening sense of belonging to something both new and familiar. As I allowed myself to become more involved with my classmates, I could see and honour them as kindred spirits on an ancient journey. That may sound an idealised, romantic notion but for someone who has long guarded his individuality and was never one of the crowd, there was a warm, satisfying buzz about being there, as if I had found my long-lost tribe.

Overseas students sometimes presented their countries to a wider audience. Attendance wasn't compulsory but these occasions drew a fair number of people. Being something of a showman, I dressed up in my Highland finery as I presented the great attributes of Scotland, the multiple world-changing inventions that emanated from that small nation as well as its negative qualities such as chronic ill-health and social problems, its difficulty in letting go of old grudges.

As I lay down my *sgian dubh* or ceremonial dagger in a gesture of surrender, a few small gasps arose from the audience. Later, a couple of people told me they had seen images of tall tartan-clad Highlanders lined up behind me. And the next day, when I was receiving a healing, I would swear I saw the outline of a big red-bearded man as he leaned over me and whispered: "We're with ye, laddie." Or maybe it was my imagination… but it straightened the hairs on my neck.

– 34 –

A long and winding road

WE GATHERED in the ballroom where the Beatles played during their 1964 visit to Miami. There were pictures of them on the walls, along with others of regular performers Frank Sinatra and Dean Martin. The Deauville Beach Resort had its best years behind it but it was comfortable enough and right on the beach, so much could be forgiven. It was certainly big enough to house the 700 students attending the Barbara Brennan School of Healing.

Our large class of around 150 students stood or sat on the floor, some of us in a little anxiety, as we waited for whatever was to come. No teachers were in evidence and we really didn't know what to expect, other than this was to be what was called an 'experiental.'

In other words, the teachers were going to act out a defence, how we protect ourselves from life. They were to do this five times in that year because there are five basic platforms or defences based on negative events or traumas in our childhood and each one is quite different.

We have elements of several in our make-up but one is usually dominant. My primary defence is the psychopathic one which was the focus of this particular gathering. Although I'm not out to kill anyone, I apparently need to be in control for fear the parental betrayal I suffered as a child will be repeated.

The doors suddenly opened and an ancient king marched in accompanied by soldiers and camp followers whooping and dancing, all of them dressed appropriately. Where they got the outfits I have no idea but they were pretty neat.

The students rose, cheered, laughed and applauded. I found myself standing grim faced, my fists clenched and both arms extended above my head. As the queen waited and the king mounted the stage, I said to myself: That's my place.

The king made a speech about conquering far-off lands and bringing back great treasures. "None of this would have been possible without the support, courage and wisdom of my brother, the general," he said, putting an arm across the shoulders of the teacher beside him.

Then, as he placed a crown on the queen's head, the general pulled out a short sword and stabbed the king in the back. The class gasped. I screamed. I felt the sword enter my back below the shoulder blades and emerge through my chest. I fell to the ground and continued to scream, easing off only when self-consciousness took over and I realised I was the only one doing so. A couple of teachers came to my side.

The point of these exercises was to bring the wound, the defence, out of the unconscious and into awareness. It certainly worked for me. But none of the other characterology plays – spread over the first year – had anything like that effect on me.

A few years ago, I ran a workshop on Meeting the Needs of the Inner Child. I explained these wounds and belief systems and one participant said none of that applied to him. He is not alone in routinely claiming his childhood passed uneventfully while unconsciously exhibiting the signs that it hadn't. I tend to believe that all children suffer wounding to some extent, regardless of how thoughtful and enlightened their parents may have been. Philip Larkin put it this way in his poem *This Be The Verse*:

They fuck you up, your mum and dad.
They may not mean to, but they do.
They fill you with the faults they had
And add some extra, just for you.
(from Collected Poems, *Faber & Faber)*

It's an angry verse, no doubt reflecting the brilliant Larkin's troubled life.

There was a discernible flow to my time at the Brennan school.

As the work deepened and the teachings became more complex, the awareness and skills of the students somehow managed to advance accordingly. While there were frequent punctuation marks in the passage of progress, one year seemed to merge into the next without the clock falling off the wall.

That was largely due to Barbara and her team, led by school dean Laurie Keene, and a cleverly designed curriculum. But what essentially drove the whole charabanc was the longing of the students themselves to heal their emotional wounds and to overcome their fears and resistances. Enticed by continuing self-discovery and supported by the faculty and each other, we shared an eagerness, even an urgency, for more – and a readiness to stand in the fire.

Warmth and a sense of safety are embedded in a good community. Once my initial suspicions of others and concerns over what they might think of me had abated, once the embarrassment of making a fool of myself had been shredded by enough episodes of me doing just that, I could allow myself to trust. It was a very unusual feeling.

SOME HEALING techniques were fairly easy to master but others demanded great attention and a belief that they would actually work. Most healings involve hands-on work with the client lying on a table but there were some that defy normal logic. One of those is called distance healing.

The idea is that you can focus on a client even thousands of miles away, read their energy field and carry out a healing, knowing that he or she will receive and benefit from it as if they were in the same room. For anyone new to this business, it's a hard one to absorb even if you accept that at these levels there is no such thing as time or space.

The teachers separated us into two groups of around seventy-five each. One group lay on tables in a large room. In the other room, the healers in the exercise took a number from a pile. Each number would relate to someone lying on a table next door. I got fifty-nine.

"Now see what you pick up about your client," said the teacher, "and do an appropriate healing. When you've finished, go and find your client and talk about it."

Some of the healers sat on chairs to do the work. I preferred standing by an empty table, imagining that number fifty-nine was lying there. Well, it was a woman. I could be fairly sure of that anyway: the school was probably about eighty per cent female, women being far more willing to be in touch with their feelings than men. She was short, not even five feet. And quite sturdy.

I scanned her 'body' with my hands. At her second *chakra* which emerges from the abdomen, I found a great tangle of relationship cords. These are energy cords attached to people in our lives, sometimes to people who have physically moved on – former partners, for example.

Hers were in quite a mess, intertwined and even knotted. So I spent the next half-hour trying to undo the confusion. I didn't want to cut any of the old ones because I didn't have the confidence and I wasn't sure of the effect that might have on the client. But I got them kind of straightened out and went off to find number fifty-nine.

"Ian!" said this short, sturdy woman, sitting up. "It thought it was you! Thank you so much for all the work you did on my cords. I can really feel the difference."

And so it went on – new healings, new understandings about myself and others, wonderful new friends. And all of it set against the delightful backdrop of Miami Beach where we played games in the sand and swam in the warm waters of the Atlantic.

ON BALMY evenings we would grab a cab down to South Beach with its amazing art-deco architecture and long, lazy streets of pavement restaurants like Sushishamba, Yuca, Nexxt and the Frieze Ice Cream Factory and sometimes hit the clubs where all the bright young things danced like the demented. Unashamedly, we joined in.

Some students were older than me, most not. They came in all shapes and sizes and from about forty countries. And as time went by we began to feel the freedom of being authentic, of allowing ourselves to be vulnerable and undefended and to feel real love for those around us.

I guess it was love that really kept us all going, as well as the longing. But as I developed a love and appreciation for all things, I really had to work on feeling that for myself.

Given our life experiences, it's not remarkable that many people don't like to discuss love or even mention it at all. Oh, it's fair enough to say 'I love my child' or my partner or dog or garden but deeper than that there's often a resistance, a discomfort. And where we tend to fail miserably is in the love we need to give to ourselves.

Here's a little exercise I sometimes do. In the bathroom mirror I notice everything – the wrinkles, the cracked lips, the skin blemishes, the nose hair, the drooping eyebrows and the far-from-perfect teeth – and I say aloud to myself in full voice and with real meaning: 'I love you. I truly love you.' Try it.

I used to find it incredibly difficult and embarrassing. I would cringe. (It would have helped to have been a narcissist). While it was relatively easy to profess love for family and friends, the idea of loving myself was completely alien. Even attempting the words brought up unbearable sadness and all I could see in those accusatory eyes looking back was the lost, betrayed child.

THERE WAS, obviously, a serious spiritual side to the school. People understandably connect God with religion, yet there are many spiritually-inclined folk, myself included, who are basically non-religious. There's a preference among some to swap the word God for Universe. I guess it makes them feel better but I'm easy with either.

I do, however, dislike the way religious leaders through the ages have used God as a weapon to keep the people under control. I object to the language in the Church of England prayer which tells us: "We are not worthy so much as to gather up the crumbs from under your table." Or in the hymn *Amazing Grace* when we thank God for saving "a wretch like me". I think we punish ourselves enough without believing we are so inconsequential.

I don't recall ever feeling I belonged to a particular religion, even when I went to church or studied with Buddhist monks. Ah, there was a time in my very early teens when I attended a church weekend camp and came back a born-again Christian. It didn't last. Around the same time I discovered masturbation and you can't be a good Christian and do that sort of thing.

SHE WALKED through the outer office leaving turned heads and a subtle perfume in her wake. She was blonde, tall, elegant and quite stunning.

"Come in," I said. "What can I do for you?"

She sat, crossed her long legs and smiled. My cigar fell off its ashtray.

"I'd like to hire you," she said. "I hear you're good at what you do."

This is weird, I thought. I'd seen Humphrey Bogart in The Maltese Falcon *and read enough of Dashiell Hammett to recognise the scene.*

Déjà vu *aside, it turned out to be the start of a beautiful friendship – entirely platonic. And a reasonable business relationship too. Carole Parker was a damsel in distress only in the vaguest sense. She wanted to start an upmarket executive recruitment agency and understood the value of good PR. She was new to Dubai but she'd run a similar venture in the UK.*

Months later, she asked me if I knew where she could raise some funding without paying extortionate interest rates. "It's taking longer to get going than I thought," she said, "and clients are slow to pay."

I had a lot of faith in what Carole was doing and how she was doing it. I took a look at her books and they were okay. She offered me fifty per cent of the business for what I thought was a reasonable amount.

Clarendon Parker became one of the biggest players in the market but just as we were moving up another gear, Carole told me her marriage had collapsed and she wanted out of Dubai. I would have bought her out if I'd had any idea how to run the business along with Bain Communications. So we sold to a British firm and I got back a little more than what I'd put in.

Carole moved to Florida where she opened a different business but, tragically, died from cancer before she was fifty. It didn't go unnoticed by me that two good friends with whom I'd gone into business – Carole and James Osborne – both died far too early.

– 35 –

Out of the game

FOR NEARLY five years from the age of seventeen, David, my healing client, hardly left his bedroom in his parents' home. He would play an internet game into the early hours, sleep until noon then start again, up to eighteen hours a day. He ate his meals in his room and drank several litres of Coke or Pepsi a day.

He suffered terribly from irritable bowel syndrome (IBS) and fought with his mother and sisters, throwing tantrums and threatening violence if others were using the internet and reducing the speed of his connection.

David was, quite clearly, addicted to gaming. A prisoner to one particular game, he and a dozen or so individuals from around the world teamed up to defeat monsters or whatever. They could apparently message each other at the same time, the players I mean. These were David's only friends.

Twice he tried to escape, enrolling in college to study engineering but both times had to abandon the course within days when his IBS flared out of control. So he continued to shut himself away, leaving the house only to attend the job centre and collect his benefits or to go to the corner shop for cigarettes. It was a dreadful existence that caused him enormous pain, anger and shame. He was caught in a trap, as I had been with alcohol, and, like me, he could see no way out, although he knew he was wasting his life. The point was approaching, I feared, when he would become unemployable and his health might collapse, even if was receiving medical help.

David and I began working together – mainly on Skype – while I was in advanced studies at A Society of Souls in New Jersey, a school I joined after four years at Brennan. It taught very different healing skills, at another level altogether, although these were also aimed at resolving the personality flaws we develop in childhood.

The school was run by Jason Shulman, a spiritual teacher of great knowledge, wisdom and understanding, a modern guru although he wouldn't like that particular label. He taught us not to seek to defeat our difficulties but to embrace them, to allow the 'bad' to exist alongside the 'good,' the lesser qualities with the finer. In this non-dualistic way, these flaws would lose their impact and our lives would become easier. But that's a lot more difficult than it might sound.

So was working with David. He was initially a reluctant client, persuaded by his mother to give it a go. But he persevered. He was a man of few words, not because he was angry or completely disinterested but because he had so little to say. He was also very shy.

"So how are you feeling today, David?"

"Fine."

"How's your IBS?"

"It's okay."

"Have you had a flare-up this week?"

"Only once."

"It's a beautiful day. Have you been outside?"

"No."

"Are you planning to go anywhere?"

"The job centre."

"Do you walk there? Get out in the fresh air a bit?"

"Mum takes me."

David wasn't looking for a job. He couldn't have held one down. The severity of his medical problems excused him but he had to sign on to collect what was called a job-seeker's allowance.

The old trick of getting the client to fill the spaces didn't work with David. It was me who was finding them difficult. I noticed how I needed to keep the conversation going, no matter how one-sided it was. I couldn't just sit in the emptiness. It looked too much like my old friend failure.

Other than at school, I hadn't done a great deal of healing work. That's not to say that I wasn't good at it. Some of my fellow students went on to have very successful healing practices but my interest was mainly in resolving my own life issues and I didn't want a new career. I had as many healing clients as I was willing to handle, mainly folk like David who were troubled emotionally and physically.

One of the dangers in this kind of work is the healer's need to fix things. It's a natural and understandable desire but it doesn't make for a good relationship with the client because expectation leads to frustration and there's a tendency to judge the client – or oneself – if there appears to be little or no discernible progress.

Nor could I push David into what I wanted him to do, although reducing his hours at the game and his intake of fizzy drinks seemed to be priorities. It had to come from him. Sometimes we just talked about unrelated subjects such as football or the weather or the beauty contained within the changing of the seasons. I would ask what he could see from his bedroom window or about his dog. In this way he began to open up and we could have real conversations. Well… almost. At the end of each session I would do an appropriate healing.

As time went by, David reduced his intake of Coke and Pepsi. After about nine months he gave them up entirely. He began to eat meals with the family, not always but with encouraging frequency. He stopped throwing tantrums and started to appreciate his mother more. He shortened his hours on the computer and took to reading books and watching TV. He still played the game, however, and decided that his IBS had cleared enough for him to visit a convention built around the game in Eastern Europe. He had never before been out of the country.

There, in a kind of fairy-tale way, he met a girl who was also a player, his first-ever girlfriend. She eventually followed him to the UK where they live happily together, not in his parents' house, and he enrolled again in the engineering college, this time without the destructive intervention of his IBS. What courage that young man showed and how blessed I felt to have worked with him.

I STUDIED with Jason for seven years, the latter four as an apprentice teacher at the ASOS school in Europe. While students were conducting practice healings on each other, he would sometimes test my understanding of how they were doing.

"What's going on at that table?" he would ask.

"Mm…not enough. She's not in contact with the client."

"Okay," he would say, "and over there…?"

Although he was a few years younger than me, it was inevitable that I would see Jason as a father figure and there were times I would rebel against his sometimes authoritative ways, but I learned an enormous amount from him and other teachers, particularly Eileen Marder-Mirman.

While I was teaching in Europe, I was also attending an advanced studies class in the US. Sometimes Jason would give us an assignment deliberately designed to challenge and confuse. On one occasion we were asked to consider the Great Bear Mother and to put together some words about our understanding of her. I had never heard of the Great Bear Mother. Was he talking about the constellation of Ursa Major? Or a grizzly in Alaska? Other than that, it didn't mean a thing to me. All I could sense was that she was not to be taken literally.

I sat with an image of her and tried to feel into what she might represent – many things or only one thing. I wondered if she was the shamanic power animal that springs from the world of spirit to feed our resolve. Perhaps she was the uncompromising protector of us, her cubs; maybe another name for God – or was she the greater universal consciousness of which we were all part?

In my journey through this life, in times of great emotional pain, I had occasionally felt a presence, a comforting, loving presence, not necessarily an external one. It seemed to come from within as much as without – one and the same. So I sat with that too and with all I had learned in my years of searching for myself and something began to take form. I wrote this:

> For me, the Great Bear Mother is the all-enduring promise.
> She is the antidote to my fear and separation although she

> holds both as easily as she does my courage and wholeness. She is the nurturer of my willingness to dare and the forgiver of my readiness to flee.
>
> The Great Bear Mother is the bringer of the profound realisation that I do not have to give up who I am to be who I am.
>
> The sadness that has threatened for so long to overwhelm me has been my refuge from life, from awakening. And yet, that sadness is a vital part of me.
>
> The Great Bear Mother asks me to consider where I would be without the ravages of my childhood, the life-sapping traumas, the heart-breaking betrayals of parents, friends and lovers – the anger and the despair, the shame, the guilt and the self-hatred. And the absolute grief for myself.
>
> The Great Bear Mother allows me to see that all the potentially crippling aspects of my life's experiences have helped to bring me to this place and this moment.
>
> She helps me to recognise – through these same eyes – the bodhisattva that I am with my capacity for love and compassion, my innate goodness and godliness. And she holds with grace and equanimity where I have felt so cursed – and where I feel so blessed.

On reflection now, I suppose the Great Bear Mother could be seen as one of many doorways into the mysteries of life and beyond – a way of thinking and questioning and imagining that leaps the barriers of conventional logic and supposed common sense. I remember Jason saying once that the question mattered more than the answer and it took me a little while to see that.

To meet the requirements of the assignment more precisely, I wrote that what had helped me in my journey through the belly of the beast, from the known to the unknown and back again – what some call the long dark night of the soul – were many wonderful people, spiritual teachers, fellow students at different schools, guides and mentors. And ordinary people. The person who shows me anger and resentment, I said, is as great a teacher as the one who knows only kindness. Sometimes I need to remind myself of that.

There was a question in the assignment on whether or not I was choosing to change my life. It made me smile. Was there a choice? I wrote that on the journey of self-discovery there was an early point of no return, a point where one understands that the process of meeting one's longing, the need to heal our existential pain, had a momentum of its own and could not be denied.

Yet it was essential to remain grounded, to go about business and life and relationships in the normal way but with more awareness and kindness and compassion and self-regard.

– 36 –

Goodbye Dubai

WE'LL CALL my employee Mona and the client Best Enterprises. To give their real names might be to embarrass either or both and I don't particularly want to do that even if it all happened long ago and everyone will have moved on.

Based on a recommendation by my wife, I had taken Mona on when she was out of work. She had no PR experience but she was smart and efficient and quickly picked up the administrative side of client relations. I was concerned she was a little short on humour but the clients found no fault with her.

A year or so after I'd promoted her to account manager for Best, I was approached by the client.

"How would you feel," asked the general manager, "if we offered Mona a job? She knows our products and our people and we need someone like her on the marketing side. We'd be grateful if you would let her come to us."

Damn. She and I had never got on well but I didn't want to lose her. Neither did I want to create any hard feelings. Best was a big client and it's not easy for an agency to reject a request like that. And I'd rather have them grateful than not. At the same time, this would be a good career move for Mona.

"Let me think about it," I said, "and I'll get back to you."

I called the general manager the next day. "Okay," I said, "but I need your absolute assurance that she'll never become involved in PR."

"You've got it," he said, "and thanks."

As an international company, Best changed its senior expatriate personnel on a fairly regular basis. A year or so later, a new GM told me he was making Mona PR manager. That was, he said, where her real expertise lay. I protested vigorously but I had nothing in writing about our agreement. I could have threatened to sue but that would have been the end of the relationship. As it was, the end wasn't that far away.

I don't know if she held a grudge or if she felt her new position gave her absolute power over us, but it seemed that Mona was undermining her old firm at every opportunity. She knew, of course, that I had fought her appointment as PR manager.

It came to a head at a meeting at the client's offices involving Best management, the advertising agency and Bain people. I can't remember the details but it was about a promotional plan for a particular product. The more I heard, the more I believed the plan wasn't right, that if it couldn't be improved then it had to be abandoned and a new one worked out. So I disagreed gently with what was on that table.

"I don't care what you think, Ian," said Mona. "You will do as you're told."

I looked around the room. The Best folk were examining the papers in front of them; the youngsters from the advertising agency also had their heads down, one of them trying to suppress a giggle. The atmosphere was filled with embarrassment.

I was nearly sixty years old, the grey-haired doyen of the PR industry in the Gulf, chairman of a well-established company, the man who had pioneered it all. I said nothing, picked up my papers, nodded in a general direction and left.

Going down in the lift, I said to myself: 'You really have to get out of this game.' I had much more important things to do. There was a new urgency to go. It wasn't just pride. Of course there was pride, but it was mainly the disrespect, not so much of my position, but of me personally.

I could have complained to the general manager and demanded an apology but what would that have gained? A small satisfaction? I was learning a lot in my healing school studies and I was aware that everyone has, to some degree, their own issues from childhood. Whatever Mona's were, they contained a lot of anger and bitterness. Regardless, with Mona in charge, we would have lost the account at some point and we eventually did. It went to another PR firm that, if I remember correctly, kept it for less than a year.

While I prefer the soft-hearted response, there was a slightly earlier occasion when it brought me no reward and actually proved very costly. I had taken on a deputy who was neither bad nor particularly good at his job but he was certainly inept at stealing from the company. Among other things, his fraudulent expenses and the forgery of my signature as guarantor for a bank loan were easily discovered.

I didn't go to the police for the simple reason that I didn't want to see him languishing in jail, possibly for years. But my failure to do so inspired him to lodge a complaint for unfair dismissal with the Labour Court. That's when I called in the cops. Too late. The judge decided that since I hadn't gone to the police immediately, I was only retaliating against the employee's claim. Even though the police evidence was solid, he dismissed the charges.

"What about forging my signature on a financial instrument?" I asked.

"Well, he didn't get the money, did he?" was the response.

I wanted to ask if, in that case, it was okay to run a red light as long as you didn't hit anyone, but I didn't want to go to jail myself. It took more than a year to resolve fully and was an expensive exercise.

THE DECISION to leave Dubai and the business was a big one. The city had been my home for a quarter of a century. I felt, at times, part of the fabric. I had helped it and it had certainly helped me. Back then there was one PR firm, mine. Twenty-five years later there were nearly fifty.

Around that time I was asked to chair a debate about public relations. The hotel conference room where it was held was filled to bursting. There must have been three hundred people and that was far from the total employed in the local industry. What a difference.

Having led the market for so long, by the turn of the millennium Bain Communications was on a gentle slide. That was due to a combination of fierce competition as more international PR giants moved in, some of my best people leaving to take up the newly available senior positions (saying you'd been trained at Bain was a fast ticket to a new job), bad appointments, plain poor judgement and my own loss of interest. Even so, we still had some great clients and profits were actually rising.

But the buzz and excitement that was once a hallmark of Bain Communications, especially in the pioneering days, had gone and I found a buyer in Euro RSCG, an international advertising and PR group. The price I'd agreed for the business, far from a vast sum, reflected my eagerness to go. Unhappily, too many clients followed me out. It was a sad day when the company was absorbed into another and the Bain name abandoned.

It would be fair to say that I had a love/hate relationship with Dubai. The city had been a fun place and it probably still is in a different way. The population when I arrived was around 200,000. When I left it was close on two million. Fewer than ten per cent of its inhabitants were UAE nationals and I often wondered how it felt to be strangers in your own land. In the passing of the decades, the city had been transformed from a place of quiet business and simple pleasures into a kind of Marvel movie set. Or maybe I'm being a little unkind.

Oil had helped Dubai compress centuries of natural development into sixty years or so – from its dependency in the Forties on dhow-trading, pearl-fishing and, later, gold-smuggling to the giant shopping centre and holiday destination it is today, better than anywhere else on earth, even if it says so itself. With the oil running out, Dubai turned to tourism, banking, free trade zones, aviation, real estate, service industries and anything else that would keep it in business and in the world's eye.

Desert sands and rough bush gave way to glass and concrete canyons, long empty shorelines were suddenly exclusive beach resorts, the old roads became twelve-lane highways and thirty-year-old hotels were demolished to create towering new ones.

I wasn't against the dramatic progress but I thought it could have been more measured with greater awareness of environmental issues. Even so, I feel some pride in having played a part, however small, in the extraordinary growth of Dubai. I had, for example, started working with Emirates Airline when it had two borrowed aircraft and three routes. At the time of writing, it had nearly 260 aircraft with almost as many on order and 140 destinations. It's now one of the biggest airlines in the world.

During the first Gulf War when Emirates was the only airline to continue operations, I came up with the 'Business as Usual' slogan for another client, the Dubai Promotion Board. At that time, we often had half a dozen international TV crews hanging around, waiting for visas to get into Saudi Arabia. I found them all kinds of interesting stories that had little to do with the war but gave them something to send back to their hungry networks.

I recall sitting one evening with an Italian crew in the lounge of the Hilton Hotel when an enormous bang shook the glass doors and windows. The crew leapt to their feet and grabbed their equipment.

"Scud! Scud!" they cried, believing an Iraqi missile had landed, and dashed for the door. I tried to tell them it was just an American F-16 going through the sound barrier but they were too excited to listen.

So many memories, good and bad, but mainly good.

ON A beautiful early morning in the spring of 2003 and with the dew still on the grass, Sharadha and I went into the large garden of our villa near Safa Park, our haven of peace and nature. We took a last look around at the flame trees we'd planted, the extravagance of bougainvillea overhanging the walls and the rising towers of the city beyond. We put our arms around each other and I wiped away a tear. Then we made our three little dogs as comfortable as possible in their special cages, loaded them and our luggage into a small convoy of vehicles and set off for Dubai airport.

What an adventure it had been!

– 37 –

French leave

THE MICE didn't just run up the clock. They scaled the stairs, the tables, the curtains – even a friend's leg – and just about everything else in the old *manoir* we had rented in the Dordogne region of France. It wasn't unusual for one to sit on the edge of the large kitchen table and stare at me over breakfast while another peeked out from behind the kettle. They even put in a combined effort and made off with a roll of my indigestion tablets.

Our cleaner, Marie-Ange, had been recommended by the owners who lived abroad and she knew the house. One morning she arrived with a carrier bag full of boxes of poison, then dug around in the cellar for mousetraps so ancient they might have sold as antiques.

"*Voilà*!" she said, dumping it all on the table.

"*Non*!" Sharadha, the French speaker in the family, said firmly as I nodded affirmatively. "We will not kill the mice."

Marie-Ange looked at us incredulously. She shook her head and decided the village had gained not one new idiot, but two.

Sharadha and I had a little talk with the mice, asking them to vacate the premises and return to the barn and the fields of grape vines and sunflowers that lay beyond and to the side of our extensive garden with its established fruit trees. That sort of animal communication sometimes works but it didn't on this occasion. The mice just looked at us and shrugged.

Okay, we decided, we will help you move. We laid some humane traps and the next morning took our captives into the field and released them. I'd swear they got back to the house before we did. There wasn't a room they didn't occupy. At night, Sharadha usually asked me to check around the bed. She wasn't afraid of mice but she didn't want them in immediate proximity. Looking behind the headboard, I often noted two or three of the little creatures clinging to the hessian.

"All clear," I would say.

It took a single event to resolve the problem. Well, that's what I tell myself. The weather had something to do with it too. Actually, it was never truly resolved but it was certainly made more bearable. The incident happened shortly after I switched off my bedside light. One of our dogs, little Baba, was snoring softly on the bed and the other two, Usha and Toffee, were asleep in their baskets nearby. Just as I was drifting off, I felt a presence in the room, something moving in the darkness. Whatever it was, it was much too big to be mice. This was a spooky old house and I was beginning to feel uncomfortable. Then I heard a sound.

"Meow..."

To say simply that all hell broke loose would be to minimise the explosion of chaos that followed that plaintive feline cry. The three dogs leapt in the air and, still in darkness, tore frantically around the room, barking their outrage, while the terrified animal screeched continuously and took to the curtains.

I switched on the light just as the curtain rail, the curtains and the cat collapsed in a heap on top of the dogs. We managed to grab our little guys before they laid a paw on the cat which bolted from the room and escaped the house through whichever point it had entered.

The presence, albeit a fleeting one, of a cat in the house did not go unnoticed by our tiny friends. After the nuclear bomb in the bedroom, the essence of scalded cat must have permeated the whole *manoir*, at least as far as sensitive little nostrils were concerned.

The incident coincided with a considerable improvement in the weather. Morning frosts disappeared and the sun had warmth in it almost from the dawn, giving the mice more incentive to seek food and shelter elsewhere. The arrival of these warmer days and nights was probably the primary mover of the mice but their happy abode may not have seemed quite as safe and comfortable as it previously had.

We had left Dubai just a few weeks earlier. Instead of heading directly back to the UK, we came to France primarily because of the dogs. At that time, the UAE was not considered rabies-free and our animals would have had to spend six months in quarantine. That simply wasn't acceptable. So we decided to stay in France for six months or for as long as it took to get the pet passports that would allow them entry to Britain. And if we liked it enough, we'd find a permanent home in the very beautiful Dordogne region.

St Meard du Gurcon was a working village. Unlike others in the area, it was not a particularly quaint one, the buildings a little too modern. It had a couple of grocery stores, a butcher's, a delightful *pâtisserie*, a very good bar/restaurant and even a ladies' hairdresser. There was a small roofed market place in the main square next to the church and opposite the mayor's office that seemed to be an irregular meeting place. Once, in the middle of what appeared to be a semi-formal event, Usha wandered over and did a couple of little twirls in front of a man who was addressing the small gathering and defecated at his feet. We steered clear of meetings after that.

Most mornings, I would wander up to the grocery and tobacco shop to buy yesterday's *Guardian* or *Times* – whichever was available – and drop in at the *pâtisserie* for a couple of large fresh-from-the-oven *croissants* and maybe a pastry or two. Sharadha and I would sit in the back garden with our morning coffee and look out across the fields of green and yellow and feel blessed to be there. It was a different world, in its own time. Even so, I missed the pace of Dubai, the constant noise and the hubbub of malls and meeting places, not to speak of the office.

At times, I caught myself falling into misery – how I might have saved Bain Communications, how I should have stayed on, reproaching myself for my foolishness with money and more. It felt as if an important part of me had been lopped off, a limb severed. But I recognised that as self-flagellation, honoured it and let it go.

St Meard de Gurcon would not have been our first choice but it hadn't been easy to find a house for long-term rental. Most properties were being offered on short holiday lets that produced a much greater income. But the owners of the *manoir*, a British couple working in Singapore, didn't want the hassle. And, with its proximity to Bordeaux, it was handy for my travels to school in the US.

Our ideal village, actually a small town, was Brantôme, one hundred kilometres to the north-east and near the city of Périgueux. It represented all that was wonderful about the Dordogne with its medieval and renaissance architecture, its ancient Benedictine abbey and the River Dronne which encircled a large part of the town. There can be few better experiences than eating a superb meal on the open terrace of the delightful Le Moulin de l'Abbaye as you watch fat trout slurp flies from the surface of the river and Mallard mums gather their ducklings.

The dogs were a major part of our enjoyment of being in France. They delighted in the green fields and woods and loved their walks along winding country lanes and through the trees. It was on one of those that tubby little Usha fell in love. She'd been spayed a long time earlier so it was an emotional, rather than hormonal, attraction. The object of her affection was a jaunty but fickle little Hungarian puli called Jazz. Passing his house, Usha would rush to the wire fence and bark and whine until Jazz deigned to make an appearance. A little nose-rubbing might follow but Jazz didn't hang around and usually dashed back indoors, leaving Usha to whimper endearments. Sometimes, when he wouldn't even bother to come to the fence, Usha was distraught in her abandonment. It took a decent treat to cheer her up.

In that summer's dreadful heatwave – the worst in nearly 500 years, we learned – we worried that Usha would not survive the forty-degree temperatures. The dogs, like us, were used to air conditioning. Now they lay panting heavily on the kitchen floor. Usha seemed to be in the greatest distress and we used towels soaked in cold water to help keep her cool. I bought a large fan into which you poured ice or cold water and that seemed to help.

Still getting used to their very different environment, it was clear that when Sharadha and I went out by ourselves the dogs suffered separation anxiety, particularly Toffee, the youngest of the three. We didn't realise how great it was until one Sunday evening as we walked

Toffee gave little indication that she'd ever had a problem.

up the road with a couple of old Dubai friends to the local restaurant. Suddenly I heard a thud and a yelp.

Toffee came whimpering out the drive on three legs and with blood dripping from her nose. After we had left, she had run upstairs and leapt fifteen feet from a bedroom window onto hard-packed clay. It nearly broke our hearts to see that little figure hobbling up the road to reach us, fast as she could go, tail wagging.

Our friends, Ian and Maggie Longhurst, who lived nearby, were quick to find an emergency vet who was quite brilliant. There was, thankfully, nothing broken and the bleeding was superficial but the ligaments of a front paw were badly damaged. The vet warned that she might need surgery that would leave her unable to bend the leg. He bandaged it tightly and covered it with a cast.

In the weeks that followed, Toffee chewed away happily at her cast, for her the only fun part of this whole awful experience. Sharadha and I gave her a lot of healings. She was able to avoid surgery and, over the years, there was little indication that she'd ever had a problem.

Leaving Toffee at home as we took the other dogs for their daily walks was out of the question. She limped along happily. We kept the three firmly on their leads and avoided the multitudes of hunters who, particularly at the weekends, would blast away at anything that flew or moved. Their hounds were not, from their appearance and manner, inclined towards making friends. If I were to point to one reason why we decided against staying in France, it would be the hunting.

We also knew that we would never be a part of this community and I didn't imagine it would be much different elsewhere. On our walks we occasionally met an elderly lady who liked to make a fuss of the dogs.

"I came here from Paris twenty years ago," she told Sharadha, "and I'm still waiting to be accepted."

So, we were going back to Scotland. Oh, I'd visited plenty of times but I hadn't lived there for fifty years. I remembered well the day of my departure in 1955 and the eleven-hour journey on a steam train from Perth to King's Cross. Then it was an electric train from London Bridge Station to poor old Gravesend. The noise it made crossing points terrified me.

On a very cold January morning about nine months after we arrived in France, we loaded ourselves and the dogs into our new British-spec Volvo estate and set off for Calais, a distance of nine hundred kilometres. We had already shipped most of our stuff ahead so there was plenty of space and reasonable comfort for the dogs.

Just after Paris, and already very tired, we ran into a great storm that stayed with us for the remainder of the journey. In the darkness, strong winds threatened to push high-sided trucks against us and the windscreen wipers could hardly cope in the torrential rain. With a right-hand-drive car and the terrible conditions, it was almost impossible to overtake in two-way traffic. So we crawled into Calais behind a convoy of lorries and eventually found the Holiday Inn. Baba and Co sauntered through the hotel lobby and into the lift as if they'd been doing it all their lives.

The storm was unrelenting. Waves crashed over the seafront and the empty streets. It was as well we had booked Eurotunnel since the ferries had been cancelled.

By the morning, the winds had diminished and, with the minimum of formalities, we crossed to the UK and hit the road north. England lay under heavy cloud that threatened rain but failed to deliver.

I've always enjoyed the undulating countryside of the English south in any weather and even when it's spliced by a motorway. The gentle

Chiltern Hills of Buckinghamshire and the rich red soil of Warwickshire were familiar to me, places with happy memories. I resisted a momentary temptation to take the next exit left.

Spaghetti Junction seemed a lot more simple than Dubai's complex intersections and we were soon through the Black Country, up into Cheshire and crossing the Manchester Ship Canal where, forty years earlier, the ship I was on damaged a propeller and had to be towed out.

Over Shap, it was downhill all the way to Penrith, only a couple of miles from Matterdale Church where my brother-in-law, the Rev David Crook, was once vicar and where we buried my mother.

In the car, talk of the long journey behind us – measured more in decades than in miles – was subdued. There was no sense of exhilaration. It was as if it was all just too big for words. Sharadha and I spoke of practical things like the house we'd bought in Argyll overlooking the Holy Loch. It was going through a major refurbishment and we hoped that its new roof would be completed by the time we arrived.

We stopped overnight at a scruffy Travelodge near Carlisle and crossed the border early the next morning. There was snow on the hilltops and the rivers were fat with winter rain. A splash of sunshine brightened the landscape somewhere between Gretna and Lockerbie and I felt my heart open.

Ah, Scotland. I have come home.

Epilogue

Look to this day
For it is life, the very life of life.
In its brief course
Lie all the verities and realities of your existence.
SANSKRIT TEXT

WHEN YOU'RE getting old, when physical ailments become a daily consideration and visits to the doctor, consultant and physiotherapist fill more space in your diary than social events, there are times when the past might appear more attractive than the future.

When you have to get up in the night to pee, when your left knee replacement proves less successful than your new right hip, when the impingement in one shoulder begins to be mirrored in the other, there's something to be said for the soft glow of the good old days and the memories of ourselves as fit and healthy and free of care.

Except, of course, I was never fit... perhaps in my childhood. From my early twenties, running for a bus was about the extent of my exercise and, when I recall how much I smoked and drank, it's a wonder I ever caught one. And as for free of care... well.

A life-time of self-disregard inevitably exacts a price but I have to admit that, in spite of my multiple complaints, I don't believe what I'm paying now is a particularly heavy one, especially when I think of friends and former newspaper colleagues I have substantially outlived and the dreadful illnesses many have suffered.

It would be wonderful to report that after many years of healing work and psychoanalysis I have overcome procrastination. I haven't. The wounds run too deep. But there is a perceptible difference. In achieving a far greater awareness of myself, I reached an agreement with my procrastination. I allowed it to exist, accepting it as part of me and, with that understanding, it has played a lesser role in my life. I can live with it without the self-judgement. And maybe that's what healing is all about.

The days of retirement had been drifting unremarkably into years and I didn't like the idea of just waiting for the shadows to close in. So at the age of seventy I enrolled at Edinburgh College to study counselling, as much for myself as for others, and for some time now I've been a kind of mentor to a young Barnardo's lad. At seventy-four I took up Transcendental Meditation.

I also joined a writers' group to whose members I owe a debt of gratitude. Without their regular encouragement and invaluable but sometimes uncomfortable critiques, I don't know if *Singing in the Lifeboat* would ever have been completed.

Memoirs, of course, are all about reflecting back, an exercise that can be as painful as it is pleasurable. I've certainly shed tears in the writing of these ones. And at this age I'm not doing an awful lot of forward planning, except for my next book – the remarkable story of one of our little rescue dogs that came from the backstreets of an Indian city, via Dubai and France, to roam the Highlands of Scotland. It is called *Baba – The Original Slumdog*.

So, if yesterday is pretty well nailed down and I'm not terribly concerned about tomorrow, what I have left is today which is, of course, the most precious of all days. It is here, right now. What a gift it is to be aware of what exists in the moment instead of being off somewhere, caught up in another time.

Afterword

THIS IS where the author, like the intrepid reporter exposing a vice den, makes his excuses and leaves. There are, undoubtedly, numerous errors in this book. And I cannot say that all the events described are chronologically in order. Memory, thank goodness, is never precise. But I have tried to be as factually correct as possible. It has not been my intention to distress anyone who appears in these pages but that may be unavoidable in some instances. Where I felt it appropriate, I have changed people's names.

Edinburgh
April, 2018

CPSIA information can be obtained
at www.ICGtesting.com
Printed in the USA
BVHW04s1531270618
520208BV00013B/239/P